The Dark Sides of Empathy

The whole of the mind is greater than the sum of its parts; configuration of simpler elements produces a new quality.

The Dark Sides of Empathy

Fritz Breithaupt

Translated by
Andrew B. B. Hamilton

Cornell University Press

Ithaca and London

Originally published under the title *Die dunklen Seiten der Empathie*, by Fritz Breithaupt. © Suhrkamp Verlag Berlin, 2017.

First published 2019 by Cornell University Press

Library of Congress Cataloging-in-Publication Data

Names: Breithaupt, Fritz, 1967– author. | Hamilton, Andrew B. B.,
    translator.
Title: The dark sides of empathy / Fritz Breithaupt ; translated by
    Andrew B.B. Hamilton.
Other titles: Dunklen Seiten der Empathie. English
Description: 1st edition. | Ithaca [New York] : Cornell University Press,
    2019. | Originally published in German under the title: Die dunklen
    Seiten der Empathie. | Includes bibliographical references and index.
Identifiers: LCCN 2018053226 (print) | LCCN 2019010604 (ebook) |
    ISBN 9781501735608 (pdf) | ISBN 9781501735615 (epub/mobi) |
    ISBN 9781501721649 (pbk. : alk. paper)
Subjects: LCSH: Empathy. | Social interaction. | Interpersonal relations.
Classification: LCC BF575.E55 (ebook) | LCC BF575.E55 B73813 2019
    (print) | DDC 152.4/1—dc23
LC record available at https://lccn.loc.gov/2018053226

Contents

Acknowledgments

O ne should not dedicate a book about the dark sides of empathy to anyone. However, one can thank those who helped in the making of the book. This starts with my family, who had to endure the long process of writing and rewriting and all the emotions that go along with that. Thank you, Leela, Kira, Lara, and Noah.

The book is the result of many conversations with family, friends, colleagues, and students. Many of their ideas or formulations found their way into the book. Even better, they set me straight when my thoughts were off target. If it would not sound like a backhanded compliment, I could say that they offered me much empathy. Some of them may be astonished that "only" five dark sides made the final list. In particular, I would like to thank Colin Allen, Aleida Assmann, Claudia Breger, Christopher Chiasson, Daniel Cuonz, Jean Decety, Wolfram Eilenberger, Kevin Houser, Phillip Hölzing, Philipp Kanske, Suzanne Keen, Sarah Konrath, Binyan Li, Lauren Lu, Christoph Paret, Eyal Peretz, Cassidy Sugimoto, Johannes Türk, Arne Willee, and Lisa Zunshine.

The book started as a translation of my book *Die dunklen Seiten der Empathie* (Frankfurt: Suhrkamp, 2017). My translator, Andrew B. B. Hamilton, gave the original book a new spin and infused it with his endless wit and energy. But somehow in the process it morphed into a new book. This is due to the fabulous editor Mahinder S. Kingra from Cornell University Press, who shook down every word and idea until they fell into place. Having started as an accessory, he ended up an equal partner in crime. Julia Cook gave the text the final touches as the exceptional copyeditor who remembered every twist of my arguments until the end; I fear she understands the book better than I do.

A few ideas from my other texts also found their way into the book, including some thoughts from my earlier book, *Kulturen der Empathie* (Frankfurt: Suhrkamp, 2009), and speculations about the development of sadistic empathy first developed in "Empathy for Empathy's Sake: Aesthetics and Empathic Sadism," in *Empathy and its Limits*, ed. Aleida Assmann und Ines Detmers (New York: Palgrave, 2016), 151–65.

The translation of the book was generously supported by a grant-in-aid from Indiana University's Office of the Vice Provost for Research. My previous work was supported by a grant from the Templeton Foundation that allowed me to lay the foundations for the ideas presented in this book.

The Dark Sides of Empathy

Introduction

This book is about the terrible things we do because of our ability to empathize with others. Sometimes we commit atrocities not out of a failure of empathy but rather as a direct consequence of successful, even overly successful, empathy. Empathy, as we shall see, plays a central part in a variety of highly problematic behaviors. Such behavior falls on a spectrum that ranges from mere callousness all the way to terrorism, exploitation, vampirism, and sadism, including along the way false pity and persistent oppression. In many cases, empathy not only fails to stop such negative acts but in fact motivates and promotes them. In short, these malicious acts happen not in spite of empathy, but because of it.

This point of view contradicts the common understanding of empathy. Usually, we assume that empathy leads to morally correct behavior. And certainly, there are many highly positive sides of empathy. As a social species, we are shaped by empathy. However, we should not use an overly simplified and glorified image of empathy. Let us take a look at two empathy-related instances that may help us to widen the spectrum.

In an online Reddit forum devoted to serial killers, a user named "Just_that_random_guy" published the following commentary in December 2015:

> There was this quote made by "Bedelia" a doctor and psychologist character from the tv series *Hannibal*. "Extreme acts of cruelty require a high level of empathy". I believe this to be true. Whenever I look at someone and I start imagining sadistic thoughts, I am able to understand and feel what the person would go through and the kind of pain and fear the person would experience and that's what actually turns me on. The stronger and more intense the pain and suffering I imagine to inflict on the person, the higher the gratification I derive.[1]

The anonymous author of these lines, who claims not to be a psychopath but just a "random guy," draws a connection between empathetic understanding and extreme emotions of another ("pain and fear"). This empathetic coexperience of pain arouses him (or her). Apparently, he can understand others and share their emotions precisely because he experiences the very pain that he attributes to them. In fact, that is the reason why he imagines their pain in his sadistic thoughts: to understand the other and share his or her feelings. Sadism is not the product of a lack of empathy but rather emerges from the wish for its intensification. Horrible fantasies (and perhaps actions as well) are possible *because of empathy*. Later on, we will describe this form of empathy as "empathy for empathy's sake" and will suggest that it encompasses extreme acts of violence as well as many forms of accepted everyday behavior.

As we shall see over the course of the book, such aberrations are not limited to a few problematic individuals but in fact touch upon many phenomena of our social world. There is a "normal" or "tolerated" form of sadism that takes the form of pressuring, exposing, or embarrassing others in order to predict and understand their feelings. There are also general practices that structure human society, including possibly our tendency to think in categories of good and evil, that can be considered as effects of empathy, as will be suggested later.

Here is a second, less radical case of a potential malfunction-
ing of empathy, something that happened to me somewhat regularly when I was around twelve or thirteen years old. At that time,
I lived on the outskirts of the North German city of Hamburg.
The city offered a subscription for public school students to all
public theaters and concert halls (nearly a dozen in the city), and
I am still grateful that my mother allowed my friends and me to
take the subway into the city unaccompanied and armed only with
our stack of tickets. However, something bizarre would regularly
happen to me in the middle of the performance. I would start
sweating and get nervous, imagining myself suddenly on stage,
standing in the shoes of the musician or actor, but without any
skill or training. I saw myself holding a violin, or dressed for some
role, only I was no artist and had not studied the lines. I imagined
myself unable to produce a single sound or utter a single word.
Inevitably, I would be mortified as I imagined seeing myself from
the outside; I felt confused and became so flushed that I had to
rush off stage to escape the confused audience. In my imagination,
I would even accidentally bump into a fellow musician sitting in
the narrow rows during my escape, making my embarrassment
and pain even worse. These fantasies were so intense and vivid that
on at least one occasion I actually had to leave my seat in the audience to catch my breath outside the hall.

This experience taught me that I cannot always control when
I will find myself transported into the world of others. Certainly,
this "wandering stage fright" is not one of the dark sides of empathy that this book deals with. According to most definitions of
empathy, this experience would not even be called empathy. If it
were empathy, one would expect an awareness of the difference
between me and other on the one hand and a possibility of nevertheless sharing some of the other's experiences on the other

hand.[2] Instead, I found myself, without preparation and while still remaining myself, transported into the other's situation: "I as myself in the situation of another." Hence, my case involved neither a sharing of emotions nor an understanding of what the other was doing. In this sense, one could characterize my experience as an incomplete form of empathy, perhaps as an early phase of its development. A special feature in my transportation experience is that it involved a stage with onlookers. Throughout this book, we will come back to this phenomenon of the "glowing skin"—of someone in the spotlight on stage who invites identification and empathy by virtue of being singled out as "larger than life." Our investigation will include both the literal stage, with the artists and politicians who perform on them, and the imagined stages in the minds of helicopter parents who wish to bask in the success of their children.

Some readers may wonder what qualifies me to write this book. My confession to a wandering stage fright may not do much to boost the reader's confidence. My academic training is in various disciplines from art history to law. After my studies were over, I added cognitive science to the mix of my professional interests, and I am now an affiliated professor of cognitive science. However, my main focus in the academy lies in literary criticism and cultural studies. Although this is not a work of literary criticism, I hope it nevertheless retains some of that field's sensitivity.[3] As a scholar of literature, one learns that every form of human behavior can be presented in the form of a narrative and can thereby be imagined by most people. Stories from real life and from fiction seem to follow similar trajectories.[4] And as a scholar of literature, one learns to imagine the circumstances under which one could commit even the worst crime or have seemingly absurd emotions. Based on this experience, it is more difficult (but not impossible) to demonize "bad" or "irrational" behavior. Hence, the main object of the book is not to condemn the dark sides of empathy but rather to understand how they come about and how many so-called perversions are part of being human. Of course, understanding how actions come about does not mean to approve of them or to excuse them before the law.

The Argument

The title of the book seems to promise an attack on empathy. Can we say that this book is *against* empathy? Such general attacks have recently been waged by the psychologist Paul Bloom and the philosopher Jesse Prinz.[5] In a more specific fashion, the philosopher Peter Goldie has also recently critiqued the concept of empathy as being too vague, and he coined the term "Anti-Empathy."[6] In previous decades, scholars suggested that empathy might lead to problematic results in certain domains, such as legal justice and in aesthetics.[7] What connects all these attacks on empathy is that they quixotically take aim at a false concept of empathy, not empathy itself. If one expects from empathy a full understanding of others, as Goldie does, one will surely be disappointed. However close empathy brings you to someone else, it cannot offer that much. If one expects absolutely fair moral judgments, as Prinz does, one can lament loudly that empathy is a poor ethical compass, falling short of such expectations to the point even of obstructing justice. Nor is empathy required for morality. Similarly, Bloom rejects empathy because it does not deliver fair judgment. But love doesn't either. Should we now be against love? No, neither love nor empathy are designed for fair judgment. To be fair to these brilliant authors, increased empathy has been prescribed as a solution to numerous social ailments and political problems, and that does call for some debunking. (In addition, neither author can be reduced to so simplistic a critique of empathy.)

Bloom's book *Against Empathy*, which was published in English at the same time this book first appeared in German, is the most interesting and persuasive attack on empathy so far. Bloom's main point is that empathy spotlights one aspect of a crisis, inspiring a rush to action (to help one person, for example) without any context or a long-term plan. If one expects sound moral judgments and actions, Bloom tells us, empathy should not be one's guide. Nor, Bloom argues, does empathy lead to the development of moral feelings in children. His book also aims to correct a major thrust in psychology research today: that our behavior is deeply informed by irrational biases. Bloom counters that we are more rational than often appears. I agree with his basic suggestions concerning empathy, though I remain more skeptical about rationality. But like Prinz's and Goldie's critiques, Bloom's condemnation of empathy only works by first setting up a straw man, namely empathy as the motor of moral and just behavior. If, however, one does not buy into this claim about empathy, one does not need to be "against" empathy. As I will suggest, the main point of empathy is not fairness. We will come back to Bloom's ideas at several places in this book.

My book is not "against empathy." It has a different and, I believe, more substantial goal: namely to consider the terrible things we *do* with and because of empathy. Empathy makes us human and it would be naive to imagine we should just get rid of empathy, even if we could. (There are specific instances, for example in medical or legal contexts, where limiting empathy-based decision-making might be advisable.) Instead, I argue that humans are what we are because we have the capacity for a wide spectrum of empathetic forms of behavior, including the dark sides of empathy—because we are "homo empathicus."

Homo Empathicus

One of this book's guiding assumptions is that empathy is not just one among many features of humanity but rather one of the central forms that shapes what we are as human beings. Empathy cannot simply be subtracted from who we are, leaving our identity intact.[8] Our experience of our social environment is not only colored by empathy but structured by it. Empathy is like a sixth sense by which we perceive the world. As soon as we are in contact with other people (or other beings that we anthropomorphize), we begin to see and experience the situation from their perspectives. This perspective-sharing can be frightening, as Jean-Paul Sartre suggests in *Being and Nothingness* when he describes how he was happily sitting alone on a bench in the park until he suddenly realized that someone was looking at him and he was compelled to imagine himself being seen. The main effect, however, is a duplication and multiplication of our perceptions: we perceive what we perceive *and* we participate in the experiences of someone else. Likewise, we extend the depths of our feelings when we feel what someone else feels. We participate in many ways in the emotions, ideas, thoughts, and intentions of other people. It is by means of others that we see ourselves as if from the outside; we perceive our environment differently because we note how others feel about it. The emotional states that we register in others become for us a fact that calls for a reaction; often they compel us to be concerned for the other's happiness.

Even so-called sociopaths or psychopaths who seem devoid of empathy can understand others to an astonishing degree and are able to coexperience, even to the point of caring, but do not usually do so. People on the autism spectrum certainly show deficiencies of empathy, but they are not entirely without empathy.[9] If there were people lacking empathy completely, we would not recognize them as people. In fact, among all personality transformations, changes in empathy and morality are seen as more fundamentally personality altering than anything else, even complete memory loss.[10]

Against Empathy?

At the end of the book, we shall face a dilemma. To be simply "against" empathy would be simplistic. But to uncritically embrace empathy without caveats would be equally problematic. Let us consider the arguments for empathy first. We live in a social world. We live in groups or clans, we observe others, we are affected by the experiences of others, we resonate with them and participate in the world to a degree via others. The suffering of others is our suffering; their happiness can be ours as well. Conversely, our emotions and moods affect others, too. Perhaps seeking such resonance in others is the core structure of being prosocial, as the German sociologist Hartmut Rosa suggests.[11] It is no surprise that empathy has been described as a balm or even as the "better angel of our nature" amid the horrors of war, injustice, slavery, and suffering.[12] Empathy can save lives, whether by connecting emotionally with a suicidal teenager, for example, or by motivating humanitarian aid workers, donors, peacekeeping soldiers, and those who work for organizations like Doctors Without Borders. Probably everyone has experienced a situation in which empathy made a possibly life-changing, if not a life-saving, difference. Through empathy, we also become increasingly sensitive to more subtle forms of oppression and masked forms of violence (as Steven Pinker aims to show in *The Better Angels of Our Nature: The Decline of Violence in History and its Causes*).

We also know that empathy needs to be learned and practiced. While biologically we are highly prepared for empathy, for it to flourish there needs to be a culture that supports it and provides models for its practices.[13] Should we then teach empathy? Empathy's most prominent advocates—including Barack Obama, who as a senator publicly voiced his concern about an "empathy deficit" and living in "in a culture that discourages empathy"—suggest that in an age with seemingly insurmountable rifts between groups sharing different worldviews (whether religious, ethnic/racial, nationalistic, or political) in addition to increasing disparities of wealth and poverty and the paradoxically isolating effects of social media (to diagnose only a few social ailments afflicting the contemporary world), empathy may perhaps be a positive counterforce.[14] People who hold this view lament the data that suggest that younger generations today have significantly less empathy than previous generations, while narcissism is on the rise.[15] While empathy loss may be a concern, I will suggest that we also have much to fear from empathy.

How can one object to empathy? To present the counterargument, we need to start with a more sober assumption: Like most other human abilities, empathy probably serves the empathizer first and foremost and not the target of empathy. This assumption is certainly no great insight but it inoculates one from the idea that "more empathy" alone is the best guard against egocentrism, narcissism, and self-interest. By coexperiencing, the empathetic person enriches first of all his or her own experiences and knowledge before possibly also helping the other person. In this sense, we could say that this book is devoted to the egotism of empathy and the aesthetic pleasure of the empathizer.

Defining Empathy

I define empathy as the coexperience of another's situation, though I do also consider and discuss research that leads to different definitions. The concept of coexperience has a wider (though in another sense a narrower) range of meaning than another common definition of empathy, namely that of emotion-sharing. I use emotion-sharing as shorthand for the idea that observing another's emotions activates in the observer the neural mechanisms responsible for the production of a similar emotion, with an awareness of the difference between self and other.[16] Emotion-sharing has emerged as a working definition of empathy in brain research over the past decades, especially as new technologies have made it possible to measure similar brain routines in observer and observed (as we will discuss in the next section). However, I argue that these empirical measurements alone do not define the phenomena adequately and that the emotion-sharing between observer and observed is an incomplete proxy for what we should call empathy. Further, the similarity of the brain routines of observer and observed are limited to a few strong emotions like fear, anxiety, and disgust, along with just a few social emotions, namely embarrassment, pride, and guilt. Empathy with complex or social emotions has so far escaped brain imaging. What does an empathetic observer do, for example, when she observes someone who is in love? Will she also fall in love? And with the same person?

In contrast to emotion-sharing, coexperience emphasizes the situation of the other. Of course, emotions are central to the situation of the other, since important situations are usually emotionally loaded. Bodily reactions are also of central importance since we experience situations in a bodily fashion. Coexperience also involves cognitive processes for which emotions are secondary, such as anticipation, consideration of circumstances, weighing of arguments, and strategic thinking. Coexperience means assuming the perspective of another in their specific situation and thus sharing their real or imagined reaction to the situation.[17]

In the context of empathy, coexperience is a psychological phenomenon in which one is mentally transported into the cognitive/emotional/bodily situation of another. The emphasis here is on the situation *of another*. There is a wide range of degrees of "transportation," from mentally sharing in another's actions, as if watching a film or reading a literary narrative, to an active (though imaginary) participation by the observer in another's decision-making, allowing the observer to experience the observed's conflicts and emotions.[18] Empathy thus means that one lives up to the demands of the other's situation in some or all of its emotional and cognitive aspects. The question of what the other should or could do—that is, decision-making—plays a large role for coexperience. Decision-making is another aspect not captured by emotion-sharing.

To be sure, coexperiencing another's situation does not mean literally being in the same situation. One core difference is that the observer is usually conscious on at least some level of the difference between themselves and the other. A second difference is that the observer does not actually have to react to the other's situation; they merely imagine how the other might react to the situation. Indeed, considering the future is a key component of empathy. A third difference is that the empathetic observer usually has greater clarity about the situation by virtue of being outside of the situation.

This last point deserves some explanation. When we coexperience another's situation or are transported into their unique circumstance, we tend to reduce that situation to a few key features. When we actually face a challenging circumstance of our own, however, we are usually more distracted by the range of possibilities and considerations, even when the situation is quite pressing and specific. Our feelings and impressions are rarely simple and unequivocal. Instead, we tend to have mixed emotions and ambiguous feelings. Even in important situations, we often do not know what we feel and think. (This is why one of the major tasks of counselors and therapists is to help us sort out our feelings and help us understand our reactions to crises.) If, however, we coexperience the situation of another, we reduce their situation to a few major features and can more easily abstract from direct perceptions. We also can perceive things the other cannot yet see but ought to: the tiger lurking in the bush!

In a word, the empathetic observer has an *aesthetic* advantage. The concept of aesthetics is used here in the sense of the German philosopher Alexander Gottlieb Baumgarten (1714–62), who introduced the term in the mid-eighteenth century to denote the clarity of sensual perception (of which beauty is just one possible version). In this sense, the situation of the other is *clear* to us, the observer, because we can simply perceive it. More specifically: we can imagine ourselves into the shoes of someone else precisely because their situation seems clear to us. Put in yet another way: we can empathize because we can aestheticize—clarify—the situation of the other. We owe this clarity about someone else's circumstance—a clarity we lack when facing it ourselves—to a *medium*: the other person, who becomes a character in a play we watch and experience. Emotionally intense situations, dramatic actions, and decisive moments are especially well suited for empathy since in these instances, the pressure on the other is exceptionally clear.

Coexperience is enhanced when the individual differences between the self and the other are collapsed: most people feel more or less the same way in these types of loaded situations.[19] To be sure, coexperiencing does not necessarily mean anonymizing the other or dispensing with their idiosyncrasies, oddities, and experiences. The empathetic observer may consider all the features of the other as elements of the situation being coexperienced. For example, witnessing a shy person or a stutterer speak in public can be especially intense, since we also coexperience their embarrassment or their pride at overcoming their difficulty.

Does this coexperience mean that we accurately experience or feel what the other is feeling? Of course not. The intensity of the coexperience correlates to the intensity of the situation and to the actual feelings of the other person. However, what someone feels in a situation and what the empathetic observer coexperiences can be quite distinct. We may imagine that a stutterer feels tremendous embarrassment but we cannot *know* what they feel or how they experience the situation. Both the observed and the observer bring their life stories to bear. In every situation, certain elements will resonate with each person differently depending on their past encounters, open wounds, traumas, and happy memories.

Perhaps, in this sense, the other is more or less made invisible in the act of coexperiencing, overshadowed by the observer's own empathetic experiencing. But the other does not disappear. The observed other can exert influence over our sympathies. We may feel close to them and want to become even more like them. Or we want to increase the difference or the gulf between us and them. These are some of the complications the book will develop.

This example may help us better understand this gulf. Someone trips loudly in a restaurant. Perhaps he bumps into a chair,
falls down, breaks some glass in the process, and cuts his hand on
the shards. This person, one can assume, feels a rush of emotions
and has various thoughts flashing through their brain simultaneously. If they feel embarrassed for having caused such a ruckus,
they may want to downplay the pain in their hand. Perhaps they
hardly feel the pain, given the slight shock and the shame. In that
case, they might be tempted to undo the commotion as quickly as
possible—they may try to clean up the broken glass with their
bleeding hand, only making matters worse. Or they might try to
divert attention from themself by blaming whoever put the chair
in their way, maybe needing to vent their emotional distress by
yelling at the waiter, even though that also only makes things
worse. Perhaps they are mostly concerned about their compan-
ion, an important business partner. Or they might be thinking that
they recently had several minor accidents of this kind and might
remember how their siblings used to tease them about their clum-
siness. If the accidents all happened recently, they may also think
that they might need to go to a doctor, given something they just
read about Parkinson's disease.

The empathetic observer, however, is less distracted and can easily imagine one or another solution to the situation. The observer
need only consider two aspects of the situation: the actual accident
and the embarrassment resulting from it. They might imagine the
pain from the broken glass, even if the observed has not felt it yet.
And they register the social scene with more clarity and can therefore more easily set aside the embarrassment.

The empathetic observer can from their vantage point resolve
the situation. The injury requires only the correct medical treatment; the social embarrassment dissipates with a quick return to

normalcy, perhaps with a joke. By contrast, the person who tripped is probably less goal-oriented because they are overstimulated by the events. The way forward is never as clear for the person in the midst of the situation.

As this example illustrates, coexperiencing comprises an emotional and cognitive reaction to the other's situation in all its perceivable facets. The observer assumes the position of the other (whether by means of involuntary transport or conscious effort), feels and reacts to the other's situation, and imagines a resolution or way out. The other's situation is *projected* (from the Latin, "to throw in front") in front of the observer, appearing both real and not real. In many cases, this leads to the observer and the observed having similar or overlapping feelings, especially when strong emotions—fear, for example—are part of the observed's situation. Even in such cases, however, there remains a gulf between both parties: in their perceptions, emotions, activation of past experiences, and plans for resolving the situation.

The empathetic observer does not always see a clear path forward. For example, when my close friend is in trouble, I may be just as desperate and therefore unable to react rationally. Not knowing what to do can intensify one's suffering; it can also block empathy, as we will see in chapter 2. Even so, the observer tends to have a more unimpeded, clearer view of the dilemma, however hopeless.

One corollary to this understanding of empathy is that coexperiencing depends on having life experiences that make it possible to read situations and anticipate future scenarios. Although children can do this, their experiential repertoires are more limited, which explains the importance of fairy tales and other stories in expanding them. At the same time, too much life experience can also limit empathy: When someone can always anticipate outcomes, he or she may be much less involved in another's plight.

Situations primed for empathy involve anticipating future trajectories; connected with this future-oriented identification is another aspect of empathy: the imagined self-interest of the other.[20] Coexperiencing another's situation means facing an open future, shaped but not fully determined by the situation. This future has some urgency—and we will discuss how only specific situations are well suited for empathy, namely those that present themselves as clear, relevant, and decisive—otherwise the circumstance is not interesting and unlikely to draw empathetic attention to itself. By assuming that the other possesses self-interest, the observer gains an idea of which future developments the other hopes for and which ones they fear. Actual self-interest is not straightforward, nor does it follow a single or universal standard, so this perspective is necessarily a projection on the part of the observer. Without this projection and sharing of self-interest, the observer can easily slide into a state of uninvolved apathy.

Now we are in the position to sharpen our definition of empathy as the coexperience of the other's situation. Coexperiencing means projecting oneself into another's situation emotionally and cognitively, typically with a clarity not available to the other. The phenomenon involves anticipating future developments by assuming at least minimal aspects of self-interest from the other's perspective. A direct simulation of the emotions of the other is not a necessary condition or a result of empathy (although it can be either of these). Critically, empathy does not necessarily lead to altruism, though it can and often does, and it is these exceptions and objections to the empathy-altruism hypothesis that are the focus of this book.

The Five Dark Sides of Empathy

The dangers arising from empathy are grouped into five trends, each of which corresponds to one of the book's five chapters.

1. Empathy can lead to self-loss, while also delivering aesthetic pleasure to the empathizer. Via Friedrich Nietzsche, I will discuss the definition and implications of "self" and "self-loss." Moving on from Nietzsche, I will embark on a discussion of the latest studies suggesting a decline in empathy and ask: Is that such a bad thing?

2. Empathy can lead to perceiving the social world in black and white, thinking in terms of friend and enemy. As I will suggest, conflicts may emerge not despite but because of empathy. Human beings tend to quickly take sides in conflicts and use empathy to glorify their chosen side while condemning and demonizing the other side. Providing a general architecture of empathy, the second chapter will propose a *three-person model* of empathy. I will suggest, using case studies (including a school experiment in Northern Ireland), that we do not act morally because we feel empathy; rather, we moralize to justify our quick and empathetic side-taking.

3. Many people associate empathy with altruism and helping behavior. However, I will suggest that this process is often flawed. A common pattern emerges: Instead of empathizing directly with a person in need, we identify with a benevolent helper figure (sometimes an imaginary one). While this self-identification may boost our own ego, it is at the expense of the person in need. Chapter 3 will discuss cases of humanitarian aid and Angela Merkel's refugee politics.

4. Empathy can be used to enjoy the pain of others. This *empathetic sadism* may not motivate so-called psychopaths (who probably feel less sadistic empathy than other people); instead it describes the emotional and intellectual enjoyment that most people feel in situations of altruistic punishment, watching tragedies, and such common events as embarrassment, bullying, and domination. I will consider in chapter 4 the degree to which sadists (including the sadistic aspects of our own personality) may actually wish for the discomfort of others in order to empathize with them. The chapter also includes a discussion of the familiar Hollywood trope I label the "empathetic rapist."

5. Empathy encompasses another morally dangerous variant I call *vampiristic empathy*, which occurs when a person expands their own life experiences by over-identifying with another person's experiences. Milder forms of vampiristic empathy can be found in helicopter parents, stage mothers, and fans; more dangerous strains are exhibited by stalkers.

In the conclusion, I will take up the question of whether empathy should be taught and promoted and, if so, how. My answer will be *yes*, though less because of moral reasons and more for the sake of increasing the complexity of our perception and awareness of social situations, which occurs when we consider and share the various cognitive and emotional perspectives of others.

There are, of course, other dark sides of empathy that I do not consider at length here. Empathy can run out. People in caregiving professions, like doctors, might suffer from this kind of burnout.[21] Empathy can also be easily manipulated (which I do address in discussing other aspects of empathy's negative aspects).[22] And empathy often falls short of the effects attributed to it—generating understanding of others, arriving at just verdicts, even promoting morality in general—though this is less an undesirable facet than it is an inaccurate conceptualization of what empathy actually is.

Every book overdetermines its subject. In the case of this book, that subject is the aesthetics of empathy, with an emphasis on clarity of vision. I will stress that for many empathizers, more important than the accuracy of their impressions, which they do not question, is the way the feelings of the other person become a fact to them, appearing transparent and perceptible in some way or another. This perceptual clarity is desired and valued. Painting the world in black and white makes such perception easier, as does the stage view afforded by vampiristic empathy. This book's emphasis on such aesthetic effects might be its bias, but it is one that I hope will provide new insights into our understanding of empathy—especially given the near absence of aesthetics in most other empathy research.

Four Approaches to Empathy Research

When I was a student, nothing fascinated me quite like the methodological premises of different disciplines. My assumption, part of the spirit of the nineties, was that once the methodology and technique were set, the results would take care of themselves. The methodological perspectives determine the results, I thought, and so they are the only things worth arguing about. Today, twenty years later, the opposite seems true to me: I am after the results. The methods, it seems to me more and more, march to the beat of the results and the findings. The same is true for some theoretical distinctions, which may make sense on their own terms but which seldom if ever come into play.

To argue about methods often seems to me like a waste of time. Only when you have results in hand can it be useful to look back at the methods used, to understand what conditions brought the results to light. And this is precisely the situation when it comes to empathy research. There are so many remarkable results and conclusions, and not all of them fit together. This makes a glance at methodology necessary, to understand how one arrives at this or that result.

The goal of the following overview is not to present the current state of the research but rather to describe which methodological approaches lead to which conceptions of empathy and what kind of results support those claims. There are four major approaches:

1. Evolutionary deliberation and speculation
2. Modeling of the minds of others (mind reading, theory of mind)

3. Brain research using empirical measurements (such as fMRI)
4. Phenomenological approaches.

Evolutionary Biology

Evolutionary biologists begin by asking what advantages or disadvantages a property or ability such as empathy offers a species when it comes to their chances of survival. Social cooperation and social intelligence emerge as central factors in the success of species and groups. Biologists ask what is necessary for cooperation within a group. Empathy is one candidate. From this perspective, the definition of empathy as intellectual or emotional driver for cooperation emerges.

A creature with empathy is in the position to perceive the needs of others and to react to them. Such abilities are especially important for raising the young of a species. Reciprocal altruism can also be inspired by empathy, when an individual helps another, and thereby increasing the chances of being helped in turn at another time. Such behavior can promote stability within the group. Empathy may allow for the expansion of groups beyond family clans and can contribute to the de-escalation of conflicts. This begins with individuals understanding the difference between genuinely aggressive behavior and an inadvertent offense. Animals capable of empathy, we would assume, should make a distinction between mere accidents and malicious acts. We can therefore assume that empathy and cooperation mutually reinforce one another, and may even depend on one another.

But there's a catch. The capacity for empathy appears to require a great deal of energy. For a brain to simulate, understand, or share the experiences of another, the entire "energy budget" of that brain's owner must be built around feeding an expanded brain. Such a path comes at a steep price. For humans, the disadvantages include birth prior to full brain development, slow development towards sexual maturity, physical weakness compared to animals of similar size, and higher caloric needs. The fact that humans and some other species have such large brains suggests that the advantages of empathy, paired with other benefits of a large brain, outweigh these costs.[23] Nevertheless, the possible advantages of empathy for cooperation are not as clear as we might hope. Cooperation is obviously possible for many species, which, even though they seem to have little or no empathy, nevertheless live in organized groups, coordinate in searching for food, raise their young collectively, and communicate important events through vocalization.

The particular questions that evolutionary biologists are asking determine how they define empathy, where to look for it, and what kind of experiments they can develop to measure it. From the evolutionary biologists' point of view, empathy requires both a cognitive act and a certain kind of prosocial behavior that need to go together. In order to show that empathy is advantageous for survival, they need to pin it down in concrete behavior. Primates who live in social groups are the preferred objects of study (but also dolphins, elephants, dogs, and, most recently, certain birds).[24] This means that some species—such as the orangutan, which is quite close to humans evolutionarily speaking but does not live in groups—have largely been ignored. And it is probably anthropocentrism that has caused evolutionary biologists to neglect species more removed from us, like octopuses. Of particular interest are dogs, which have been bred as human companions for more than ten thousand years.

One evolutionary aspect of empathy may be competition. An individual with a greater ability to empathize may have an advantage over those without that quality, though it is question-able whether this individual ability helps the species as a whole, since competitive conflicts produce both winners and losers. The net balance for a species might be neutral. Still, competition be-tween individual humans might produce an overall cognitive ad-vantage for the species.

Researchers are particularly interested in so-called altruistic be-havior. One famous experiment model puts two animals of the same species in adjacent cages. The animals are fed only when they both pull on a lever. Another typical experiment gives one ani-mal what it wants only when the other one pushes a button from which it gets nothing. The individual with the button could even have a disincentive to push the button if it is painful or requires work to do so. The question posed by such experiments is this: Which animals, under which conditions, are prepared to act, work, or suffer for another?[25] (Experiments have shown that rats, for ex-ample, will free other distressed rats from cages, even if this comes at a cost for themselves.[26])

The focus on action is a particularly interesting aspect of many the-ories based in evolutionary biology. Mental processes only become relevant when they are translated into observable behavior. This is an important measuring stick for someone who wants to teach people to be empathetic. Yet many aspects of cooperation are not easy to observe, either because reactions ensue after a delay or because inten-tions are difficult to determine. One difficulty for someone trying to learn about human empathy is that concepts like cooperation are not an explicit part of our direct self-awareness or experience. We rarely use empathy with so particular a purpose in mind that we could say, "I am using empathy now in order to better cooperate with others," or "By using empathy now I will expand our group." And the mental processes of other species are even more mysterious.[27]

There are many obvious limitations, difficulties, and challenges in using the approaches of evolutionary biology to understand human empathy. A great deal is uncertain here. Instead of the long processes of evolution, we see only its results in the species around us today. It is therefore unclear whether empathy (in one of its forms) is even an important factor in evolution or whether it may just be a side effect of other abilities—such as, for humans, linguistic communication. In this context, Michael Tomasello and his colleagues have proposed that pointing gestures are the precursors to linguistic communication.[28] In these gestures, two or more beings coordinate their attention onto an object. This is not empathy, and it requires no deep theory about the otherness of the other, but it does imply a consciousness about what the other has in view and therefore in their mind.

Theory of Mind

A specific line of inquiry has emerged from evolutionary biology, turning into its own branch of research under the term "theory of mind." Some primate researchers, beginning with Emil Menzel, David Premack, and Guy Woodruf, have asked whether primates can understand that others do not share their point of view—whether they can imagine what other primates think and feel.[29] Theory of mind—sometimes referred to as cognitive empathy—could be defined as the *understanding* of the other's emotions, thoughts, states, desires, and preferences.

Experiments to test this question make use of "false belief tasks" to determine whether the subjects understand that another does not have the same knowledge that they do. In a now-classic study, a group of children are shown a Smarties brand candy wrapper containing not Smarties candies but pencils. When a new child enters the group, the other children are then asked what the new arrival thinks will be in the package. They succeed not by applying what they know but by considering what the new arrival does not know and correctly answering, "Smarties."[30] Most children can do this at around four years of age, but other experiments, less reliant on language, suggest that children possess a theory of mind much earlier.[31] Chimpanzees also seem capable of this task, based on the results of other experiments in competitive situations, though the evidence remains disputed.[32]

These experiments reveal an understanding that specific knowledge is discrete and not shared by all. This difference of knowledge or belief between two individuals concerns a single item, rather than a general understanding of their consciousness or thinking. Still, theory of mind research has produced major insights, raising a number of provocative questions: Does the fundamental differentiation of self and other find expression in theory of mind? Does theory of mind depend on the capacity to take on another's perspectives and thus to possess a mobile consciousness? If so, is there a mechanism for sharing and simulating experiences that make this possible? (This is usually called *simulation theory.*) Or is theory of mind instead based on a collective knowledge of how people typically behave and feel, upon which an individual draws under certain situations? (This approach is often called *theory theory* or "folk psychology."[33]) Or do we assemble mental files into which we assign knowledge to others? To what extent is past experience a requirement for recognizing when others are in similar situations?

This research has led to rich discussions within several disciplines over the past decades, in which different strategies for solving the theory of mind problems have been proposed, such as those based on simulation or on so-called common sense.

Of particular interest in such cases are people with autism, who often fail at "false belief tasks," or manage them only later in life than others. A now-outdated hypothesis suggested that people with autism have trouble simulating and cannot register others as independent beings.[34] (This is known as "broken mirror" theory.[35]) Still, people with autism can develop a theory of mind eventually, perhaps by accumulating enough personal experiences and skills of deduction to do so.[36]

Theory of mind is ultimately about correctly attributing knowledge and mental states to others; sharing emotions is either absent or incidental. Theory of mind is therefore more clearly delineated than other forms of empathy and, through experiments like "false belief tasks," empirically testable. This focus on testability sidesteps the principal questions about when someone begins to understand the other as an independent being with their own mental processes and what this means.

What can be tested—whether someone knows that others do not have the same knowledge as they do—becomes the base definition. This model is then expanded by analogy to include conditions, intentions, imaginations, preferences, wishes, and similar mental states. Whoever possesses a theory of mind can make justified claims about others, such as "Person A thinks x about person B or object C" or "Person A thinks or feels y in this situation and therefore will probably not do z." The provability of such concrete statements (which, however well justified, can be true or false) is part of the typical conception of theory of mind, distorting our view of the more complex question of what it means to have a consciousness at all or to discover one in someone else.

A much-read but contested study has shown that reading works of "high literature" improves the capacity for a theory of mind immediately afterwards in members of the test group. (The control group read popular bestsellers.)[37] The production of a theory of mind seems to be an intellectual process that proceeds on its own, without emotional judgments. People with a theory of mind can understand others more accurately, but this does not lead them to be more prosocial or morally good. As an intellectual process, theory of mind can be applied to help or to better compete with others.[38] But sociopaths, psychopaths, and bullies also score high on theory of mind tests.[39] Developing a theory of mind does not inculcate a sense of pleasure, nor does it result in a bond between two people. There is also no risk involved: One simply learns something about someone else.

Philosophers and information scientists turn to theory of mind because this form of *intellectual empathy* expresses itself in the ability to ground claims and assumptions. In this regard, theory of mind is an important element in computer learning, in the development of artificial intelligence, and in processes involving moral decisions.[40]

Brain Imaging

In recent years, we have seen huge leaps in our ability to measure brain activity. Imaging techniques have improved especially drastically. MRI and fMRI technologies makes it possible to measure the oxygen levels in the blood and to localize blood flow to particular regions of the brain. The leading assumption is that the regions with more and more oxygenated blood are active and being put to use in some process. These images show that while individuals have marked differences in their brain functions, they tend to follow similar patterns during similar actions. (In typical trials, all the subjects are given the same stimulus, so that their reactions can be measured against one another, as can those of different population groups.) From this work, the definition of empathy as the sharing of emotion or affect emerges as introduced above.[41]

MRI and fMRI's have the advantage of measuring brain activity in real time but they do so in unnatural circumstances, requiring subjects to keep perfectly still in a narrow scanning tube while loud, whirring machinery generates an electromagnetic field around them. (Participants in empathy studies usually receive acoustic signals or video clips; sometimes a story is read aloud, a readable text is projected before them, or a video sequence is played. In any case, there is no way to be lost in the action and one is unavoidably conscious of the artificial apparatus of the experiment itself.)

We can now measure whether similar cranial routines are activated in different individuals when, for example, "false belief tasks" are solved. While this does indeed appear to be the case, there is no consensus so far as to whether such routines are specific to a theory of mind or if they are also applied in other thought processes.[42]

A working hypothesis has emerged that an empathetic brain carries out similar neural routines to those of the brain of the person being observed. This is true for actions as well as for emotions and feelings such as pain.[43] When a person being observed shows a particular emotion, we anticipate that the parts of the observer's brain associated with this emotion will also be activated. This is called *sharing of the affect*. More generally speaking, this hypothesis assumes that brain activity during an action in one individual is similar during the observation of that action by another. This model is variously called *perception action coupling, perception action model,* or *common coding theory*.[44] (Precursors of this idea, although without empirical evidence, can be found in the work of Eduard Beneke, Hermann Lotze, and William James.)

Treating action and observation similarly has an economic advantage in brain architecture, since it avoids redundant mechanisms. One of the predictions of this model is that a person who lacks the ability to feel a basic emotion is likewise unable to perceive this emotion in others. This presumption has been confirmed with regard to some emotions, such as disgust and fear, but not in all cases.[45] Situations in which someone performs an activity while observing someone else performing the same activity present interesting possibilities for further research.

(A note on *mirror neurons:* When these neurons were discovered in 1993 in macaque monkeys, there was great hope that a neural basis for empathy had been found. In these monkeys, certain matching brain routines seem to be triggered by specific neurons in the brain when they observe goal-oriented hand movement. But researchers have become appreciably more skeptical since then.[46] The execution of complete routines of action and observation as predicted by the perception action coupling model seems more promising to many researchers now, and the role mirror neurons could play in that process, perhaps as a catalyst, is unclear.)

The use of fMRI imaging has led to one fascinating insight concerning empathy and the difference between the sexes. Tania Singer and her colleagues have registered highly similar reactions among men and women in virtually all situations—except in relation to punishment. When someone innocent was punished, men and women reacted equally empathetically, observable through activation of the pain center. But when the one being punished had committed some violation (playing unfairly at a game,) the brains of female subjects still consistently showed an empathetic (that is, pain-activated) response, although a weaker one than at the punishment of an innocent person. Men, on the other hand, tended to show appreciably less empathetic brain activity, often close to none; instead, this punishment activated regions of the brain associated with satisfaction and reward.[47] This specific difference is more remarkable because in no other case has so fundamental a difference between men and women in empathy-relevant situations been found.

What may be true about theory of mind–based concepts of empathy is also true for brain imaging: its definition of empathy follows its testing methodology. Researchers both use in their studies and derive from those studies a definition of empathy that centers on the similarity in brain activity between the one acting (or feeling) and the empathetic observer: empathy comprises simulating or sharing the brain activity of the observed party.

We can test the limits of the definition of empathy as emotion-sharing. As we already discussed, this form of emotion-sharing does probably not include empathy for another's decision-making, since the weighing of the other's decisions is not so much an immediate affect, even though it involves emotions. The intellectual process of understanding another's thoughts or feelings also does not meet this definition of empathy. Accordingly, people who routinely experience the situations of others, such as doctors and caregivers, as well as more rationally calculating people, would according to this definition be less apt to feel empathy. Also, people on the autism spectrum, who acquire an understanding of others more through the collection of experience, do not show empathy according to this definition but rather exhibit theory of mind. Empathy understood in this way also does not include situations where someone is stoic about their suffering; instead, the observer feels something that might be more typical or appropriate to the situation. Situations in which the observed person sees their own situation differently than the observer are likewise not included in this definition but are rather considered as effects of imagination and sympathy. This definition makes a clear distinction between sympathy and empathy, with sympathy being an affective reaction to the benefit of someone in need: "I feel for you but not like you." To be sure, according to this model sympathy can, but does not have to, emerge from empathy.[48]

Social and other more complex feelings pose a problem for such definitions derived from brain activity measurement. If you empathize with someone who is in love, as we wondered before, do you also need to love the same person? These definitions also allow many more problematic cases to be included under empathy, such as emotional infection, swarm behavior, and similar involuntary reactions. Additionally, these definitions suggest that life-like, ultra-realistic films, although fictional, will arouse hyperempathetic responses in the viewer because so much is being seen and experienced onscreen, even if they show little empathy and sympathy in real life. In fact, film seems to be the prime medium of this empathetic response; but how much of this is due to how these studies are conducted—by having participants watch films in a scanner while being immobilized?

Brain-imaging researchers tend to use this strict (but consistent) definition of empathy— the sharing of feelings—within a rather elastic or heuristic broader conception of empathy, in order to avoid unwanted exclusions or other conclusions. Or they speak of two empathy systems in order to integrate the phenomenon of theory of mind.[49]

Brain research has yielded astonishing results. This is why it is so important to be clear about its limits. We already mentioned the need for the test subject to be immobilized in the MRI machine. And because of this, test results apply to a laboratory setting, not to everyday life. The majority of cases explored in this book could therefore not be verified by brain scans at this point.

Furthermore, even the most precise scanners can currently only reveal approximate pictures. For a long time, it was assumed that the brain had just over eighty functionally distinct regions. This classification underlies all the studies discussed here. But in July 2016, a new and improved map of the brain was proposed, which posits 180 functionally differentiated regions.[50] It is clear that some prior results were thus rendered obsolete, since many adjacent areas have simply been lumped together. Among the areas most relevant for this book is the rediscovered region 55b, which is especially activated when people hear narrative stories.

Even with improved maps and equipment, these tests only measure a general blood flow pattern, and if we think about the speed of the flow and diversity of thoughts, another limitation becomes clear. It is unlikely that we will ever be able to look at images of brain activity and determine what someone is thinking or experiencing. Still, general patterns of feeling and activity will become even more clearly discernible. To put it simply, we are able to tell whether the person in the scanner is reading high literature or something less demanding, and whether it is suspenseful or not.[51] But we will probably never know the contents of the story they are reading and what they think about it through such technology.

Another inherent limitation of these findings is the incongruence between brain reactions and actual behavior. For example, consider the study by Tania Singer and her colleagues mentioned above, which showed (like most others) largely similar empathetic brain activity between men and women. In spite of these neural similarities, there are presumably considerable differences in how men and women express empathy. Various cultural influences may have a bearing on this. We might explore whether women employ the vocabulary and facial gestures of empathy more often than men, since most western cultures tend to code empathy as feminine. However, there may be no significant difference when unobtrusive observations are used; or perhaps some men act more empathetically than some women, but only when they think they are not being observed.[52] An fMRI image cannot give us any insight here.

Based on the findings of brain research, some psychologists, such as Daniel Batson, have focused less on empathy itself than on cases when empathetic concern leads to actual altruistic behavior. Such an approach sees empathy as a reaction to the distress of someone else and encompasses compassionate behavior, bringing us to another methodological approach for understanding empathy.

Phenomenology

The fourth approach to empathy research is also the oldest. I will call it the phenomenological method. Phenomenological investigations are based on distinctions that can be observed by humans.[53] The central questions for a phenomenological approach to empathy are when, how, and under what circumstances someone shares the experience of another being. Phenomenological approaches are therefore well suited to individual cases (and case studies) in which empathy plays a role. The definition of empathy derived from this approach is the one I gave above: coexperiencing the situation of another.

In practice, this means that the catalyst of empathy is understood as a component of the empathy process. Phenomenological reflection does not stop at the markers and signs of empathy, nor at brain routines; rather, it is concerned with the behaviors and situations that begin without empathy but soon lead to the "activation" of empathy, which is then integrated into other processes. In other words, this approach tends to be concerned with the triggers and the expressions of empathy, and it is influenced by older investigations into such concepts as pity and what the Germans called *Einfühlung* (literally "in-feeling," though commonly translated as "empathy"). Pity, for instance, suggests both an empathetic response and its triggers, though the list of possible empathy triggers or catalysts goes beyond human pain and suffering.

This book will discuss numerous examples of such triggers or catalysts of empathy, including spontaneous side-taking in conflicts, social tensions, or competitions. (Central to this discussion is the three-part architecture of empathy I present in chapter 2.) In general, then, phenomenologists observe the course of the conditions and processes that culminate in empathy and pursue the subsequent forms of behavior. Put differently, phenomenological approaches consider the larger contexts of empathy.

The shared experience of another's situation begins the moment we participate in someone else's fate, no matter how large or small. This participation includes an emotional reaction to the other's situation and the calculation (or even the affective anticipation) of what the other will experience next. This is more than simply sharing another's feelings and involves anticipating their future. Frans de Waal, a primatologist and pioneer of empathy research, has defined empathy (although without the future-oriented component) as "feeling one with another's state" and "shar[ing] in the other's state of mind via bodily communication."[54]

One complication lies in the different perspectives that an observer can assume. We can share the experience of another's situation without sharing their perspective; for example, by imagining being a friend of the person in a challenging situation. In theory, phenomenological research can provide the tools to observe this difference in perspective, but it remains consistently difficult to pin down such fine distinctions with these methods. The observer can, of course, quickly change their point of view. Nevertheless, it bears emphasizing that generally only one perspective is possible at a time. This insight is not unique to the phenomenological approach. Theory of mind research also points in this direction. The phenomenological method does, however, contain the observation that taking on a perspective contains a certain risk: *self-loss* (which I will consider in the next chapter).

The phenomenological method reaches its limits in the subjective nature of its observation. Such observations are not directly grounded in rigorous empiricism, though the results can be tested; but because it offers no claims about neural processes, methods of verification are limited. Without borrowing data from other methods, the phenomenological approach can uncover intersubjective patterns in empathy triggers, their processes, and their content; these patterns are informed by numerous factors, including the position of the observer and the cultural context. The advantages of this method, however, are not insubstantial and include closeness to the individual's experience and the possibility of connecting empathy to other practices.

This brief overview should be sufficient for showing the different methodological approaches towards empathy and the definitions and research aims that emerge from each. It is possible to distinguish more conceptions of empathy, as Daniel Batson does.[55] I have already hinted at some of the possible prerequisites for empathy. Each research approach takes different prerequisites into consideration, such as the separation of the self and the other, the recognition of feelings in others, self-awareness, or sympathy.[56] (There is an ongoing controversy about whether self-control is a specific precondition for empathy or just a general precondition for the working of the mind.[57])

Methodological approach	Evolutionary biology, behavioral sciences	Theory of mind, philosophy	Brain research and imaging	Phenomenology
Prerequisites for empathy	Emotional infection; involuntary emotional transference; coordination and groups	Separation of self from other; processes of understanding; self-awareness	Simulations; strong emotions; emotional infection; imitation of body language	Active intuiting into position of others; sympathy; transportation into narrative and fictional worlds; involuntary participation
Definition of empathy	Cognitive acts leading to cooperation (altruism) or competition	Theory of mind, understanding the emotions, beliefs, and mental states of others	Similarity of brain activities between observer and observed	Coexperience of the situation of others
Relationship to emotion	Reaction to emotions	Understanding emotions	Copying, sharing, or simulating emotions	Sharing the experience that leads to emotions
What empathy leads to	Prosocial behaviors (helping, cooperation)	A more precise understanding of others	Neural basis for intersubjectivity	Cultural basis for intersubjectivity
What do researchers look at? (Examples)	Forms of cooperation, communication, and altruism by primates	Autism; human development; accurate intersubjective understanding	Patterns for some emotions; difference between the genders	The relationship between aesthetic form and empathy (catharsis, anagnorosis)

Returning to my childhood experience in the theatre, when I suddenly, involuntarily, and traumatically coexperienced the situation of the actors on stage: while none of the four approaches laid out here would categorize my experience as empathetic, each would attribute to it aspects of "preempathy." Evolutionary biology and brain science could speak of an emotional transfer of stress and tension. There is no developed theory of mind at work here (for then I would have understood how the situation looked for the actors), but rather a simulation of the situation of the other, without knowledge of their knowledge. Phenomenologically speaking, I was stepping into the position of another, while ignoring the professional training of the other, and so misreading the situation.[58]

These four approaches can be neatly separated, methodologically, as can their various (mostly implicit) definitions of empathy. But that does not mean that evolutionary biologists, philosophers, psychologists, teachers, brain scientists, and phenomenologists abide by these distinctions. Frans de Waal, as we saw, offers a more or less phenomenological definition that was based on the findings of evolutionary biology, behavioral science, and brain research. This book, too, will gather the findings and conclusions of each field, even when they reach beyond the lessons of phenomenology.

1

Self-Loss

Empathy, the Enemy of the Self (Nietzsche,
Beyond Good and Evil)

In August 1973, Jan-Erik Olsson, a parolee, entered a bank with a gun. He took four hostages, one man and three women, and arranged to have an accomplice brought into the bank. Together, the two men held the hostages captive for more than five days. When they were released, the hostages would testify in support of their captors and one of the hostages entered into a long-term romantic relationship with the accomplice. The hostages saw the world through the eyes of the hostage-takers and adopted their imagined self-interest—a classic scenario of empathy. The place was Stockholm and the phenomenon became known as Stockholm syndrome (also known today as Survival Identification Syndrome or Hostage Identification Syndrome).

What is especially conspicuous about Stockholm syndrome is that the empathetic or identificatory relationship of the hostage to the hostage-taker can outlast the hostage situation. The hostages take on the perspective of the hostage-takers in such a committed way that they fear and fight the police, that they continue to support the hostage-takers after their defeat, and that they testify for the hostage-takers in the court proceedings (all of this was the case in 1973). In the process, the hostages suffer a loss of self.

Stockholm syndrome and its relationship to empathy will be treated in more detail below; I will start our discussion by considering how empathy itself can lead to a loss of self. What qualifies as a "self" that one could actually lose or leave behind when one slips into someone else's shoes? This question is less an empirical question than a conceptual one, relating to how we define a term such as the "self"—a question that leads us back to the nineteenth century and the German philosopher Friedrich Nietzsche, whose insights I find helpful in clarifying the notion of the "self" in the context of "self-loss."

Nietzsche may have come to his questioning of the self and of empathy via Schopenhauer. Schopenhauer, who arrived at empathy through the concept of compassion, valued empathy more than almost any other thinker. Unlike almost every thinker of recent centuries, especially the German idealists, he did not ascribe any systematic meaning to the self or to individual consciousness, arguing that the emotionally and intellectually isolated self is nothing more than vain illusion. Schopenhauer's goal was to break down the "wall between You and Me" with compassion.[1] But at the same time, he emphasized that such a breakdown could only last a short time in concrete actions of empathy or compassion. For Schopenhauer, the illusion of the self is the opposite of empathy. (The architecture of his thought also allows for the possibility that it is the illusion of the self—with all its interests and experiences, such as envy—that represents a barrier or filter that controls and subjugates empathy. We will discuss such filter or blockers in chapter 2.)

We will see that for Nietzsche, too, the self is not to be taken for granted and that for him it is also a kind of illusion. Nietzsche also positions the self and compassion as being in opposition; unlike Schopenhauer, however, Nietzsche saw compassion as something dangerous.

Nietzsche's thinking about self-loss can be found in paragraph 207 of *Beyond Good and Evil*. He does not use the term "compassion" explicitly; nor does he use the German aesthetic notion of *Einfühlung* that in its 1909 translation into English resulted in the neologism "empathy." Nevertheless, the discussion is about precisely the question of intellectual and compassionate understanding of other people and sharing the feelings of others. The objective man, whom Nietzsche has in mind here, is characterized by his perceptive abilities, the central form of which is what we would today call empathy. The previous paragraph (206) ends by asking what "compassion" is (the German word *Mitleid* mirrors the Latin root of "com-passion" or "suffering with") and what it means to understand the other.

I would like to quote the passage in its entirety before analyzing it in detail:

> However gratefully we may welcome an *objective* spirit—and is there anyone who has never been mortally sick of everything subjective and of his accursed ipissimosity [self-referentiality]—in the end we also have to learn caution against our gratitude and put a halt to the exaggerated manner in which the "unselfing" and depersonalization of the spirit is being celebrated nowadays as if it were the goal itself and redemption and transfiguration. This is particularly characteristic of the pessimist's school, which also has good reasons for according the highest honors to "disinterested knowledge."
>
> The objective person who no longer curses and scolds like the pessimist, the *ideal* scholar in whom the scientific instinct, after thousands of total and semi-failures, for once blossoms and blooms to the end, is certainly one of the most precious instruments there

are; but he belongs in the hand of one more powerful. He is only an instrument; let us say, he is a *mirror*—he is no "end in himself." The objective man is indeed a mirror: he is accustomed to submit before whatever wants to be known, without any other pleasure than that found in knowing and "mirroring;" he waits until something comes, and then spreads himself out tenderly lest light footsteps and the quick passage of spiritlike beings should be lost on his plane and skin.

Whatever still remains in him of a "person" strikes him as accidental, often arbitrary, still more often disturbing: to such an extent has he become a passageway and reflection of strange forms and events even to himself. He recollects "himself" only with an effort and often mistakenly; he easily confuses himself with others, he errs about his own needs and is in this respect alone unsubtle and slovenly. Perhaps his health torments him, or the pettiness and cramped atmosphere of his wife and friend, or the lack of companions and company—yes, he forces himself to reflect on his torments—in vain. Already his thoughts roam—to a *more general case*, and tomorrow he knows no more than he did yesterday how he might be helped. He has lost any seriousness for himself, also time: he is cheerful, *not* for lack of distress, but for lack of fingers and handles for *his* need. His habit of meeting every thing and experience half-way, the sunny and impartial hospitality with which he accepts everything that come his way, his type of unscrupulous benevolence, of dangerous unconcern about Yes and No—alas, there are cases enough in which he has to pay for these virtues! And as a human being he becomes all to easily the *caput mortuum* of these virtues.

If love and hatred are wanted from him—I mean love and hatred as God, woman, and animal understand them—he will do what he can and give what he can. But one should not be surprised if it is not much—if just here he proves inauthentic, fragile, questionable, and worm-eaten. His love is forced, his hatred artificial and rather *un tour de force*, a little vanity and exaggeration. After all, he is genuine only insofar as he may be objective: only in his cheerful "totalism" he is still "nature" and "natural." His mirror soul, eternally smoothing itself out, no longer knows how to affirm or negate; he does not command, neither does he destroy. "*Je ne méprise presque rien*," he says with Leibniz: one should not overlook and underestimate that *presque*.

Neither is he a model man; he does not go before anyone, nor behind; altogether he places himself too far apart to have any reason to take sides for good or evil. When confusing him for so long with the philosopher, with the Caesarian cultivator and cultural dynamo, one accorded him far too high honors and overlooks his most essential characteristics: he is an instrument, something of a slave though certainly the most sublime type of slave, but in himself nothing—*presque rien!* The objective man is an instrument, a precious, easily injured and clouded instrument for measuring and, as an arrangement of mirrors, an artistic triumph that deserves care and honor; but he is no goal, no conclusion and sunrise, no complementary man in whom the *rest* of existence is justified, no termination—and still less a beginning, a begetting and first cause, nothing tough, powerful, self-reliant that wants to be master—rather only a delicate, carefully dusted, fine, mobile pot for forms that still has to wait for some content and substance in order to "shape" itself accordingly—for the most part, a man without substance and content, a "selfless" man. Consequently, also nothing for women, *in parenthesi.*—[2]

Nietzsche brings the capacity for objective perception into direct relationship with a particular kind of (metaphorical) preparation: a thinning out of the person:

> ". . . and *then spreads himself out* tenderly lest light footsteps and the quick passage of spiritlike beings should be lost on his plane and skin."
> "His mirror soul, eternally smoothing itself out . . ."
> "The objective man is indeed a mirror . . ."

This thinning out is the precondition for the objective person—that is, the perceiving person—to receive the imprint of the other.

In order to be receptive, the person must cast off, or flatten out, their own scabs and bumps:

> ". . . lest light footsteps and the quick passage of spiritlike beings should be lost on his plane and skin."
> "Whatever still remains in him of a 'person' strikes him as accidental, often arbitrary, still more often disturbing . . ."
> "[He is] only a delicate, carefully dusted, fine, mobile pot for forms that still has to wait for some content and substance in order to 'shape' itself accordingly."

These metaphors imply that this perceptual capacity influences a person's identity at a fundamental level. According to these passages, it is *not* true that a person uses only a sensory-cognitive apparatus to perceive things and people, and then shares this information with other mental systems. The implication is rather that one must prepare one's *entire self* for the act of perceiving and recognizing. To be an objective person, one has to be fundamentally "receptive." That does not mean that we possess something called a "perceptive self" or a "receptive self." For Nietzsche that would be an oxymoron, a nonentity. There is no such thing as a "receptive self" in Nietzsche's view since selfhood and reception exclude each other, as we will see.

The fundamental property of the objective person is perception. Nietzsche seems to be as unyielding as ever on this point. You can only perceive and recognize if it is your primary objective to do so. At the very least, a person cannot be simultaneously perceptive and assertive. This impossibility—to both perceive and to assert oneself simultaneously—cannot be resolved simply by doing them one at a time—that is, by observing and perceiving others at one moment, and articulating and expressing oneself at another. Rather, the ability to perceive rules out the possibility of being assertive at any point. The ability to perceive others—the capacity for sympathy and empathy—speaks to the structure of the person as a whole.

The ability to perceive, to have empathy, has its price. Nietzsche counts the following among its costs:

> His love is forced, his hatred artificial and rather *un tour de force*, a little vanity and exaggeration. After all, he is genuine only insofar as he may be objective: only in his cheerful "totalism" he is still "nature" and "natural." His mirror soul, eternally smoothing itself out, no longer knows how to affirm or negate; he does not command, neither does he destroy. . . . Neither is he a model man; he does not go before anyone, nor behind; altogether he places himself too far apart to have any reason to take sides for good or evil.

The objective-perceptive-empathetic person loses their capacity to take a stand of their own, to judge and evaluate the actions of the other. The perceptive person is passive. This passivity consists of more than just not acting. It is rather a passivity that proceeds from observation and perception. The person who perceives, according to Nietzsche, cannot judge. To give a judgment means to take a position and show strength. And this is just what is unavailable to the objective person. The objective-perceptive-empathetic person cannot judge, show strength, lead, act, or show passions.

Nietzsche's argument is not that empathy leads to a narrowed range of vision, such that one only feels empathy with people similar to oneself, or in the sense of Paul Bloom's narrowing of attention or spotlight vision.[3] Rather, the very *habitus* of receptivity makes it impossible for people to take a stand for themselves. And without this ability, there is no such thing as the self. The identity of the objective person is an absence of identity. They are (almost) nothing, leave no trace, have no self. Indeed, the perceptive-objective-empathetic person, because they have no identity or no self, cannot themself become an object of observation or of empathy.[4]

Empathy, Nietzsche suggests, requires that one be selfless and wait for an external stimulus. Here and at other points, he insinuates a dualism between the self and the selflessness of the empathetic person. Some readers of Nietzsche will hear echoes of other dualisms throughout his work, such as between active and passive, masculine and feminine, the blond beast and the crippled weakling. But rather than yielding to the temptation to try to nail down such possible parallels, let us stay focused on this passage from *Beyond Good and Evil*.

Self-loss is further developed in paragraph 207:

> "The 'unselfing' and depersonalization of the spirit"
> "Whatever still remains in him of a 'person'"
> "He recollects 'himself' only with an effort and often mistakenly;
>   he easily confuses himself with others, he errs about his own
>   needs . . . He has lost any seriousness for himself"
> "The objective man is . . . a 'selfless' man."

What exactly is this thing called the "self" that the person with empathy casts off or else never had in the first place?

According to this paragraph, selfhood expresses and asserts itself in its actions. The list of such actions includes love, hate, agreement, rejection, judgment, and domination. The emphasis is therefore not on physical actions but rather on those that contain a decision and a choice: it is about predilections (saying yes and no), judgments (making decisions between good and evil) and emotions (expressing love and hate). Such a decision requires no "free will" (this is an important point for Nietzsche in the second part of *Beyond Good and Evil*). Instead, every decision draws a line between before and after: After the decision is made, the world of facts has changed. It implicates another person and determines how one relates to that person. To act in Nietzsche's sense (again, according to paragraph 207) means to be a ruler, decider, possibly a tyrant over someone else, and perhaps to be caught up in passions. Such actions therefore have nothing to do with the free consideration of different possibilities. (But we do not yet know whether the action creates the self or the action merely expresses the self, or some third option.)

A person acting in such a way would have a strong identity, a self. If such a person were to observe others, following Nietzsche's argument, they could only praise or condemn, love or hate them. This would be no empathy or understanding but some form of overpowering the other. Empathy is impossible for a *self* (someone acting "as a self" or "like a self") because that self would have to express itself by judging, ruling, dominating, being passionate. Hence, the self would dominate others and therefore feel no empathy. Empathy keeps the self from being a self.

Nietzsche situates the empathetic or objective person at the opposite end of the spectrum from the self. The empathetic person must exercise self-control in not judging or forming any feelings of their own so that they may understand, emotionally and rationally, the other. The self, on the other hand, carries out strong, impulsive actions, making the decisions that the objective person cannot, and is therefore able (perhaps even compelled) to love, to hate, to judge, to rule.

It would seem that the perceptive-objective-empathetic person tends to feel their way into the very situations that they cannot manage themself: the strong actions that bestow on others their self. The selfless, objective person feels empathy for that which they must give up in order to be able to feel empathy: a strong self.

This means that unless one is thinned out, without a loss of self, there can be no perception of the other's self.

From these observations, we can formulate our first thesis about Nietzsche's argument on empathy: *A person becomes capable of empathy when they cast off or lose their self. Empathy in turn allows them to recognize a strong self in others. The strong self, observed with empathetic precision, has what the empathizer lacks: a self. There may be a direct causal relationship here: the objective, empathizing person relinquishes the idea of their own self in order to discover (or rediscover) a self in others. According to Nietzsche, one has empathy with the other as a self.*

This last formulation bears repeating: the "other as a self." We have not yet really determined whether the decider (or ruler or passionate individual) actually has a self. We have simply claimed it, based on Nietzsche's paragraph 207. From the perspective of the empathizer, it does, however, seem likely. It is the other, the observed other, who loves, hates, rules, and acts. Can we not assume that anyone who acts in this way, who has properties marking them as a strong, natural, or unmediated self, is a being with a strong identity?

But Nietzsche gives us reason to call into question the strong identity of the observed self. The first sign of doubt stems from the fact that the observed other as a being is secondary to their observed behavior. It is not the person who loves, hates, and rules but rather the acts of loving, hating, and ruling that the objective person observes. It might just be a habit of assuming that in these actions a strong self is expressing themselves. It could be that the agent is secondary to the act: The agent might just be a grammatical convention to make the act intelligible. When we hear of decisive actions or feelings, we tend to assume that a strong self is making these decisions with some kind of will or somehow feels these emotions. Nietzsche, however, draws attention to a different possibility, namely that strong emotions lead to decisions, not because of the mastery of a self but simply because emotions in themselves are strong declarations and thus are decisive.

The assumption of a firm identity and the existence of the other as a self is further complicated by a closer look at the metaphor of "thinning out." Nietzsche appears to have a technical apparatus in mind here. It is no coincidence that his formulations recall a camera: "He waits until something comes, and then spreads himself out tenderly lest light footsteps and the quick passage of spiritlike beings should be lost on his plane and skin." The short text makes frequent use of optical metaphors. Mirrors are mentioned four times. The German word for the silver halide surface used in nineteenth century photography is *Silberspiegel*, or "silver mirror." The mirror is tightly bound to the metaphor of thinning out, which suggests that the objective-receptive person is like a photosensitive slide of glass treated with dried gelatin and a silver alloy, giving it the appearance of a mirror.[5]

These metaphors of film and camera do more than reveal the essence of the objective person as purely reactive, receptive, and protean. They describe what the empathetic person is doing. This person with camera-like qualities is drawn towards certain behaviors: loving, hating, ruling. But a strong self is not inherent to such actions. The actor might only *appear* as if they were a strong force of nature and would seem to the observer to be a hero of Caesar-like proportions. The objective person is therefore not simply a receptive film cell that captures impressions neutrally, but rather a surface like the film screen onto which the other is projected as a heroic being, as a self (that exists only in the eyes of the observer). The achievement of objective observation—of empathy—is therefore to operate as a projection apparatus that glorifies the other and elevates them to the status of a self.

The counterpoint to the objective person is the hero, the force of nature, the alpha-animal: one who rules, loves, and hates but does not exist as a self. At the very least, there is no way of knowing because this personality can only become a self through empathetic observation. Now we can articulate a second thesis of Nietzsche's conception of empathy: *Empathy brings about a self-effect: the empathetic person bestows a self on the observed other. The self is transplanted from the empathetic observer to the observed object. While the observed strong person (the one who loves, hates, judges) may not have a self, whatever that may be, they appear to the observer as though they did. The price of empathy is the loss of the self; its reward is the (re)discovery of the self in the other. The self only exists from an external perspective. It is a projection by an observer.*

In Nietzsche's worldview, there are no free selves and strong identities. Rather, there are certain actions that conjure up *the idea* of a self. For the external observer, because they have no interior view of the acting person, these actions constitute something strange and unfamiliar. Where they may have doubts about themself, they see strong positions taken by others. They are incapable of seeing themself *as a self* and are correspondingly more strongly drawn to the actions that seem like expressions of strength. The objective, selfless, empathetic person and the projection of a strong self depend on one another.

Paragraph 207 presents actions (loving, hating, judging) only from the perspective of the observer. In fact, all the work in this section is done by the empathetic observer, who thins themself out, and in so doing loses their self (if they had one in the first place). In this way, they become receptive and able to recognize and project onto others the self that they are lacking.

Self-Observation and the Feminine in Nietzsche

Before we continue with the discussion, we should briefly unfold two aspects of paragraph 207 that would otherwise get lost. I will address the second, Nietzsche's analysis of women and the feminine, below; first, I want to examine the impossibility, according to Nietzsche, of self-observation.

The objective person, Nietzsche writes, "recollects 'himself' only with an effort and often mistakenly; he easily confuses himself with others, he errs about his own needs." We may ask ourselves why his excellent sensory apparatus does not display more competence at self-observation. Today most people would assume that there are all sorts of connections between the observation of others (empathy) and self-knowledge.[6] Following Nietzsche's metaphor of the camera, we can see that while one may take a self-portrait in a mirror, the camera can never photograph its own internal mechanisms; it is its own blind spot. (Had Nietzsche used the metaphor of the eye instead of the camera, the "inner eye" of self-observation would be an apt descriptor.) But why, according to Nietzsche, is self-observation impossible—or, at least, so difficult—for the empathetic person?

The dynamics of perception and empathy for Nietzsche lead to a paradox when it comes to self-observation. This becomes clear when we consider the dynamic constellation of the strong individual (the self) and the objective (empathetic) person more closely.

Someone who behaves as a strong subject, Nietzsche says, cannot help but judge, rule, love, hate, reject, etc. A direct consequence of this is that such a person is not very good at observing others, since they are already categorizing, evaluating, and thereby dominating the other before they have processed all the sensory data about them. Today we would call this implicit bias. They skew the data and do not give the other a fair hearing. The self, whose strength is first visible in action, cannot show anything but strength, cannot help dominating the object of observation, and therefore fails to understand others. In short, the hero has no need to be just and objective.

The objective person, on the other hand, is perfectly equipped for perception. The price for their perceptiveness, however, is that they must strip off their self (if they ever had one), dilute it, empty themself out. After this, there is virtually no substance left that they could register in an act of self-observation. Because the objective person is so flexible and adaptive, they can fit into anything, like the container that Nietzsche describes at the end of the paragraph; but by doing so they become void of any content and lose their own profile. There is therefore no object for self-observation.

So neither the strong self nor the objective person can possess self-knowledge. The person with self-strengthening, self-reinforcing actions (loving, hating, ruling) would have to become an object in order to observe themself—and they hate, love, or rule such objects.

The actual problem of self-observation is not the failure of the inner eye but rather that this eye always changes what it sees. Self-observation would make action in the strong self impossible. Indeed, Nietzsche tells us that we should not expect rulers to have any capacity for self-observation. (Writing these lines in the middle of the 2016 US presidential election, and revising them during the early presidency of Donald Trump, I cannot help finding a certain relevance here.)

The second aspect of paragraph 207 that I wish to highlight is Nietzsche's discussion of the objective person in the context of his analysis of women and the feminine. (It can be found both in paragraph 207—see the final line, in parentheses—and in later paragraphs of *Beyond Good and Evil*.) For Nietzsche, women play a particular role in the relationship between the strong self and the objective person: they take a third position. In the world of Nietzsche's thought, women are masters at manipulating the way they are seen by others. They understand how they are observed but, unlike the objective person, they do not comport themselves purely receptively or projectively in the face of observation. Rather, they stake a claim to the observations of others by disguising, masking, beautifying, or withholding themselves. Nietzsche addresses the strategies of women under the category of "shame"— that is, their awareness of being observed. In this sense, women are the true masters of empathy, who fall victim to neither subjecthood nor objecthood.[7] They are the manipulative, second-order observers, who observe how others observe them.

Empathy as Resentment (Nietzsche: *On the Genealogy of Morals*)

There is another idea we need to add to the previous analysis. Readers of Nietzsche will see echoes of paragraph 207 of *Beyond Good and Evil* in his next book, the closely related *On the Genealogy of Morals*, which continues the earlier study of morality's cultural roots. The later text presents an astonishing origin story for Western culture as the scene of a power struggle between two "races" that ends in the defeat of the stronger, wilder barbarians. The wild barbarian, who was once glorified as "the predator, the mighty blond beast lusting for victory and pillage," is the epitome of the master race. But the blond beast becomes the victim of the trickery of the crafty underclass, who convince the more powerful beast that it would be good to show some morality and thus to have sympathy for the those weaker than themself, which in turn has the effect of enslaving the master race to morality and its enforcers.

The terms "master" and "slave," and others like them, are the analogues of the relationship between the objective-empathetic person and the one with a strong self as presented *Beyond Good and Evil*'s paragraph 207. I am primarily interested here in the similarities, not the differences. The central parallel, which requires some interpretation, is that the slave and the objective person *project* or *invent* the strong individual as a worthy creature to observe, to adore, and to follow. In the eyes of others, the strong self (lord, aristocrat, ruler) appears to be at peace with themself and content.

To quickly summarize the argument in the first part of *On the Genealogy of Morals*: Morality is the product of the conflict between two political classes (or races), namely masters and common people or slaves. The origin of the word "good," Nietzsche claims, is bound up with terms for the aristocrats. The word "bad," on the other hand, is derived from the defining characteristic of the people as "simple" or "vulgar." (The German words are *schlecht* [bad] and *schlicht* [simple].) The trick the underclass pulls, inspired by Judeo-Christian priests, is to reverse the hierarchy of the concepts, and declare "good" to be a property of the poor and powerless (*On the Genealogy of Morals*, paragraph 7). This is the famous "slave revolt in morality" that turned moral reasoning upside down.

While masters approve of life, affirm themselves, and accept even their enemies, the clever slaves deny and negate everything—most of all the independence and identity of the masters. The slaves even have a negative relationship to themselves, to the point of hating themselves. (As paragraph 207 of *Beyond Good and Evil* has it: The objective person, if he is even capable of hating, hates only himself. He hates "almost nothing" [*presque rien*], that is, his very nothingness.) The slaves are not at peace with themselves, but rather keep looking to the others, just as the objective person observes the strong beings.

To be sure, Nietzsche himself does not explicitly equate the slaves of *Genealogy* with the objective person of *Beyond Good and Evil*. He does not even use the term "objective person" in the *Genealogy*. In fact, the contexts of both passages indicate a number of important differences. The objective person thins themself out and is receptive, but it is unclear whether or not they hate themself (they hate, after all, "almost nothing"), whereas the clever slaves in the *Genealogy* are consumed by hate. However, the structural proximity implies that the objective person is just as fixated as the slave is on stronger beings with their (apparent) independent selfhood. Their efforts are solely aimed at the strength of the other *as a self*, whether it is to admire them, or to weaken and poison them. (See *Genealogy*, paragraph 11.)

If we read these two texts together in spite of their differences and use them to understand each other, it turns out that the slaves in the *Genealogy* can only reach their goal of poisoning the spirit of the masters by turning themselves into sharp observers with no identity. Sharp, objective observation transforms the strong individuals into stunted, shriveled, crippled, weak beings. This stunting can be the direct goal or just a side effect; it can destroy the rulers or reverse the roles of master and slave, such that the newly minted slaves regret their former existence as masters; or it can take the form of reeducation of the master into an empathetic observer.

In *Genealogy*, the formerly free masters internalize the value judgments of the clever slaves. Nietzsche is unclear on how exactly this internalization or absorption works. It is a major lacuna in the argument of the *Genealogy*. But by looking at paragraph 207 of *Beyond Good and Evil*, we see that compassion (empathy, objective observation) appears to be the prime candidate. When the slave succeeds at teaching the master to observe, the master can see the suffering of the weaklings, have empathy for them, and thereby understand their own part in the suffering. When the master develops pity, they are bound by it, becoming unfree and selfless.

In this process, empathy turns into pity, which for Nietzsche represents a perverted form of observation—perverted because it is not directed at strong models, from which one could learn something. Rather, pity projects suffering as an ideal. When empathy is reduced to pity, the master turns into a slave. True pity, Nietzsche warns, doubles the amount of suffering (paragraph 134) and leads us to forget human strength (paragraph 135). And pity only actually helps the other in a limited number of cases.[8] Empathy— and even more so its perverted form, pity—are the revenge of the weak, a means of punishing and enslaving the ruling class.

There is another way in which *On the Genealogy of Morals* goes farther than paragraph 207 of *Beyond Good and Evil*. The attitude of the underlings, it says, is one of resentment, and this attitude influences their careful observation:

> The slave revolt in morality begins when *ressentiment* itself becomes creative and gives birth to values: the *ressentiment* of natures that are denied the true reaction, that of deeds, and compensate themselves with an imaginary revenge. While every noble morality develops from a triumphant affirmation of itself, slave morality from the outset says No to what is "outside," what is "different," what is "not itself"; and *this* No is its creative deed.[9]

The slave, unlike the self-involved aristocrat, turns outward and takes aim at those with a strong self. The main occupation of the aristocrat is to feel "good"; the slave's focus, on the other hand, is the other, the aristocrat, who, viewed through the slave's "venom-ous eye of *ressentiment*," is evil.[10] In short, the empathetic observer *lives in pursuit of others*. They experience and feel what the others might. This is the literal meaning of resentment: re-sentiment, a secondhand feeling, the condition of being always in pursuit. The empathetic person has no feelings of their own, at least not strong ones full of passion. Instead, they relive the feelings of others. In this sense, as Nietzsche sees it, empathy is, structurally, resentment.

This is Nietzsche's actual claim: the empathetic observation of the slave is not simply driven by admiration and awe of the aris-tocrat but also by resentment and hate—that is, merely derived feelings rather than free emotions. (Sigmund Freud would a few years later characterize the ambivalence and the double bind of the Oedipus complex as the love-hate of the child, who admires the symbolic father, wants to be like him, and therefore must get rid of him.)

Of course, it is necessary to add here that the situation of the *Genealogy* is different from that of *Beyond Good and Evil*. In the *Genealogy*, the underlings are actually oppressed, which is a good cause for resentment. While this is the not the case in *Beyond Good and Evil*, the objective person is operating in a similar situation as that of the slave in the *Genealogy*: they look outside themself at what they are not and, in this moment, become selfless. It there-fore seems plausible that they also come to regret this process of thinning out and to hate the strong individual whom they think is to blame.

We have now arrived at the third thesis about Nietzsche's argu-ment concerning empathy: *The price of empathy is the self—to be more precise, the belief in one's own self. Correspondingly, empathy feeds into resentment, in the form of rage at having sacrificed one's own self. Even in the admiration and awe that the objective person feels for the strong self, there lurks jealousy, quiet rage, and bad will. The mantra of the objective person, the person with empathy, could be as follows: Everyone who has a self should be stripped of it because I lost mine, or else never had one to begin with. Every self is worthy of its own demise. In fact, each self is likely a lie anyway.*

There is obviously a chicken-and-egg problem here: Does the objective person have empathy because they have thinned themself out? Or do they thin themself out because they have empathy? Or are they thinned out from the beginning and therefore able to master the art of receptivity? Do they use empathy as an excuse for their silent rage, their absence of self as an excuse for resentment, their doubt about their own self, or their fear of showing a self? Or do they wield empathy and admiration even when they know that there is no such thing as a self, desperately attempting to save the idea of a self in another person? Is it really the case that empathy hollows out one's self, or is it instead that one uses empathy to compensate for an already weak identity?

Nietzsche himself answers this question in different ways at different points in these texts. The structure that applies here, however, is that a person with empathy sacrifices the idea of their own free and strong identity in order to perceive, project, admire, *and* hate the strong self. *This is what Nietzsche means by empathy.*

Nietzsche's Cure for Empathy

Before we summarize Nietzsche's claims and start to test how correct they are, we should at least mention how Nietzsche himself tries to solve the dilemma of paragraph 207.

Nietzsche may have been one of the earliest thinkers to reckon with the costs of empathy. While most thinkers on empathy, including those in the present day, celebrate it as a positive and prosocial force, Nietzsche sheds light on what actually motivates people to empathize. That motivation may, according to Nietzsche, be a form of compensation for what the empathetic person lacks.

This insight reveals Nietzsche's own bias that there is a contradiction between empathy and a strong identity. A person cannot cultivate empathy on the one hand and a free, strong self on the other. Nietzsche adds to the stakes when he suggests that the *entire person* is altered by empathy; empathy and receptiveness change one's total personality structure in such a way that the objective person can only recognize a strong identity in someone else. With this hypothesis, Nietzsche the philosopher has subjected himself to the authority of psychology. He proposes a mechanistic conception of the psyche that has a one-dimensional apparatus in the center. Whoever exhibits empathy once will always be under its influence.

As soon as Nietzsche has taken this radical position, he diagnoses it as terminal so as to discard empathy and receptivity in general. For Nietzsche, there is no hope to be found in empathy, identification, or pity and so he sets out looking for ways to abolish them. (In fact, he does so in many of his works.)

One such method is to be found in irony, which appears under different names in his works: critique, rhetoric, and philology. In *The Birth of Tragedy out of the Spirit of Music*, a text famous for its duality between Apollonian and Dionysian forces, irony emerges at the end of the book as a third force, under the name Socrates. While Socrates does at first appear as a follower of the Apollonian man, Socratic irony later manages to escape art's dilemma between Apollo and Dionysus. In a similar way, I suggest, Nietzsche looks for a third position to resolve the dualism between the empathetic person and the strong self.

Irony runs through paragraph 207. To cite a single example: consider Nietzsche's quotation from Leibniz, "Je ne meprise presque rien" (I hate almost nothing). Nietzsche comments, "One should not overlook and underestimate that *presque*." What is so important about this *presque rien*? Nietzsche leaves no doubt that it is the objective person himself who is meant as an *almost-nothing*: he is "in himself nothing—*presque rien!*"

This is Nietzsche's joke: We already know that the objective person cannot hate or negate. If they cannot hate, then we could also say that they could hate *nothing and no one*. And here, Nietzsche slips in the same joke that Odysseus pulled on the Cyclops. Nietzsche has already suggested that the objective, empathetic person transforms their self into "no one." This means, since they are a selfless nothing, that they *can* hate themself because they can hate "nothing" or "no one"—they can hate something after all, making the *presque* (almost) necessary.

The original context of the letter from Leibniz that Nietzsche quotes here shows that Leibniz had something entirely different in mind: "Je ne meprise presque rien (excepté l'Astrologie judiciare et tromperies semblables)" (I hate almost nothing (excepting judicial astrology and similar trumperies [deceits])). Nietzsche's joke suggests that the self of the empathetic person is just as arbitrary as astrology.

For Nietzsche, irony is a way out because it is capable of charting a path that avoids the weakness of the empathetic person without glorifying the unreflective barbarism of the self. Irony appears as a possibility in every word, and in every act. In the case of pity, irony expresses itself as the distanced observation of its effects. The ironist distances themself, using empathy to remove themself from the action by one degree and observe how others are affected by pity and receptivity.

Nietzsche, Discoverer of Stockholm Syndrome

Clearly, Nietzsche is at odds with how we typically think of empathy today. The objective person in Nietzsche's model does not feel compassion for every single suffering person. In fact, Nietzsche does not name a single instance of compassion for the weak in paragraph 207. Instead, the objective person reacts to the strength and the powerful expression of preferences: "He waits until something comes, and then spreads himself out tenderly lest light footsteps and the quick passage of spiritlike beings should be lost on his plane and skin." The "light footsteps" and perhaps also the "spiritlike beings" have a minimum of strength or substance, for which the objective person develops a sensitivity. They are even more alert to stronger forms of expression: irrational behavior, firm decisions, loving, hating, tyranny. The empathetic person reacts to strength of decision and of feeling—to that which they do not allow themself.

The objective person sees every action as that of a strong and self-determining self. At the same time, they are blind to similarly selfless beings. Nietzschean empathy, therefore, would seem ill suited to humanitarianism. (Recall that Nietzsche is speaking of the objective person and their powers of perception, of which empathy is only a particular case.) Is Nietzsche's version of empathy, then, more akin to Stockholm syndrome than it is to our current conception of empathy?

Stockholm syndrome occurs when a hostage is so overwhelmed by the personality of the hostage-taker that they turn their captor's wishes and imagined beliefs into their own. Nietzsche certainly evokes a phenomenon similar to Stockholm syndrome, even if it does not perfectly match its features. (For example, Nietzsche's objective person is not physically or psychically overwhelmed by the other, but instead, as a selfless being, opens themself up to them, etc.) But we can still read Nietzsche's account as a contribution to the modern understanding of the phenomenon in his attribution of the primacy of the victim's action.

Modern analyses generally emphasize the traumatic dimension of hostage situations and their long-term impact on the hostage. Nietzsche, on the other hand, emphasizes how the victims have helped to shape the structure of the hostage situation themselves by subordinating themselves, casting off their selves, and taking on the self of the other. Obviously, "victim" is not the best word to describe the agency of the objective person. Nor do I think that Nietzsche is suggesting that the hostage-taker is somehow justified or excused by the possible subconscious complicity of the victim or by their unconscious desire to be taken hostage. Nietzsche's scenario, after all, is not about an actual hostage taking.

To summarize: Nietzsche does not suggest that humans are equipped with a strong sense of self that we lose when and because we develop empathy. Nor does he argue that empathy is simply a loss of one's own perspective. Rather, Nietzsche's thesis is that empathy engenders an asymmetry that empowers an (imaginary) other; the empathetic person is at the same time emptied out and weakened.

Today we would say that Nietzsche's psychology is overly simplistic. Instead of positing a radical divide between empathy and strong self-awareness, we would probably assume a dynamic balance between self-awareness and empathy. Nevertheless, Nietzsche's model retains contemporary relevance and his contribution to the discussion of empathy can be summarized as follows:

1. The empathizer falls into an admiration trap. They invent a strong, free self to admire (such as a tyrant, wild man, or passionate being, who simply does whatever they want). This invented self is an *Übermench* or superman, as Nietzsche's *Thus Spoke Zarathustra* famously articulates. Compared to him, the empathetic person is flat, empty, pallid, and selfless.

2. The selflessness of the empathetic person is not a result of losing a self one once possessed. Rather, the empathetic person digs a trench between themself and someone they observe, whom they categorize as superior by attributing to them intensity, spontaneity, immediacy, and freedom; the empathizer, in turn, sees themself as not having a self in comparison. (You might call this an observation bias.)

3. Loss of self in the objective person means assigning to the other those mental qualities that wither because of empathy and diminishing oneself by comparison. Stockholm syndrome is an example of this dynamic, in which the observed is seen by the observer as exceeding their actual physical or mental strength; as a result, the observer's position is emptied out.

Moving beyond Nietzsche's examples, we can consider a range of empathetic projections of passion, strength, power, and mental characteristics such as authenticity, independence, or "coolness." The figure of the star, which emerged in the early twentieth century, and the charismatic politician are related forms of empathetic projection. This effect that we could call an *empathetic endowment effect* combined with the specific account of self-loss is how Nietzsche enhances contemporary discussions of empathy.

I have introduced Nietzsche to clearly illuminate the connections between receptivity, empathy, and personality change. But he is only one source underpinning the thesis of this book. Diverging from Nietzsche, this book will argue in chapter 2 that self-loss is more likely a result of empathy than its precondition, though the two are so closely related as to be perhaps inseparable. I will go on to argue that empathetic reception does not lead to emotional neutrality or coldness; observed and observer tend, rather, to "warm up" to one another. I will also show how empathy regularly appears in conjunction with judgment and that rather than leading to an inability to judge, empathy results in positive judgments for the observed and negative judgments for their adversaries.

However, before we move on we should pause to reflect on the significance of Nietzsche's negative assessment of empathy. While he might implicitly describe the modern condition (of people being trapped in a selfless state of observation, weakness, and resentment), he also opens the way for us to consider that less, not more, empathy could be a good thing. This provocation stands in square opposition to what most commentators believe today. Hence, it seems appropriate to consider the case of empathy decline in the following section.

Living for Oneself: Do Today's Students have an Empathy Deficit Disorder?

Is empathy on the decline? In particular, are young people today less empathetic than earlier generations? A widely publicized study from 2011 made the case that they are. "Changes in Dispositional Empathy in American College Students Over Time: A Meta-Analysis" by Sara H. Konrath, Edward H. O'Brien, and Courtney Hsing concluded that American students have largely lost their capacity for empathy over the last three decades. These findings were widely discussed in the media, especially the fact that the greatest decrease in empathy had taken place in just the previous decade. What are we supposed to do with such findings? How are we supposed to react to these changes? Will coming generations have even less empathy than this one?

A number of countries have undertaken initiatives to counteract this alleged loss of empathy. For example, the Canadian project rootsofempathy.com has worked to embed empathy by means of promoting emotional literacy in the classroom.[11] Barack Obama famously deplored the "empathy deficit" in our time.[12] And while Europe receives millions of refugees from Syria, Iraq, Afghanistan, and northern Africa, its intellectual leaders are asking how school children should react to new classmates arriving from war zones and refugee camps.[13] But before we join in this call to empathetic activism, it is worth taking a closer look at the study itself. While in fact a few reservations about the study are in order, our attention will be focused on how to evaluate its conclusions: Would a decline of empathy be an entirely bad thing?

The study is actually an impressive metastudy that evaluates a total of seventy-two other studies carried out between 1979 and 2009. In total, 13,737 students were evaluated using the same personality test, making the results highly comparable. The test is the most widely used empathy test to date, the Interpersonal Reactivity Index (IRI), which was developed in 1979–80 by Mark H. Davis. It concentrates on four aspects of interpersonal relationships: empathetic concern, perspective-taking, fantasy, and personal distress. For each, participants were asked seven questions that asked them to rate whether a statement concerning a sentiment would describe them well. The data found that empathetic sensitivity fell considerably in the decades in question, most steeply in the years right before 2009. There was also a measurable decline in perspective-taking skills.[14]

What exactly was being measured? The IRI is a survey that students (and other groups not evaluated in this study) filled out. The tasks are not directly about empathetic ability, and not about the actual use of empathy, but rather attitudes towards empathy. It is a self-assessment. Each participant indicates the extent to which particular attributes, expressed in short sentences, apply to them. There are no direct data here about brain activity or altruistic behavior.

This distinction between attitudes *about* empathy and actual empathetic behavior is important, which we can illustrate by considering gender. For example, can the claim that women have more empathy than men be verified? It depends on how empathy is measured. In surveys about personal attitudes towards empathy or opinions about who has more empathy, women come out as more empathetic. In their IRI metastudy, the authors determined that women, on average, performed higher in all four categories.[15] However, using fMRI technology to look at brain activity results in a different picture: gender differences in empathy are marginal or at least not pronounced.[16] In general, the strength of self-assessment is that people know themselves best. The weakness is that such tests are subject to various beautifications and adjustments. The gender difference discovered by the 2011 metastudy remains significant, though. It shows that women articulate empathy more clearly while men tend to downplay it. In other words, the survey reveals how important and valuable people think empathy is for them. A decline in this measure over the past three decades should indeed be meaningful because attitudes have an influence on our actual behavior, on our self-image, and on our political positions. But whether empathy itself has declined—on that question the study is silent.

The study's use of comparative historical data is also questionable. While the students used the same survey between 1979 and 2009, can we rule out the possibility that at different times they might have understood the same questions differently? Over the course of three decades, the range of meanings, associations, and connotations of words can change appreciably, especially among the young. In fact, our baseline assumption should be that words have different contexts in 2009 than they did in 1979.

There are several outdated expressions that feel more polarizing today than before. For example, one question reads, "I often have tender, concerned feelings for people less fortunate than me." Even though most American students today understand the word "tender," it definitely sounds old-fashioned. At least, none of my students know what to do with the word outside of the kitchen. The male students, in particular, are put off by it, even those who have shown relatively high levels of empathy in general.

There was another IRI phrase that some of my students didn't understand at all: "ill at ease." Another struck them as being feminine: "I am often quite touched by things I see happen." That was probably not the case in 1979. My students also have difficulty with the expression "I go to pieces." Not every question has aged this noticeably, but these examples urge caution.

The study's authors did consider but then rejected the possibility that the American student population could have changed demographically. This is remarkable, as they simultaneously point to the data that show the proportion of ethnic minorities in American schools rising from 12 percent in 1979 to 25 percent in 2009. This, too, must have some significance, as does the rise in the number of economically underprivileged students.

In a conversation in December 2015, Sara Konrath, whom I consider a friend, suggested another possibility for the changes in attitude: that people today are more self-critical when it comes to empathy and for this reason give themselves lower scores than in previous decades. In that case, the lower scores in attitudes about empathy may actually reflect higher awareness of empathy and therefore maybe even *more* empathy in 2009 than in 1979.

Nevertheless, Konrath and her coauthors give us reason to take the data seriously—and indeed all these suggestions cannot entirely explain away the results. Let us therefore assume that the changes in the attitude of students towards empathy between 1979 and 2009 do, in fact, go hand in hand with a loss of empathetic feelings and actions. How should we react?

This question was raised with no small urgency by the study's authors and by the media. A *New York Times* article comments, after summarizing the findings, "Low empathy is associated with criminal behavior, violence, sexual offenses, aggression when drunk and other antisocial behavior. Depressing news."[17] The *Boston Globe* ends its article about the findings with a quote by W. Keith Campbell: "So if you have a society where a lot of people are narcissistic, the whole thing blows up."[18]

The authors were careful not to propose an overly simplistic explanation or to be too quick to assign blame. They consider possible reasons, such as growing prosperity (which appears to correlate to increasing self-centeredness), stronger competition at universities and workplaces (which leaves individuals less time for empathy), rising narcissism (as embodied in "generation me") and smaller families (with fewer siblings and therefore opportunities for empathy per child).

Ahead of these possible factors, the authors cite the rise of social media as a central influence and likely culprit: "This growing self-interest is further reflected by the meteoric rise in popularity of social networking sites such as MySpace and Twitter, by which people can broadcast their own personal information, pictures, and opinions to the online world. Facebook's 'Doppelganger Week' is just one example of the ways in which people today can lionize their own lives and, as a result, potentially isolate themselves from reality and actual social connections."[19]

As a scholar of literary history, I can't help but smile at this. For centuries, critics have been claiming that the new media were spoiling the youth and would lead to increased narcissism. Three hundred years ago, the new media were the novels that emerged in England, France, and Germany, which quickly captured the imagination of the youth. Eighteenth-century critics feared that these novels would spoil the young, turn them into narcissistic addicts, and lead them to suicide. Famously, Goethe's first novel, *The Sorrows of Young Werther*, in which the young protagonist commits suicide, was alleged to have tempted its readers to suicide as well. Today, this "new medium" of yesteryear, the novel, is what we hope our children will read—in part, at least, for the sake of inculcating empathy. (Incidentally, Lynn Hunt has argued in her book, *Inventing Human Rights: A History*, that the novels of the eighteenth century contributed to the emergence of empathy and universal human rights.[20]) Go back two hundred years before Young Werther's tragic death and reading itself was decried as a dangerous pastime. Shakespeare's Hamlet is shown as a misled young reader: "But, look, where sadly the poor wretch comes reading." The usual suspects for social degeneration are always new media, whether novels or social networks. Bashing them is easy; proving they are responsible for increased narcissism, for example, is far more difficult. It's also worth debating whether narcissism is even a bad thing—or whether increased empathy is an unalloyed good thing.

Oppressive Empathy and Liberating Narcissism?

Contemporary social and cultural values define such qualities as understanding others, sympathy, and empathy as being good, while such traits as self-centeredness, narcissism, and a lack of empathy are defined as bad. In light of our reading of Nietzsche's arguments about the price of empathy, however, is the loss of empathy among today's youth really a crisis? Could it have some positive implications? Following Nietzsche, perhaps the decline in empathy reflects the emergence of a new self-confidence. Put starkly: Does increased self-focus, egoism, and narcissism pose a danger to society and the self by reining in empathy or is it an overdue liberation from the claws of a Stockholm syndrome culture defined by obedience to authority?

This duality is surely troubling in several ways. One could point out that it introduces or repeats false dichotomies from Nietzsche or the 2011 Konrath, O'Brien, and Hsing study; or that Stockholm syndrome is a rare, exceptional, and disputed phenomenon that has little to do with empathy in general. Or one could dispute that phenomena like Stockholm syndrome, narcissism, and self-focus even have cultural dimensions and instead speak only to individual personality disorders. But there is no question that empathy and altruistic behavior are in no small measure bound to cultural processes.

This then means that different historical periods and national cultures have developed quite different practices of empathy and can be distinguished accordingly. That is not to say, of course, that it is easy to find these differences, let alone quantify them. To better understand how cultural developments and tendencies affect the practice and value empathy, let me turn once again to Nietzsche, who seeks liberation from empathy.

By thinking in the broadest terms, it is possible to understand phenomena like Stockholm syndrome as a part of our culture and not a deviation from it. I am not speaking here of the individual trauma that a hostage or kidnapping victim undergoes, which according to some experts manifests itself as overidentification with their captor. (It should be noted that other psychologists see such identification as a rational strategy for survival that becomes pathological.[21]) Instead, I am deliberately and perhaps provocatively creating an analogy between the structural function of Stockholm syndrome and the way in which dominant institutions employ intensive training scenarios (as in corporate or military training) or confining intellectual and cultural strictures (as in graduate school or marriage) to enforce at least a partial surrendering of the self.

It would, of course, be absurd to describe militaries, corporations, or marriages and families as hostage-taking institutions inculcating Stockholm syndrome. But at the same time, the subservience of women to men and children to fathers in legal, social, and political contexts is an indisputable historical fact that invites us to think about the psychic process of acceptance of such gross asymmetry. Stockholm syndrome might describe one extreme of the range of possible forms a marriage can take.

In feudal societies, vassals were not only bound to their feudal lords but participated vicariously in their lives and, through public mourning, their deaths. Even in modern institutions, leaders and figureheads are routinely elevated, empathetically speaking. Dictators, for instance, depend on this tendency. But many institutions that we would consider more benign—state, church, party, corporation, club, or clique—also use a human face to embody the institution. The members of the institution have a relationship with, identify with, and share their feelings with this public face. At a minimum, many people seem prepared to give up part of their identity to an institution in order to integrate themselves into it. They often do so not before some sort of abstract ideal or because of a rational calculation; rather, they submit their personalities to the more or less imaginary personality at the top. Corporations, for example, continue to circulate anecdotes and myths about their founders or CEOs. Indeed, we may ask to what extent the empathetic relationship to one's boss remains an important factor in the cultivation of workplace loyalty today. (Understanding the iconography surrounding the CEO as a modern incarnation of Nietzsche's "blond beast" certainly warrants further study.)

Building on these admittedly speculative points, I now want to explore the extent to which the formation of complex institutions may only be possible because of a rudimentary empathy, the willingness of the individual to place themself in the shoes of a leader and immediately subordinate themself to this figure at the same time. Sigmund Freud supposed as much in *Group Psychology and the Analysis of the Ego*. The moment when empathy binds an individual to an institution allows the size of a social group to grow immensely and makes it possible for political structures to take shape.[22] Problems naturally emerge when a leader dies and the empathetic binding force must be transferred to the successor. In his influential study *The King's Two Bodies*, Ernst Kantorowicz viewed the rituals accompanying the death of a medieval ruler through this lens. In spite of the bodily death, he found, a representation of the ruler had to be kept "alive" until a successor was named.[23]

While these models (and others such as Max Weber's charismatic revolutionary or Joseph Schumpeter's creative entrepreneurial genius, to remain in Nietzsche's era) primarily see active potential as a top-down process, Nietzsche suggests a bottom-up dynamic and emphasizes how the "slave"—the objective-receptive-empathetic observer—projects the idea of the leader and in doing so conceives the epistemological foundation of Western culture.

It would be wrong for any number of reasons to reduce all of Western culture to a type of Stockholm syndrome in its self-negating deference to authority, but I want to focus on two of these reasons in particular. First, the theories and practices of Western culture have changed. While Stockholm syndrome, as theorized (however accurately) by Nietzsche, may have been a cultural norm in some cultures of the nineteenth century, it is now an exception, a special case that is pathologized as a disorder. If anxiety about the loss of self is a central motif in today's world (with the caveat that the self can be lost even if it never existed in the first place) it is also immediately evident that there are strong countervailing forces that make it possible to recognize self-loss in the first place. Hence, the visibility of and discourse on "self-loss" is itself a clue that loss of self may not be an accurate diagnosis of an actual general cultural ailment. Usually, the more central features of a culture are not visible from within.

Second, viewing Western culture as Stockholm syndrome can cause us to lose sight of the possible positive sides of the (partial) loss of self resulting from empathy, even beyond the obvious benefits of pro-sociality and altruism. The empathetic person subsumes their own identity for the sake of another but is nevertheless enriched by their coexperience with another. Self-loss contains within it the kernel of self-expansion.

My argument in this chapter is not meant to simply reverse widely shared values, posing narcissistic self-involvement as good and empathy as bad. That would be not only naive but also dangerous. As I will discuss at several points later in the book, from an evolutionary point of view, empathy makes us human and goes a long way in making complex societies possible while enriching us as individuals. People with a lack of empathy live in a small, impoverished world. Instead, I want to be clear that as soon as we start weighing the arguments for and against empathy, we are in uncertain territory. No one, certainly not me, can precisely point to where empathy turns into a harmful self-sacrifice, where the alleged narcissism of today's youth becomes a negative development, or where a cultural institution demands too much emotional sacrifice from us. Every culture produces its own standards, and individuals must apply their own thoughts and values to the matter. Whether we live in a world of inadequate or reduced empathy is not objectively measurable but is rather a question of individual opinion. But I do maintain here that there is such a thing as too much empathy.

Before I explore in the second chapter how an excess of empathy can be kept in check by cultural and psychological forces, I would like to make, or at least consider the possibility of, one more intercultural comparison.

My observations so far, for all their generalizations, have focused on Western cultures. Other cultural conditions, like those in Asian countries, pose a new set of challenges. Direct comparisons using tools like the IRI survey used by the team lead by Sara Konrath can reveal similarities and differences both within and between cultures. A 2013 study by Melissa Ann Birkett indicated that Chinese students express less empathetic care than their American counterparts but share similar values when it comes to fantasy.[24] The hypothesis is that modern China displays a variety of factors that likely limit the development of empathy in the population. Among these are:

1. The one-child policy, which was in force from 1979 to 2015.[25]
2. Overpopulation in cities and some entire regions.[26]
3. Rapid economic growth, a spike in individual wealth, and high degrees of competition.[27]

4. A general acceleration of the pace of life, and a corresponding lack of time.
5. An authoritarian one-party system and censorship.

In spite of these factors, which at least in Western cultures would work against empathy, we must view the cultural context as a whole. Consider, for instance, the importance of respect for elders in Chinese culture. The complex heritage of Confucianism has been blended with modern structures to produce a plethora of new forms. To measure empathetic ability and empathetic action in China, one would have to integrate into one's research methods different social constellations and their importance for Chinese culture. That is beyond what is possible here. It is for example possible that instead of empathy, the related concept of sympathy would be more relevant for China. And it is possible that the concept of sympathy in China might be applicable not only to people but also to landscapes. (The German concept of *Einfühlung*, empathy's precursor, likewise encompasses the aesthetic reception of art, nature, and fellow beings.) If we were to transpose this idea of sympathy onto European cultures, their inhabitants would display a "sympathy deficit" by comparison. Or perhaps young people in China would show less empathy for young people of other classes, but markedly more for older people in general than American college students.

Instead of using data from China, Germany, or the United States to offer up a facile declaration that empathy is good and its absence is bad (or vice versa), we can only suggest the value of observing, from within a culture, whether people are prepared for the concrete interpersonal demands placed on them. In the case of American youth, we could ask whether they are succeeding at empathizing with their friends' widespread fear of failure. In the case of Chinese youth, we might ask whether the growing divide between the generations is offset by strong connections within groups.

Whoever wishes to pursue such national comparisons must keep in mind that the concept of empathy (and, hence, the tests devised to measure it) was informed by a particular set of cultural factors in nineteenth-century Europe, developed within the context of European and North American academic milieus, and relies on the typical behaviors and family structures of "the West" for its vocabulary. While it is obvious that these do not correspond to the Chinese (or Korean or Indian or aboriginal Australian) situation, we can no longer assert with any confidence that they correspond to the challenges of the twenty-first century in any human society. It is at least possible to consider whether empathy may not be needed as much today as it was in earlier periods.

2

Painting in Black and White

Hence the problem was how to overcome not so
much their conscience as the animal pity by which all
normal men are affected in the presence of physical
suffering. The trick used by Himmler—who apparently was rather strongly afflicted by these instinctive
reactions himself—was very simple and probably
very effective; it consisted in turning these instincts
around, as it were, in directing them toward the self.
So that instead of saying: What horrible things I did
to people!, the murderers would be able to say: What
horrible things I had to watch in the pursuance of
my duties, how heavily the task weighed upon my
shoulders!

—*Hannah Arendt*, Eichmann in Jerusalem:
A Report on the Banality of Evil

We begin with an extreme example. Hannah Arendt here describes how Himmler, among other sensitive individuals
serving the Nazi regime, was able to "free" himself from empathy
for his victims by redirecting those feelings towards himself. Empathy, clearly, cannot be reduced to a simple process that, once set
in motion, follows a particular path. Rather, it is characterized by
blockages and diversions, and in order to show such complexities

at work, this chapter will propose a general architecture of empathy and then develop in more detail some of the triggers for empathy in specific situations.

In the previous chapter, the question of too much or too little empathy led to broad cultural and philosophical inquiries. Now, I want to affix these questions to the concrete behavioral mechanisms of empathy and the controls we have developed to distinguish between a surplus or deficit of empathy and ask: What are the consequences of employing such empathy management mechanisms?

In proposing an architecture of empathy, I am working from the assumption that empathy as a whole is influenced by the risk of excess, by a loss of self. Discussing how the regulation of empathy is *a part* of empathy leads to the construction of a three-stage model of empathy with these elements:

1. A plurality of abilities and mechanisms related to empathy and a tendency to use them;
2. A variety of mechanisms to block, limit, or control empathy; and
3. Ways in which the blocking mechanisms can be disabled or bypassed to allow for empathy.

I do not suggest that parts of this model correspond to three distinct neural routines. Rather, the three-stage model offers a phenomenological description of actual uses of empathy. Mapping this architecture makes it possible to ask why we either switch empathy on or repress it—and whether or not we are aware of doing so. This focus on the actual uses of empathy then leads to one of the dark sides of empathy—the biases, prejudices, and injustices that empathy can cause.

In developing a model of the actual use of empathy, the mere capacity to feel empathy is only one aspect of the overall phenomenon.

The majority of people are equipped with an impressive range of empathetic abilities that are richly interwoven with our experiences and our identity, but the capacity for empathy does not in itself guarantee that people employ it, as the example with Himmler shows. And so it is also necessary to locate when and how empathy is activated. Put differently, this chapter examines the triggers of empathy. But before outlining the overall architecture, I want to consider the sheer variety of empathetic abilities.

The Discovery of Empathy

A glance at the early history of empathy research illustrates our strong aptitude for empathy as a species. The idea of empathy originated as a concept in German aesthetics called *Einfühlung* ("in-feeling") that signified the projection of human feeling onto the natural world. In 1909, Edward Titchener coined the English word "empathy" as a translation of *Einfühlung*; "empathy" was then back-translated into German as *Empathie* and, with slight variations, emerged in other European languages at around the same time.[1] Earlier, Theodor Lipps, a professor of aesthetics at the University of Munich—whose mentor, the German philosopher Robert Vischer, had devised the word *Einfühlung* based on eighteenth-century aesthetics—began analyzing the ways in which observers project themselves onto crudely drawn forms and figures. His work rested on the idea that all aesthetic enjoyment promotes a self-encounter by the observer. Accordingly, he suggested that observers take pleasure in a geometrical figure because they can see themselves in it through *Einfühlung*.

In his 1906 book, *Ästhetik: Psychologie des Schönen und der Kunst* (Aesthetics: Psychology of beauty and art), Lipps argued that observers give life to not only the simplest drawings but also the most complex works of art by projecting their own feelings, moods, and emotions onto them. Doing so makes manifest and objective something of themselves, which they can then confront and experience as an external object.[2] This tendency could be called an "empathy bias," namely this tendency to anthropomorphize paired with the establishment of an emotional link based on an assumed similarity with external objects and also real others. The creators of animated films have made use of this ability to imagine nonhuman and even inanimate objects as living beings, anthropomorphizing all sorts of animals and inanimate objects.

A younger colleague of Lipps, Wilhelm Worringer, gave this empathy bias a German name, *Einfühlungsdrang*, the "drive to project our feelings into another being" (an expansion of the word *Einfühlung*).[3] Worringer's project was a critique of this urge, not because he thought it was insignificant; on the contrary, he thought it was ubiquitous in human experience. In his opinion, humans constantly suffer from projecting themselves onto other beings and objects. Against this all-too-powerful "empathy drive," Worringer offered another form of aesthetic reception based on abstraction. However, in his 1907 book, *Einfühlung und Abstraktion* (Empathy and abstraction), he fails to offer abstraction as a viable alternative to empathy. Abstraction, in this account, remains a weak and pale intellectual activity. Whereas he does demonstrate the power of empathy, his argument runs out of steam when he offers abstraction as an alternative reception theory, managing only to say that we ought to be able to control our dominant urge to empathize without telling us how.

By now, the existence of an empathy drive or empathy bias is old news. Whether or not they can name the urge, nearly everyone knows the experience of having feelings aroused by a stick figure, a smiley face, or the face-like features of a robot. Vittorio Gallese and his colleagues have demonstrated that mirror neurons respond to aesthetic experience and works of art much as they do when faced with a real person.[4] To use a crass example, one doesn't need to be a marketing genius to realize that "happy" packaging can be very effective at getting customers to buy a product—at least in less cynical times. Indeed, the discovery of empathy around 1900 coincided with the emergence of a new simplicity in art, paving the way for modern design, and the invention of branding and marketing as we know them today.

Whatever Lipps's reputation is in the history of aesthetics—and he can be critiqued for reducing the aesthetic object to an instrument of the observer's desire to expand the self[5]—his thinking continues to inform much of the academic interest in interpersonal empathy and its moral promise. His influence is evident in the ideas of his contemporary Edward Titchener; the philosopher (and later saint) Edith Stein, who saw human empathy as a kind of projection; and the phenomenologist Edmund Husserl. Daniel Batson may have recently dismissed the idea of aesthetic empathy as a misguided concept, but the modern scientific study of the phenomenon still can be traced back to Lipps.[6]

Lipps highlights the idea that humans have a fundamental inclination towards animation, anthropomorphization, the projection of feelings, and empathy. The point of this short historical digression is not to defend Lipps's legacy, or even to show how relatively recent this discussion is. (In fairness, the prehistory of empathy must mention Aristotle's concept of sympathy and concepts proposed in the eighteenth century by David Hume, Gotthold Ephraim Lessing, and Adam Smith.) The point, rather, is to show that the empathy bias—the tendency to over-empathize—is woven throughout the history of the study of empathy, even if today we would not use words like "drive" or "urge," and that it should be taken seriously as an element of the empathy complex.

A second factor informs this tendency to (over)extend empathy. We human beings have not one but several techniques at our disposal for empathetically understanding others. The range of potential mechanisms that scientists have identified in recent decades stretches from the intellectual practice of purposeful guessing of feelings and the calculation of another's thoughts to unconscious emotional simulations and selective imitation, as when one mimics another's body language.

Even narrow definitions of empathy—for example, definitions limited to relying on the Perception Action Model, which describes the use of similar neural processes and routines in both observer and observed—allow for a large number of ways that the emotional coexperience can be activated. Catalysts of this kind include unconscious emotional "infection" in large crowds (as in cases of mass hysteria), the observation of strong feelings or of goal-oriented behavior, the assumption of another's perspective, and the experience of being emotionally transported into a fictional world.[7] Furthermore, it is probable that these various empathy-related reactions regularly transition from one to the other. What was initially an intellectual impulse can unleash emotional processes, and so on. There are also techniques of actively translating different forms of emotional responses into knowledge and emotions, as Rolf Reber demonstrates in his concept of "critical emotions."[8]

At the end of this chapter, we will imagine specific cultural catalysts of empathy. It is striking, in any case, that the brain's empathy apparatus can be variously activated. For now, it is enough to note that we are biologically prepared and culturally primed for empathy in multiple ways. Both biology and culture lead us towards empathy. Our social environment effectively cultivates empathy because our emotional and intellectual understanding of others gives us palpable advantages. We are incited, trained, and seduced by empathy. We also live in a world of empathetic noise. Not only other people but also various media compete for our emotional attention, further exciting our tendency towards empathetic identification. In brief, we are hyperempathetic beings.

Constructing an Architecture of Empathy

Hyperempathy

The concept of hyperempathy is the first step to building (or recognizing) an architecture of empathy. Hyperempathy might seem like a good adaptation for a social creature. We must remember, however, what evolutionary biologists call the "costs" of any feature we develop. As discussed in the previous chapter, empathy entails the risk of self-loss as an effect of taking on the perspective of another, leading to a weakening of one's own interests, feelings, self-perception, intensity, identity, self-esteem, or self-awareness. This does not mean losing a basic and existing psychological faculty like the ego (as imagined by Freud) but rather *bestowing a self* onto the other, conceived of (by Nietzsche and others) as overly powerful, more real, and more important than the idea one has of oneself. This bestowal has the effect of hollowing or thinning out the idea of one's own self. Perhaps instead of self-loss, it would be more appropriate to speak of self-*production*, but of a self that is denied to the observer and attributed only to the observed other. Through this empathetic transfer of self, the other may appear to us as if a movie hero. (We should keep in mind, too, that self-loss can be a path to a richer experience of an event or an emotional state through empathy with the other.)

On a more pragmatic level, self-loss involves losing focus on one's interests. Negotiators sometimes describe how they were (as Germans idiomatically say) "pulled over the table" once they entered personal negotiations. Empathy makes us exploitable in many ways.

The observation that humans are hyperempathetic leads to the second step in our proposed model: identifying the mechanisms or techniques that prevent or limit the loss of self. How do we manage to control, focus, or block empathy? Without this ability to filter, steer, or even turn off our emotional and intellectual identification with others, we would live in a perpetual state of Stockholm syndrome. In the most extreme cases, we might be unwillingly drawn into the perspectives of not only other people but also animals or even mythological and fictional creations, leading to a total loss of self. Empathy filtering or blocking is therefore as important to being human as is empathy.

Just as there are different capacities leading to empathy, we can tentatively suggest that there is not a single means of limiting empathy, ranging from conscious steering to learned forms of callousness and numbness.[9] At the level of neural activity, in addition to empathy-activating mechanisms (possibly mirror neurons), there are likely also suppression and blocking mechanisms, perhaps caused by a group of neurons that suppress other neurons.[10] We should be careful here, however, because the connection between mirror neurons and empathy, if there is one, is not yet well understood. We can imagine that the neural routines of mirror neurons proceed semiautomatically, prereflexively and prerationally, but this does not mean that these activities necessarily lead to empathy.[11]

At the other end of the spectrum of control mechanisms are conscious processes with which one can selectively distance oneself from others. We can learn to block empathy. A surgeon, for instance, should probably not empathize too much with the patient on which they are operating, and we may assume that other specialized occupations require the development of techniques for controlling empathy—for instance, judges (to inculcate impartiality) and physicians and other caregivers (to avoid emotional burnout).[12]

Between the extremes of non-conscious mechanistic neural controls and the learned willful techniques of empathy blocking, we can posit a variety of other suppression techniques at the physiological, psychological, and sociocultural levels. How to classify these mechanisms is largely an open question. What constitutes empathy blocking? What role is played by higher-level psychic systems, such as consciousness? What role do collective cultural techniques play? (Cultural groups and even entire societies can apparently develop exceptions to empathy; for centuries, African slaves were exempt from the empathy of plantation society in the New World.) And when is empathy allowed after all?

Blocking Empathy

It would be premature to offer a thorough and systematic overview of all possible empathy-blocking mechanisms. Instead, I will present a series of particular phenomena of blocking, control, or suppression of empathy and will ask about potential mechanisms involved in these phenomena.[13] Hannah Arendt identified one such technique used by Himmler and other Nazi perpetrators of war crimes: redirecting empathy from the victim of violence to oneself as its reluctant perpetrator.

Intuitive moral judgment. In the introduction, I discussed how we tend not to extend empathy to the suffering of people we find to be morally in the wrong. Most of us feel less empathetic when we think someone deserves punishment. The attribution of guilt, therefore, could serve as a catalyst for the blocking of empathy. An insightful study of this phenomenon has been done by the neuroscientist Tania Singer and her team. Observers of the punishment of someone who cheated in a game felt less or no empathy for the guilty person. The question is what exactly leads to the suppression of empathy for the wrongdoer.

One way to think about the withholding of empathy could be that we feel angry about the cheating and thus focus righteously on our own emotion, forgetting about the other. Negative behavior by others would lead to self-focus. This might be in line with some of the observations by Jonathan Haidt and his collaborators, who focus on intuitive emotional moral verdicts, which are subject to only a slight rational control.[14] However, we might also wonder about the process of language attribution in this context. When, for example, we call the behavior of a teenager "reckless," do we distance ourselves from them and thus feel less empathy towards them if they harm themself accidentally because we have actively discredited the other? In this case, we would not focus on ourselves, but rather build up a distancing device.

Negative attribution, stigma. This kind of distancing raises questions about the extent to which all kinds of attribution, including but not limited to retributive attributions, can serve as a catalyst to limit empathy. One case in point might be irreversible attributions—like particularly strong defamations that persist even after they are found to be groundless. This tendency of defamations to stick makes irreversible attribution a powerful tool for propaganda: in the aftermath of the 2016 US election, Hillary Clinton remains "crooked," even in the complete absence of evidence.

Attribution can take many forms beyond questions of guilt. We could speculate as to whether the mechanisms outlined here play some part in ethnic, national, or religious violence. One group may systematically and persuasively paint another group as bad, with its members being deemed less valuable. Marked by such language—though not simply by language alone—the members of this other group would be seen as deserving of less empathy, regardless of individual behavior or circumstances. Once stigmas are established, they can be hard to dispel, and such instances are all too common throughout history. The rhetoric and actions of the Black Lives Matter movement is an attempt to break a pattern of historical stigmatization. By making this deceptively simple claim, that "Black Lives Matter," the speaker overcomes underlying and often unspoken racist assumptions among not only whites but also blacks who may have to break internalized patterns of enforced self-doubt.

Marking, tracking. Another related explanation for empathy blocking could be that when a person behaves badly, they are marked in the observer's mentality as deserving of less empathy when they suffer misfortune as a punishment for what they did wrong. Such tracking does not require many aspects of language. Movies and fiction often operate this way; we expect a good or bad ending for a character simply because they seem to deserve it.

Appraising worthiness. A different possibility may be that in observing an empathetically-relevant scene, we come to an appraisal as to whether we should empathetically engage.[15] (Experiments could be devised to distinguish between this and other explanations by changing the order in which information is received or by expanding the time between crime and punishment.) Related to what we could call an Appraisal Theory of Empathy is a study that alternated payment information. Subjects were shown pictures of bodily pain. At the same, they were told how much money the pictured person received for undergoing such pain. When the sum was big enough, the subjects showed little empathy. When the same people in the pictures were said to have received no compensation, the fMRI measured increased levels of empathy.[16]

In-group bias. Membership in a group is yet another powerful and common form of empathy control. Numerous studies have shown that people on average show less empathy towards people who are not a part of their group and that similarities between observer and observed play a major role.[17] However, it is not clear whether a single mechanism or a plurality of mechanisms accounts for this dynamic. For example, we may ask whether this is a case of empathy suppression or of selective, preferential empathy.

Familiarity with situation. Sometimes I ask my students what role they imagine prior experience plays in empathy. More precisely, how does experiencing a particular situation first, before watching someone else go through it, affect empathy? My students routinely answer that shared personal experience is an important enabler of empathy. They suggest that it is easier to share feelings and emotions when one can recreate them from past experience. (These speculations are supported by empirical evidence based on the direct observation of physical pain.[18]) However, some students argue that is also plausible that familiarity with a situation may also lead to withholding empathy. Previous experience may make us less curious, preventing the formation of empathy as a means to share a situation that would otherwise be inaccessible to us. It could be that by knowing that a particular experience is "not so bad," we withhold our sympathy for others and may even be repulsed by what strikes us, in retrospect, as a pathetic excess of feeling. For example, when I show a YouTube video to my college students in which high-school students dramatize how hard they have worked for a test, implicitly begging for pity, my students tend to laugh. At the same time, I imagine that middle-school students can emotionally relate to their upper classman. An aversion to a past event may also make us less likely to want to relive it. In these cases, having previously experienced something can be a reason for callousness, aversion, or avoidance, and therefore function as a top-down blocking mechanism.[19]

The range of possible blocking mechanisms is thus wide, as even these few examples indicate. One could attempt to categorize the various forms of empathy blocking by their degree of consciousness. One could also distinguish between techniques focusing on either the subject or the object—that is, the empathizer and the target of empathy. Some are aimed at directing empathy away from a particular target, perhaps because of that person's guilt or because they belong to the wrong group. Blocking techniques aimed at the subject, on the other hand, stop an individual from forming empathy at all. Likewise, we can organize these blocking techniques and mechanisms on a scale from the individual level to the sociocultural group.

The model of empathy I construct later in this chapter calls for empathy-blocking mechanisms as a countermeasure to the tendency for hyperempathy (or empathy bias). However, there is a related but distinct way to account for the need to block empathy. Stephanie Preston and Frans de Waal have suggested an influential model of empathy in which infants, like many social animals, have a hard time distinguishing themselves emotionally from others.[20] This primitive condition of undifferentiatedness between the self and the other is observable in cases of shared emotions or emotional contagion. When an individual feels a strong emotion like fear, it can spread through an entire group, unleashing a collective panic.[21] Social creatures find themselves in a sphere of "shared manifold."[22] Preston and de Waal suggest that humans and other species learn to distinguish themselves from others, thereby keeping others' emotions at bay. Seen in this way, the function of the ego or the self is to protect the individual from emotional contagion. Empathy emerges in this model on a higher level. With empathy, the individual returns to the earlier stage of undifferentiation while at the same time being aware of the difference between the self and the other.

Preston and de Waal's model is insightful if one considers emotional contagion and herd behavior as the starting point of an investigation. But their model is problematic from other points of view. It assumes, for instance, that selfhood is an acquired faculty. Another assumption of the model is that emotional contagion delivers the impulse to develop the self. Not everyone will agree to that. Emotional contagion is limited to a few strong emotions and affects, primarily fear, aggression, and exhaustion.[23] Under this model, these strong feelings would be central to the development of the sense of self, meaning that in cultures or populations with little aggression and fear, there would be almost no sense of individuation. A further concern is that the Preston-de Waal model presents empathy as a kind of regression to an earlier stage of undifferentiatedness.

Clearly, this brief discussion of the mechanisms that restrain, block, or neutralize empathy opens more questions than can be answered here, revealing just how much research on empathy remains to be done.

Bypassing Empathy Blocks

The third step in constructing an architecture of empathy is identifying the mechanisms and techniques that bypass or neutralize empathy blocking so that empathy can take shape. If we are in fact correct that humans are hyperempathetic (step 1) but learn to suppress, control, and limit our empathy (step 2), the next question is this: When and how do we nevertheless feel empathy? *step 3*

A series of possibilities emerge for this third step. The schematic representation below allows for an initial taxonomy. I should emphasize, however, that this is intended as a highly theoretical or even metaphorical construct. Further, there are cases in which empathy-blocking mechanisms never come into play, where the external impulse to share feelings (like the sight of an injured person) leads straight to empathetic identification and intervention. Empathy, we can say with some confidence, emerges despite the blocks discussed above through a number of top-down processes and steering mechanisms:

1. An empathy-blocking mechanism may be *bypassed*, as in cases in which the mechanism does not work for a particular stimulus of empathy—perhaps the blocking mechanism "specializes" in preventing empathy in a different situation—and is thereby overcome. (One can almost imagine that such a mechanism will adapt to this stimulus and be more effective in neutralizing empathy the next time it comes up.)
2. If the catalyst for empathy is strong enough, it might *break through* the impediment. A catalyst's strength could be derived from a few different elements. Bodily reactions may come into play or it could be a matter of the clarity or precision of the experience, as in watching a film, viewing a work of art, or reading literature. These can be powerfully moving experiences when

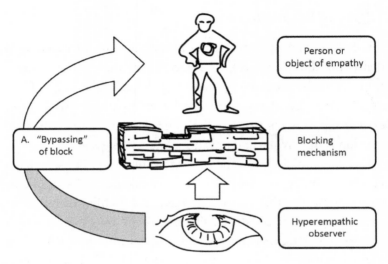

FIGURE 2.1
Bypassing the empathy blocking mechanism

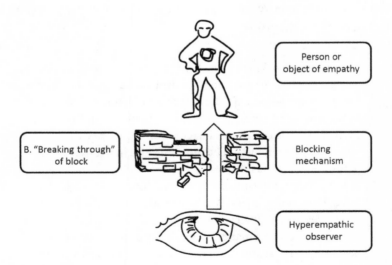

FIGURE 2.2
Breaking through the empathy blocking mechanism

they present situations that are not clouded by the messiness of prior knowledge of the specific people and events. Other strong catalysts of empathy might involve children being harmed or unjust suffering, with outrage at the fact of such unfair suffering spilling into empathy.

3. Culturally sanctioned catalysts may also be strong enough to escape from the empathy blocks. We might imagine this as a tunnel through the empathy barrier. It may be that certain situations allow for or even demand an empathetic response in a particular culture. These catalysts could differ from culture to culture and from group to group. A child who has hurt themself and is crying will arouse empathy in one culture but may be met with irritation in another. Similarly, abusive treatment towards animals may arouse sympathy in one cultural group but indifference elsewhere. Cultural codes of behavior help determine whether we should show empathy or not.

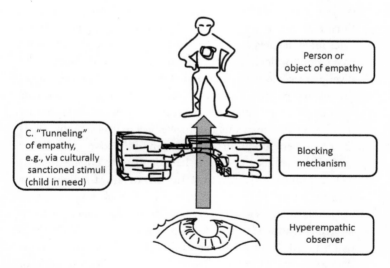

FIGURE 2.3
A culturally sanctioned instance of empathy is permitted

This leads us to a further observation, namely that we can also be consciously moved to empathy. When called for, we can "turn on" our empathy. But what seems like activating empathy may in fact be shutting down an empathy-blocking mechanism. In such a conscious activation of empathy, as in the cultural channeling of empathy, the impulse does not come from an external stimulus but rather from the observer's readiness to empathize.

4. Blocking mechanisms may also be circumvented via a *temporary allowance* of empathy. Two possibilities present themselves, distinguished by the mechanism that sets the time interval. With the first, the nature of the blocking mechanism determines the amount of time it is in effect. We might imagine this as a kind of pulse, whereby the barrier becomes passable for a short period of time then closes again. Certain moods, for example, stimulate us to "lower the gate" for a while.

The second temporal bypass features a *return-to-self structure* that depends on the interplay between subject and object. If the subject has decided that empathy is required only for a short time, it is easier to allow empathy because they know after a brief interval they can "return to themself." The ability to bypass empathy blocks for short periods of time can be seen in the diverging reactions to acute and chronic illnesses. Research indicates that people show more empathy towards acute patients than chronic patients in specific cases.[24] A person temporarily needing a wheelchair due to a broken leg may elicit more positive empathetic attention than a person confined to a wheelchair for life. While this may be problematic from an ethical point of view, it conforms to our architecture of empathy by allowing for a quick "return" to the self, thus minimizing self-loss.

Fiction provides another example of our preference for time-limited empathy. Most people are prepared to step into the shoes of a fictional character for a short time, even if that character undergoes the most terrible suffering. Why is this? Because works of fiction (and narrative in general), have an ending, at which point we can withdraw our empathy.[25] Although both of these cases are

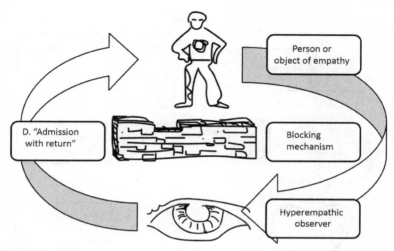

FIGURE 2.4
A time limited instance of empathy "with return"

more complex than this short overview allows (and we will return to tragedy in chapter 4), the point here is that the promise of a conclusion can provoke empathy and persuade us to lower our defenses. In addition, this interplay between the subject and object of empathy also reveals that only looking for external catalysts for empathy is too simplistic. Indeed, a subject who wants or needs to empathize can look for a suitable object or even create one.

5. *Secondary activities* in the mind unrelated to empathy may also activate empathy, "spilling over," as it were, to circumvent or shut down the blocking mechanism. Nearly all forms of attentiveness to others can strengthen our hyperempathetic tendencies: strong emotions like love and passion, for example, or the evaluation and judgment of others, either in moral cases or in competition, choice scenarios, and contests. Side-taking, which I will examine below, is one such activity. Because the impulse or secondary activity does not emerge from situations that typically demand empathy, we might visualize the blocking mechanism as being asleep and therefore easily sidestepped.

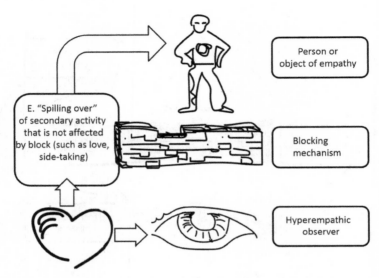

FIGURE 2.5
A secondary activity "spills over" to become the empathy catalyst

6. The *unity of the entire architecture* of empathy I am constructing
   here may also play a role in going through or around empathy-
   blocking mechanisms, such that when one element is activated,
   the entire system of empathy routines is set in motion. This is
   simple to imagine when we think of a stimulus positively connected to empathy or features associated with empathy. When
   we notice a similarity between someone we do not know and
   someone with whom we have established an empathetic link, we
   are more likely to also feel empathy for this stranger. Theoreti-
   cally, it may even be possible that the activation of an empathy
   blocking mechanism could lead to empathizing if the blocking
   mechanism is associated with empathy. An observer might become more fixated on the object of the blockade, thus precipitating a secondary empathy. This at least is how certain writers
   of the romantic era imagined it: a hero could fall in love with
   the very person they most despised since the effort of blocking

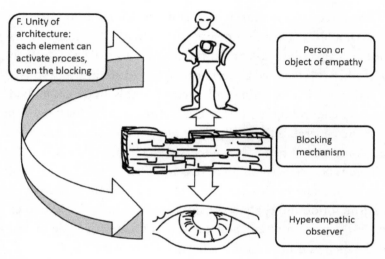

F. Unity of architecture: each element can activate process, even the blocking

Person or object of empathy

Blocking mechanism

Hyperempathic observer

FIGURE 2.6
The unity of the architecture of empathy; each element can arouse empathy

associates the other with the positive attention of love. This seeming paradox is resolved by recognizing that every component of the architecture can be part of the empathy routine. Feet find their way to familiar paths; even withholding empathy in order to administer punishment can lead to empathizing with the subject of that punishment.

At this juncture, I should emphasize once again that this proposed architecture is not a representation of the brain and its components. Rather, this model offers a phenomenological description of logically delineated processes of empathy. The brain is imagined here as a black box that we are trying to understand using only input and output. The central purpose of this model is to embed our core empathetic capacities in social, cultural, and individual processes, which determine when we actually feel or activate empathy. Put simply, this is a trigger theory of empathy.

The three-stage architecture of empathy allows us to formulate the complex balance of empathy and empathy-blocking mechanisms. It also allows us to predict that empathy will be at its strongest when it is engaged by certain secondary activities and when it is activated for a short time only. Central to this model are individual and cultural differences in the use of empathy. Starting from just the generalized capacity for empathy, individual differences in its use would be hard to understand. One could imagine that different people have different degrees of empathetic ability. This can be measured in the cases of significant empathy deficiency—autism, for example. However, differing capacities do little to explain the pattern of empathy activation for most people in daily life: When and how do those people who have a disposition for empathy use it? Or not use it? How do cultural factors influence individual cases?

By understanding blocking mechanisms as part of the architecture of empathy, we become aware of complex individual variations in the use of empathy. This frees us from the naive idea that the more empathetic a person is, the better that person is. In many cases, someone who blocks empathy can act in a morally superior way. Thus, the need to understand when, how, and why people turn empathy on and off, and in what situations. In the following section, we will examine one secondary activity that is of particular interest for the culture of empathy.

The Three-Person Model of Empathy

The three-stage architecture of empathy proposed above implies that possessing the general capacity to empathize it is not by itself sufficient for the emergence or deployment of empathy.[26] Thinking and feeling empathetically requires both an external stimulus (a particular situation, whether real or not) and, in particular, a disabling (even temporarily) of empathy-blocking or empathy-neutralizing mechanisms. We have seen the force of certain catalysts—for instance, the sight of a child in danger— but internal preparations, personal experiences, and acquired empathy-blocking mechanisms are just as important in explaining why and how empathy actually occurs.

Among the most significant catalyst for empathizing is the dynamic of *side-taking*: when the observer is witness to two parties in conflict and decides to support one. I call this the three-person model of empathy and will explore it in greater detail first by describing its general features, especially how side-taking morphs into empathy, and then by focusing on an example from the 2016 US presidential election.

I start with the human ability to take sides. This quality—and it is a quality, if a peculiar one, that seems to be rare in non-human animals—can hardly be overestimated. It is, surely, part of our development as social creatures. Humans are uniquely focused on side-taking and on the judgment of their fellow humans. While coalition-building occurs among some animal species—notably our closest relative, the chimpanzee, but also some species of dolphins—the influence of such coalitions is weaker than among humans, as far as we can tell.[27] Think, for example, of how unforgiving humans can be; how judgments about individuals or groups, once made, linger in perpetuity; how rivalries are maintained and even passed on from generation to generation; and how precisely we observe one another. These seem to be singularly human traits.

Side-taking and moral judgments are not the same thing, and the relationship between them is complex. It is often the case that we take the side of the one with whom we also feel moral agreement. Still, it is unclear whether side-taking follows moral judgment or vice versa. Do we place someone in the moral right because we are on their side? Or do we take their side because we believe they are morally correct? Both are not only plausible but, in fact, describe the structure of actual behavior in specific cases. It seems to be a compelling hypothesis that side-taking is the primary, and evolutionarily older, structure and that moral judgment follows closely on its heels. If this hypothesis is correct, it opens up many questions concerning the evolutionary and functional primacy of moral intuitions, side-taking, and reasoning/rational justifications to legitimize our position.

Daniel Batson and his colleagues have conducted experiments in which they asked participants to distribute limited goods among people in need. Those who were instructed to avoid empathy distributed the goods according to principles of fairness. But the participants who were encouraged to act with empathy contradicted rules of fairness and justice, clearly favoring those with whom, following instructions, they formed empathy. From this, the researchers concluded that empathy contradicts the principles of fairness and justice. What may be just as remarkable is that the participants who distributed empathetically apparently did not see their choices as unfair or themselves as acting against the principle of fairness. This may indicate that empathy can have primacy over rational or moral decision-making.[28]

Further evidence for this hypothesis is found in the astonishing speed with which we judge others. This is true for opinions we form based on someone's physical appearance (their face, for example), which takes place in a fraction of a second, as well as in juridical situations, in which a majority of people come to a decision long before the actual argumentations and weighing of evidence.[29]

One of the puzzles that the following reflection is meant to solve is why these quickly formed positions tend to stick, even when later information does not match the initial judgment. In political primaries, therefore, debates may not persuade voters to support one or another candidate as much as reinforce the correctness of the choice they have already made. The answer that I arrive at below is this: empathy, bit by bit, does the work to solidify hasty judgments.

By definition, side-taking occurs when there is more than one option and when more than one decision is possible. Even if the choice is more or less predetermined, it routinely appears to the decision-maker that it is purely their decision. The difference between options does not even have to be particularly significant, though it can become more so once tensions emerge between the positions because the mere existence of conflict, however subtle, suggests significance, making people feel compelled to choose. And while the side-taker may not fully understand the side they are taking, share the feelings of the person whose position they have selected, or perceive their intentions, the decision, we assume, is based on their recognition of a *tendency* in their chosen side that is derived from perceivable actions and inclinations.[30]

From these observations, I will recapitulate the three-person model of empathy: An observer sees a conflict, takes one side, sees the situation from that perspective, and thereby slowly develops empathy. This in turn leads to a strengthening and reinforcing of the initial side taking.[31]

The dynamic relationship between side-taking and empathy creates a positive feedback loop. When an observer of a conflict between A and B takes the side of A (be it quickly and intuitively or carefully and deliberately), they will tend to see the situation of the conflict from A's perspective. From this point of view,

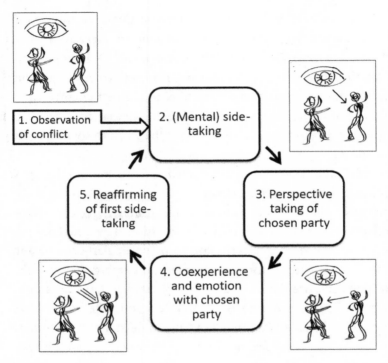

Figure 2.7
The three-person model of empathy

B appears to be somehow unappealing, wrong, or even hostile since they oppose the chosen side A. B might be seen as an aggressor who is harming A. And the more that the perspective shared by the observer and A distinguishes between the two sides (A and B), the more probable it becomes that the observer will also share the pain and feelings of A. In short: the observer experiences the emotional situation of A and develops empathy for A but apathy or antipathy towards B.

Empathy is not the end here but rather the beginning for renewed or confirmed side-taking and, therefore, a stronger alignment with the chosen side. Empathy might also stimulate a rational process of *ex post* justification of one's side-taking—and there are always rational arguments to be found to support even an unjust cause. As human beings, we are exceptionally good at finding or inventing reasons why our initial side-taking and decision-making may have been correct, and we tend to believe ourselves. It thus becomes all the more likely that the empathetic observer will take with new enthusiasm the side they have already chosen, hardening their initial judgment.

This positive feedback loop does not have to begin with side-taking; it could start at any point: adoption of another's perspective, empathy, or side-taking. What is critical is the alternating confirmation and reinforcement of these three elements (side-taking, adoption of perspective, and empathy). The dynamic stays the same. And conflict only reinforces this cycle because it creates situations in which there is a clear contrast between A and B as competitors, adversaries, or victim and oppressor. Such stark situations are uncommonly conducive to empathy because they are so aesthetically clear (to return to the concepts described in the introduction), precipitating an action, decision, or emotion.

The three-person model can offer an explanation of how different elements and forms of empathy are tied together through the empathy process and how they can transform into one another. We can, for example, distinguish between a number of capacities and empathy-like forms of behavior, from theory of mind to thoughtful care.[32] But these behaviors, including those that we do not necessarily associate with empathy, frequently work together in daily life. An initially rational observation that leads to side-taking can soon lead to a very emotional empathy. By the same token, a strongly emotionally colored and spontaneous empathy can lead to taking another person's side and mobilizing rational reasons for this choice, even if we only come up with them after the fact or make them up.

This model offers an explanation for why arbitrary, accidental, superficial snap judgments or side-taking can persist and reinforce themselves through empathetic mechanisms, even when they contradict our moral intuitions. Still, we should not underestimate human judgment. Even shockingly quick, intuitive judgments are usually correct.[33] The simplest heuristics often outpace complex calculations.[34] And according to the evolutionary psychologist, Robert Kurzban, and his colleagues, our moral judgments are relatively rarely wrong, at least.[35]

For the sake of completeness, I want to mention here that this model does not predetermine what criteria we use for our initial side-taking. That is more a matter of tendencies, including:

a) Similarities between observer and the person or people whose side one is taking.[36] (That said, people can still process experiences dissimilar to their own and develop empathy.[37])

b) Strategic calculations that serve the self-interest of the side-taker.

c) Moral-juristic decisions as to which side is more correct.[38]

d) Prior experiences with the person or people with whom one is siding.[39]

e) Bandwagon-effects of others choosing a side

f) "Self-reflexive" forms of side-taking: Since the observer as observer is more passive,[40] they might tend to be more sympathetic to the passive, acted-upon side of the conflict.

g) The strength of the emotions on display.

h) Inherited cultural frameworks.

i) Instances of victimization: Tendencies of care may be culturally reinforced by humanitarianism to have more empathy with survivors of oppression and injustice.

To summarize the three-person model, we can say that empathy functions particularly well in supporting quick judgments and the behaviors that result from them. As a highly social species we experience conflict and discord as part of our daily lives. The dynamic of side-taking, adoption of perspective, and empathy allows us to rapidly make firm decisions, to jump into conflicts, and to take clear positions. Empathy legitimizes both positive and negative behavior towards others. When I have decisively chosen one side, I am free to criticize, attack, punish, delight at the defeat of the other side. Empathy is the mechanism that turns quick and even accidental side-taking into enduring alliances and prolonged divides. Frequently, empathy not only fails to end conflicts, but deepens them.

How Empathy Fuels Division

Having established various ways in which empathy functions, we can at last begin to turn in a more sustained way to the dark sides of empathy, resulting from the dynamics of empathy triggers and side-taking. We will first look at the most polarizing election in recent US history, then turn to terrorism and an effort to use empathy to bridge divisions in Northern Ireland. We will conclude the chapter with a reflection on the evolutionary forces that might have shaped fiction.

Donald Trump, Master of Empathy

Our societies have built many institutions and rituals around the central human activity of side-taking. Some of these are designed to be enjoyable. In sports, for example, side-taking not only simplifies and focuses our experience, it makes the game fun. Fiction

follows similar tendencies. A more serious and consequential ritualized form of side-taking is the electoral process in democracies.

I first wrote this chapter in the heat of the US primary election
season in the spring of 2016, primarily with a European audience
in mind. At that point, the election of Donald Trump seemed to
be a far-fetched possibility to most observers. I nevertheless devoted a section of this book to his early success in the primaries,
which I attributed to his skillful management of strategic empathy.
I did not mean that he was himself empathetic but rather that he
displayed an excellent talent at drawing empathy to himself. And
even though I stand politically very far away from Trump and his
supporters, I was surprised to find myself reacting empathetically
to him.

This book will appear in English halfway through Trump's
first term as president, so let me go back to the spring of 2016.
Americans are accustomed to focusing more on the personalities than the policies of national political candidates; even so, the
rise of the businessman, television personality, and self-described
political outsider Donald Trump surprised everyone as Trump
took the top spot in polls and won ten of the first fifteen Republican primaries. The possibility that he might become the Republican candidate for president suddenly seemed realistic. His rise
divided voters into opposing camps within the Republican Party.
One had to be for or against Trump. This division became even
more stark in the general election. Why did Trump inspire such
deep divisions? And did he win the presidency despite or because
of them?

In the debates and in his campaign appearances, Trump be-
haved differently than people had come to expect from a politician. To all appearances, he allowed himself to be guided
by spontaneous bursts of emotion. Trump said things widely

considered politically unviable: he confessed to breaking moral taboos, railed against political correctness, made derogatory statements against Mexicans, Muslims, and journalists, and he openly mocked women and people with disabilities. He outlined an aggressive, America First foreign policy involving improbable military interventions. He promised to ban Muslims from entering the United States and build a "beautiful" wall along the country's border with Mexico to keep out migrants he stereotyped as rapists and murderers. He insulted his opponents and reversed his own positions more rapidly and often than most politicians and spread easily detectable misinformation. But what was (and still is) the most radical thing about Trump was the self-confidence he projected (and continues to project), regardless of whether or not it is justified. This is how he excited the public's imagination—whether for or against him. Every observer formed a strong, even visceral opinion about him.

In the primaries, every other candidate turned against Trump. Within the Republican Party, a "Never Trump" movement attempted to derail his campaign. And the media was seemingly obsessed with him, infamously given him hundreds of millions of dollars of free advertising through their coverage. The result can be easily described in terms of empathy. His emotions, outbursts, many violations of taboos, and self-confident presentation, paired with his image of a political outsider, led a substantial portion of the electorate to take Trump's side and see things from his point of view. The fact that he stood as "one against all" only made him a more attractive object of side-taking and empathy.

In fact, pinning "one against all," "one against the majority," "one against the apparatus," and "one against the others" has become his general strategy of presenting himself. He regularly poses as the victim of a media conspiracy ("the FAKE NEWS media"); he calls the Special Counsel investigation led by Robert Mueller into Russian involvement in the 2016 election a "witch hunt" against him ("the single greatest WITCH HUNT in American political history"); and he describes himself as the one person standing up against false elites, intellectuals, other countries, foreign influences, etc.[41] The model he uses is ancient and can be observed in both Classical and modern Western tragedies. It fits the scheme that Trump presents his opponents not as individuals but rather as part of large networks and nebulous groups (one foreign national stands in for all foreigners and so on). The one-against-all scheme uses the deep-seated American preference for the individual, the underdog who is victimized by large institutions or corporations, which might be traced to American colonists freeing themselves from the burden of a superior colonial power.

Implied in the scheme of one-against-all is that the one is the victim of the many. In this sense, Trump presents himself as the great victim who deserves support, pity, and empathy. Those who take Trump's side see his opponents from his perspective and therefore empathize with him; and they will only ever find more reasons to support him. By presenting himself as a victim, he justifies any outrage, any action: threats about censoring the press, encouraging attacks on demonstrators at his rallies, and the like. For those who have taken his side, the ugly face of his anger can be directly linked to his being victimized, thus confirming their initial side-taking.

Trump's anger attracts the empathy of his supporters because they too feel victimized by illegal immigration, multiculturalism, feminism, globalism, East-Coast elites, and unfair depictions in the media. During his campaign, Trump promised to speak up for these victims of globalization, political correctness, and the overreach of the federal government. In fact, he made them aware that they could present themselves as "victims," even though they might be part of the dominant American culture. "BUILD THAT WALL" was a rallying cry for those (white) people who came to feel they were the victims—not of a failed immigration policy but of one that deliberately targeted them.

Every fit of rage, every insult, and every lapse of judgment by Trump can be explained and excused, even celebrated. Empathy for "The Donald" among his supporters only reinforces the idea that they made the right choice, and they eagerly wait to see how he will defend himself from the next attack. Side-taking, identification, and protectiveness are all blurred together. Even as his opponents deride him as a great political baby, his supporters want to help him and will stand by him because his feelings have become, for them, facts. It undoubtedly helped him significantly that Hillary Clinton, his opponent, was portrayed in the media as emotionally cold. We are more likely to empathize with people who show emotions. In a contest between a "cold" rational player and a "hot" temperamental one, the "hot" person frequently wins because their emotions draw people to their perspective—or, due to the peculiarities of the American electoral system and of the 2016 election in particular, draw just *enough* people to their perspective to win the presidency.

Readers will hear the echo of the opening passage of this chapter in which Arendt describes the Nazi strategy to portray oneself as victim of duty while witnessing or committing atrocities. And yes, the basic strategy bears resemblance. But does this make Trump a Nazi? Certainly not; the strategy of portraying oneself as victim is far too general and widespread to refer to a specific Nazi heritage.

In fact, one aspect of the perplexing personality of Donald Trump is that he cannot be easily pinned down. Many commentators have tried to identify the basic pattern of his erratic actions. Certainly, he exhibits signs of narcissism, xenophobia, racism, arrogance, irrationality, and unconventional behavior. It might, however, make more sense to describe his strategy of presenting himself as the victim of changing constellations of conspiracies and to understand his clever use of shifting polarizations to constantly present himself as worthy recipient of the empathy of others. Indeed, if he has an identity structure, it is that of a drama queen.

Other trends and factors certainly helped Trump's victory: demographic factors within the so-called forgotten (white) America; the influence of social media (and the influence of Russia on social media); the anxieties of a lower middle class that lost economic ground under previous administrations; a rebellion against identity politics and political correctness; and a general fatigue with politics as we know it.

One of the more surprising aspects of the first year of Trump's presidency is that despite the disastrous disarray of his administration, investigations into his campaign's alleged collusion with Russia, his failure to accomplish any signature political wins (except, as of December 2017, an unpopular tax reform bill), and numerous missteps in the international arena, as of this writing Trump still enjoys the solid support of approximately 35–40 percent of voters. This unwavering support makes sense if we recognize Trump as a master of empathy who effectively presents himself as powerful underdog and thereby continually reinforces and reinvigorates side-taking in his favor.

We can use the three-person model of empathy to illustrate Trump's strategy. In fact, we can describe a specific "scene of empathy" that Trump employs (and we will give more theoretical weight to the phrase "scene of empathy" in chapter 3). Trump's scene of empathy has two core elements. The first is the witty, spontaneous, combative Trump, who knows how to react spontaneously in front of audiences and media and to counter verbal attacks. In one of the debates, for example, his Republican competitor Ted Cruz accused him of having (bad) New York values. Trump immediately turned the attack around, talked about being a New Yorker who was in Manhattan on 9/11 and how he felt the pain of the attacks patriotically as a New Yorker.[42]

Another infamous episode that oddly did not seem to substantially harm Trump's support was the release of a recording in which Trump brags that because he is a star, he can get away with groping women. One should have expected these tapes to mark the instant end of his candidacy. Trump reacted to these tapes first by denying having said any such thing and then by saying that he was "not proud of it" before settling on the response that stuck: His statement was mere "locker room talk," thereby implying that all men say things like this when in private and, most of all, that it is inappropriate to confront a man with private statements of this kind. That is, in the moment he should have had sympathy or empathy with the victims of his harassment, he redirected attention and empathy back to himself. In fact, by this line of reasoning, his statements expressed some positive appreciation of women. And as we now know, Trump still retained a significant number of female voters even after this episode.

Trump is not only good at parrying attacks; he is especially brutal when attacking and defaming his opponents and in strategies of misdirection and diffusion. After getting in trouble for his "locker room talk," he shot back about Bill Clinton's sexual behavior while in the White House, implicating his Democratic opponent in a culture of sexual harassment by association. Even though the episode is likely to have harmed Trump's candidacy (though not fatally), it also reinforced his status as a victim (of the media, of women)—even when he was the perpetrator. As a victim, Trump is rather vocal, self-confident, and aggressive. Indeed, it might have hurt his candidacy more had he expressed remorse or otherwise (in the eyes of his supporters) shown weakness.

To some degree, Trump employs strategies that one might associate with victim advocacy or, more pointedly, the #MeToo movement that emerged in the fall of 2017. Again, this is not by chance. Part of Trump's appeal is that he opens the door to the majority of white American males to present themselves as victims of political correctness, feminism, and those seeking to emasculate them. They, too, can stand "in solidarity to all those who have been hurt" (to use a phrase by actress Alyssa Milano, who played a significant role in spreading the message of the #MeToo movement) by a variety of forces supposedly aligned against them: preferential hiring practices that favor minorities and women, family courts that deny equal parental rights to fathers, false accusations of sexual assault and rape, sexual consent practices on college campuses that presume the guilt of male initiators of sexual activity. Isolated instances of such events are taken as widespread practices or a broad "war against men" (to borrow a phrase used repeatedly by men's rights activists).

Of course, there is also a large difference between Trump's self-staging and the #MeToo movement. In the high-profile cases that characterize the #MeToo movement, a specific accusation is made that points to a past scene of harassment with an (alleged) perpetrator, such as Harvey Weinstein or Dr. Lawrence Nassar, that has left a lasting emotional scar. The later scene of accusation can also be highly dramatic, as in the case with the trial of Nassar, but it does not duplicate the earlier, dark scene of victimization. For Trump, the earlier and the later scenes fall together. Trump presents the scene of his "defense" as the primary scene. By defending himself against the media and other opponents, he simultaneously alleges his status as victim and thus his right to lash back. Like few others, Trump has mastered the art of presenting himself as a victim-hero.

His first State of the Union address on January 30, 2018, successfully opened his model of the victim-hero to others. The speech was filled with theatrical references to American heroes and victims (plus one Korean victim-hero, present at the event). The performative message was, in Trump's words, "Americans are dreamers, too." (The rhetoric here attempted to take back the term "dreamers" from the children of undocumented immigrants, whose claims to US citizenship Trump's administration was challenging.) Native-born Americans, his speech assured listeners, were the victims of "American carnage" and thus entitled to participate in Trump's fiction. For Trump, seemingly, the new American Dream is to be a victim-hero like him.

The second element is the audience effect that Trump's attacks and (often petulant) parries precipitate, whether in heated, fast-paced debates or via Twitter. That Trump is attacking or being attacked is more important than any actual arguments or truths such attacks may or may not contain. Facts often follow feelings and become "felt truths," so that if one feels Trump is right, real facts are dismissed as "FAKE NEWS."

Let me add a note here: While commentators quickly coined the term "post-fact" to describe our current moment, this is actually a well-established tendency. The exceptions are not the leaders who ignore or deny facts but those with the odd restraint to let themselves be guided by the facts. It is the regime of truth that some civilizations have cultivated that is the rare flower, not the emotional disregard for the "reality-based community."[43]

Trump's empathetic advantage derives in part from putting himself into situations in which no one knows what he will say or how he will escape. Will he finally fold, or will he come up with yet another riposte? Such anxiety can be a fantastic trigger for empathy. The audience observing Trump, whether they support him or not, coexperiences the pressure on Trump to respond. When I watched the debates, for example, I often felt that I was the one being called upon to respond, not Trump. An accusation is a key trigger for focusing attention and taking a perspective. (I have suggested elsewhere that this dynamic of the accusation is a central feature that motivates narrative to provide excuses and justifications.[44]) Most people, if backed into a corner by legitimate criticism as often as Trump is, would probably crumble in the spotlight or admit wrongdoing. We have seen countless public figures do so. But Trump unfailingly comes back with a defense—strong or ludicrous, depending on whether one likes and supports him or not—usually in the form of a vicious counterattack.

Trump becomes, for the observer, a figure of empathy, not as a human being but as a victim of "unfair" or "unjust" attacks. The stronger the attacks and accusations, the more appealing he becomes to his base, and the fact that many of the accusations are legitimate paradoxically plays to his advantage. His proneness to error paired with his killer instinct for spontaneous replies make him an avatar for his supporters; they know that they, too, make mistakes and wish they could deliver comebacks like Trump.

I am honestly embarrassed to admit this but during the election, I felt myself being drawn into Trump's perspective. Was this a manifestation of my childhood wandering stage fright, in which I projected myself into another's situation just at the moment they stepped into the spotlight? Regardless, I repeatedly found myself coexperiencing Trump's situation and I could observe the three-person model of empathy occurring within me. I started to share his perspective via a process I cannot call anything but empathy.

While it failed to persuade me rationally to side with him or his (to me) terrifying positions and excesses, I was emotionally invested in his performances. There were tense moments for me: Trump is confronted with some past missteps, again, in a debate, and needs to answer, on the spot. What will he say? What could I say? Seen from his perspective, his opponents looked quite unappealing.

This dynamic revealed in a very personal way how empathy and side-taking could have resulted in his victory and his base of support, even among registered Democrats. One can imagine one of his supporters saying, "I respect Trump. He's a real person who says what he really thinks and feels. I like that. Do I agree with or believe everything he says? Of course not. I also don't believe everything my spouse says, and I still love them." By this logic, Trump's missteps and even his catastrophic errors of judgment can only help him, as long as he remains vocal about it.

There is certainly a segment of voters who support Trump's derogatory, discriminatory, racist, and sexist utterances, the people whom Hillary Clinton derided as "deplorables." The impact of their malignant opinions should not be minimized. However, it seems likely to me that a larger part of the population who voted for him did so not because of these statements but in spite of them. Trump's polarizing persona demanded from everyone a clear position, either for or against. And among those who were for him, empathy strengthened their resolve. Indeed, Trump's depressingly plausible boast that he could "stand in the middle of Fifth Avenue and shoot somebody" and not lose voters suggests how powerful a force in politics empathy can be.

Contrast this support for Trump and with the slogan devised (by a graphic designer, Ida Woldemichael) for Hillary Clinton's campaign: "I'm with her."[45] To be "with" someone means to agree with or support them; it does not necessarily mean that one empathizes or identifies with them.[46] But to his supporters, Trump was—despite his wealth and lifestyle—one of them. Even his aggressively narcissistic personality does not contradict his status as a master of empathy. In general, narcissism and empathy do not stand in conflict with each other in social contexts, since narcissists aim to attract the empathy of others and are, in that sense, gifted at manipulating them to do so.

I should note that once Trump was elected, I stopped sharing his perspective. I am liberated from his magnetic empathy, which worked on me during the election and in the debates but no longer does so now that he is in power. And even though I was unsurprised by his victory, and in fact predicted it early, I have no idea what will happen in terms of his base. Will he finally lose their support? Will they finally laugh at him rather than with him? Or will he need to keep escalating his rhetoric and actions, perhaps to the brink of starting a war, to keep alive the dynamic of side-taking and polarization?

Radicalizing Conflicts through Empathy

If Trump's rise represents one of the dark sides of empathy's side-taking aspects, another can be located in its role in fueling conflicts and deepening divides between people. Conditioned to believe that inculcating greater levels of empathy can lower the risk of conflict and ameliorate violence, we may find this counterintuitive. Terrorists, though, can act out of empathy for those in whose name they kill; ethnic, religious, and political conflicts can arise and escalate because of empathy for the victims of oppression or injustice, whether real or imagined.

In the previous pages, I just described how empathy can be used to solidify and deepen quick side-taking judgments. In theory, this can lead to polarizing feelings that turn relatively moderate tensions into acute conflicts. But how does it work in practice?

A particularly drastic instance of polarization is terrorism. Modern terrorism has its origins in the incendiary nationalisms of the nineteenth century, which coincided with the emergence of mass media. Localized acts of violence only become widespread terror when they are broadly disseminated. It is therefore not wrong to describe terrorism as bloodily effective marketing. A relatively small number of people are able, with a single spectacular event, to throw an entire nation into a state of fear and shock, thus bringing attention to their ideas. In spite of this hateful calculus and the brutality of their deeds, the people who commit acts of terrorism are rarely coolly calculating agents of hate or mindless fanatics, as depicted in Hollywood thrillers and popular media. Many of them might instead be seduced into action by their devotion to a group, a religion, or a leader, rather than a rejection of the dominant culture and ruling powers. The point I wish to highlight is that even the assassins and suicide bombers of recent history are more likely to shout "Alahu akbar" than "Fuck the West." Terrorism is, from this point of view, initially an alignment with—a decision for—one side and a reasonable degree of sympathy for a movement. In fact, this kind of siding with a group can occur in people who are not directly connected to victims and survivors or otherwise affected but instead live a comfortable middle-class life.

Clark McCauley and Sophia Moskalenko describe the typical mechanism by which people become radicalized as group identification: "We are a special or chosen group (superiority) who have been unfairly treated and betrayed (injustice), no one else cares about us or will help us (distrust), and the situation is dire—our group and our cause are in danger of extinction (vulnerability)."[47]

For these authors, the focus is on an in-group identification of the activists, be this leftist anti-poverty fighters, freedom fighters, white supremacists, or Islamist groups. Cases of Islamist middle-class sleeper cells in the West show that there can be quite a gap between the sleeper terrorist and the actual group that becomes the target of identification or solidarity. In these cases, it makes more sense to speak of actual empathy. The sleeper observes a conflict, say the tensions between Jewish settlers and Palestinians, and starts to feel deeply for their chosen side. They may only perceive the conflict via the media but they start to develop deep feelings about the injustice done to their chosen side, a side they view as suppressed by the other side.[48]

In an interview, Martin Rudner, a former Carleton University professor and a specialist on terrorism, sums up the idea of the sleeper as follows: "They come from good middle-class families. . . . In other words, they weren't alienated."[49]

One such riddle of radicalization is Mohammed Atta, the oldest of the 9/11 attackers, who is often described as the group leader. He grew up in Egypt as part of the upper middle class and did well in school. No obvious episode of discrimination or trauma has been identified as causing his radicalization. He was a loner, but not isolated. It seems that his radicalization began as a consequence of moving to Hamburg, Germany, in 1992 for postgraduate studies, but not as a direct indoctrination but rather a self-selected reclusiveness.

I sometimes wonder about his experiences in Hamburg. A year after he arrived there, I also came back to Hamburg from the United States to do postgraduate work at Hamburg University (Atta attended the city's Technical University). My experiences as a returning German must have been the polar opposite of his. They were also quite different for my then-girlfriend, now wife, an

American of part Indian heritage who also stuck out as different in the dominant German culture. The question is which of Atta's experiences in Hamburg led him to radicalize further. Was he treated like a second-class citizen? Or did he choose to withdraw?

Mohammed Atta lived first with a German family and then for years with German fellow students. He also found part-time employment for five years with an urban planning company. In that sense, he was well integrated into society and had good opportunities. However, it seems that on another level separate from his actual living conditions he actively sought out and reacted to moments of suppression of the Arabic culture by dominant Western influences. His thesis, completed in the mid-nineties, focused on the way (Western) modern architecture was destroying traditional Arabic cityscapes (and Aleppo in particular). He was especially opposed to concrete skyscrapers that would destroy not only the skyline but also the flow of traditional life. As a child, his parents had moved to a skyscraper apartment. (That he would pilot one of the planes that destroyed the World Trade Center towers is, at the very least, suggestive.)

From what we know, Atta had no obvious cause to turn to mass violence and was not alienated. He had opportunities; his two older sisters became a medical doctor and a professor, respectively. Nor was it the case that his in-group was a band of radicals. Even the cleric in the Hamburg mosque he attended may not have played a decisive role in his radicalization, since it was Atta who seems to have sought him out. Instead, the choice to become a terrorist appears to have emerged more from nostalgic fantasies about a pure Arabic world that was being violated. Buried below the aggression that led to his shocking acts of violence, then, might be an intensely positive feeling for an imaginary city, culture, and world that he could never recreate. He opted for and empathized with this fiction of a pure Arabia, and thereby ended up loathing the West.

These speculations about Atta are unverifiable and are not intended to excuse his actions. There are multiple social and psychological factors that can transform a well-adjusted individual into a terrorist. Figures like Atta, however, appear to have taken a side, as described in the previous section, and made it their own, sharing in their suffering so strongly that they see the defense of this side as their life's calling. Terrorists, in short, may act out of empathy and be inspired by its polarizing quality.

Indeed, so effective is empathy at intensifying polarization that even attempts to use it to bridge social divides and reduce tensions between groups are complicated. Keith Barton, a professor of comparative pedagogy at Indiana University, has written about a fascinating case of empathetic education gone wrong in which school authorities in Northern Ireland attempted to devise a history curriculum for grades six through eight that would promote understanding between Catholic and Protestant students and thereby lessen tensions between the two sides. All students were taught and tested on the reasons why the Catholics supported the Home Rule Bill of 1888, what acts of violence and political injustice the Catholics had suffered, and so on. At the same time, the curriculum explained the historical suffering felt by Protestants as well. The idea was a simple one: By learning to see the conflict from the other group's perspective, students would develop an empathy that would relativize and soften the hardened opposition between the sides. The effort was a success, it seemed, as students demonstrated their mastery of the new material, with the students generally succeeding in telling the story of the conflict from both perspectives.

But contrary to all hopes, several follow-up studies revealed that this new generation of students was just as strongly polarized as students who had not experienced the new curriculum. In fact, as Barton and his coresearcher, Alan McCully from the University of Ulster, discovered, "identification of students with their group's historical positions grew even stronger" after three years of the new program.[50] They concluded that while "students were highly sympathetic towards members of the opposing group . . . their sympathy consisted primarily of assimilating the experience of the other into their own frame narrative. Rather than simply ignore or disregard the alternative position, students now reinterpreted it."[51]

What went wrong? There are different ways to interpret the data. One possibility is that the curriculum neglected to directly engage the students emotionally and was instead focused largely on the intellectual appreciation of differing perspectives. In conversation, Barton told me that this is what he believes. Another possibility is that the pressure from the social milieu in which the students lived, with its widespread cultural divisions, was simply too strong to give the students any real choice. This case suggests the limits of education to make a significant difference in perspectives shaped by history.

One other plausible explanation is that the structure of empathy itself was working against this pedagogical peace process. Instead of bridging the divide, empathy here served to strengthen divisions. Barton and McCully suspect that within this well-intentioned effort were the structures of further polarization.[52] If empathy is closely interlocked with side-taking, as I suggested above, then identification with one side will only intensify after being presented with more examples of conflict, whether or not they show one's own side in a bad light (as argued earlier in this chapter). The main takeaway for the students was that every event in their history could be seen from both a Catholic and a Protestant side. This only reinforced the division the program was intended to overcome as students internalized the polarization of two sides. And the students knew very precisely which of the sides was their own. Even when the students had learned to take on cognitively (and probably also emotionally) the perspective of the other side, the curriculum consistently taught them that such a perspective was just that: that of the other side.

While this project was abandoned, using pedagogy to stimulate opposing sides of a conflict to empathize with each other should not necessarily be dismissed. However, we should not simply assume that empathy will do more good than bad. In the case of Northern Ireland, it would seem to make better sense to teach a common history curriculum, emphasizing, for example, the Great Famine of the 1840s, since hunger makes no distinction between rivals.

The case of South Africa offers a different model of resolving conflict, one that does not engage the mechanisms of empathy but rather attempted to forge a new national identity. The methods of the Truth and Reconciliation Commission are important because they reached forgiveness as a judicial verdict, independent of disposition, empathy, or side-taking. The goal of this judicial-political apparatus was to keep the conflict from growing deeper, to set aside punishment in favor of avoiding further escalation. Whoever gave a full confession was forgiven. Perhaps this principle—that forgiveness could be the result of a judicial procedure, as long as the full truth was put on the table through confessions—kept the dynamics of side-taking and empathy in check.[53]

Fiction, Side-Taking, and Weird Moralities

Fiction is a critical site where people develop and practice empathy as coexperience. In fact, the evolution of fiction and the

emergence of empathy are probably intertwined, with each feeding the other. Fiction could only develop because of the development of what I call a "mobile consciousness" that allows one to be
transported in situations other than one's own, a prerequisite of
coexperience. At the same time, the early development of empathy
most likely required constant training and refinement paired with
rewards; fiction, of course, rewards its readers with pleasure and
excitement. While it would be highly interesting to disentangle the
complex relationships between empathy and fiction, the topic of
this book is a different one.[54] Side-taking is, however, a fundamental feature of fiction, one that bears at least cursory examination.

In the following, I will first suggest that fiction trains us in empathy and side-taking by making it pleasurable. I then argue that
while pleasure in side-taking is often connected with moral cues—
we side with the good characters—morality is not the driver of
the development of fiction. Rather, I will suggest that the training
of side-taking for empathy propels the polarization of opposites.
I will close this discussion by pointing to a complication of side-
taking in fiction that prefigures our discussions of sadistic empathy in chapter 4.

To explain the coevolution of fiction and empathy, one probably
needs to begin with the institution of the stage, one of the key cultural sites that trains group coordination and encourages collective
attention. The stage, in the widest sense, has a long history prior
to the actual development of theater. It begins with performances
in front of groups of people to communicate meaningful events,
where one or more performers or narrators (re)enact a past, future, or imaginary scenario. The "stage" includes many political
speeches, educational communications, and religious services.
It trains people to "mobilize" their consciousness in ways that allow
the observer to transport into the performance. This phenomenon

is likely supported by the collective nature of the institution, in which few perform and many observe. The audience learns to co-experience the glorious death of a hero as recreated on the stage as a cathartic collective event.

Missing from this sketch is a second aspect of the role of narrative (whether fictional, historical, or mythological) in empathy, namely its emphasis on side-taking. One fundamental feature of fiction as a subset of narrative—though it is also true of other kinds of narrative—is its presentation of characters who embody opposite features: old-young, male-female, strong-weak, smart-stupid, or beautiful-ugly. Further distinctions arise along with the plot, such as courage-cowardice, honest-deceitful. Of these, the distinction between good and evil might be most pronounced. In folktales and myths from around the world (not only Western stories), good characters reveal themselves through their good actions, while the wicked commit one crime after another until they meet their just end. An astonishing number of canonical literary works retain this scheme, however sophisticated their plots, characterizations, or literary styles. To be sure, modern heroes make more mistakes and are less certain of their path; but when they recognize their mistakes and improve themselves for the next test, they (more often than not) achieve a happy ending. Even in aesthetic-emotional exceptions like tragedies, wickedness is still punished even as the hero, who perishes, finds a glorious ending and is elevated in the eyes of the audience.

Why does narrative—and fiction in particular—so strongly rely on such clear distinctions as good and evil? Clear distinctions allow for clear side-taking. Not surprisingly, I link this quality to empathy, though I also hope to intrigue the reader with a puzzling riddle derived from this insight. Before we get there, two prominent theories that explain the dynamics of side-taking will help us with our answer.

The first of these theories holds that societies need to inculcate a sense of morality to promote cooperation. The community identifies enemies (bad guys, external threats, freeloaders) who then need to be punished for violating the community's moral code. In fact, not only do these enemies need to be punished; the act of punishing needs to be incentivized in order to motivate someone to do the dirty work of punishment. (There are different strategies to incentivize the act of punishing: punishers get an emotional boost by feeling good about their work; there can a prestige effect that makes effective punishers leaders; there can also be a mechanism to punish non-punishers, thereby indirectly incentivizing punishing.) Narratives, both mythological and more broadly fictional, may have emerged to bolster support for the view that being a good guy (a cooperator) is better (more morally correct) than being a bad guy (a non-cooperator).

In reality, of course, there are seldom purely good or truly evil individuals. Yet works of fiction often depict just such clear moral categories. When we consider that stories and myths have been circulating for thousands of years—perhaps ever since humans first began to speak some 70,000 years ago—and that today we still spend our days telling stories, it is not absurd to imagine that there might an evolutionary explanation for this emphasis on morality in storytelling.[55]

William Flesch has developed this theory of fiction by adapting theories from evolutionary psychology, arguing that fiction instigates and strengthens our moral feeling.[56] More important than identification or empathy with the hero, he claims, is the punishment of evil and of those enablers who stand by and allow evil to flourish. Flesch emphasizes how much of Western literature, from the stories of the Old Testament to modernity, is influenced by images of poetic justice or *comeuppance* (which served as the titles of Flesch's 2009 book). From an evolutionary perspective, as suggested, it makes sense for a community to punish wrongdoers and also those who do not intervene on behalf of the community and thereby leave the hard work of punishing to others.

From Flesch's point of view, storytelling serves an important moral function in a society. Literature, broadly defined, creates near optimal training conditions to highlight possible mistakes and to establish them as emotional events in individual minds. The exaggerations of fiction, the caricaturing of good and evil characters, makes the audience keenly aware of the markers of immoral behavior. There are many aspects of Flesch's argument that I find quite powerful, but, for me, his framework fails to answer a basic question about storytelling: Why do we enjoy fiction? Why do we spend so many hours a day surrounded by stories? (Jonathan Gottschall calculates that it can total four to six hours per day.[57]) There seems to be some deep pleasure to be had by slipping into the shoes of fictional characters that is different from the punishment framework suggested by Flesch. The other limitation of Flesch's theory is that while it might explain moral distinctions, it does not adequately account for narratives that use non-moral distinctions, such as strong-weak or strong-witty.

There is a second theory of side-taking and narrative that focuses less on punishment and also incorporates non-moral distinctions. This theory holds that by coordinating the task of side-taking, morality has a selection advantage by reducing tensions within a group. This theory, developed by Robert Kurzban and Peter DeScioli, focuses on how the violence in conflicts can be reduced and suggests bystander intervention as a solution.[58] When conflict emerges, bystanders can quickly and peacefully suppress it by choosing one and the same side, thus overwhelming the other side, which should then quickly give in. For this intervention to work, all bystanders must choose the same side, even if it is other than one's own group.

Moral evaluations of the situation would provide the bystanders with the cues to allow for the dynamic coordination of their side-taking. For example, all will favor the innocent victim and not the immoral aggressor. Moral reasoning provides reasons for people not to automatically favor their ingroup, thereby creating the possibility for larger societies to cooperate.

The crux of Kurzban's and DeScioli's argument lies in the fact that people must then actually come to the same side of the conflict. Morality can indeed indicate which side is the right one. But does this actually work? People in conflict are especially skilled at drawing on the reactions of observers and coming up with plausible arguments for their own position in order to win over at least some bystanders. Another complication arises when we add that people make moral decisions based on different moral intuitions, as Jonathan Haidt has suggested in *The Righteous Mind: Why Good People are Divided by Politics and Religion.*[59] Haidt shows how people can disagree about their evaluation because they have different appreciations of each basic moral intuition (care, fairness, authority, loyalty, liberty, and sanctity). In short, there is a lot of ambiguity in side-taking. People certainly do take sides and do so quickly, but they may not agree as much as Kurzban and DeScioli suggest.[60]

Even if we concede that there is enough bystander coordination to draw people to the same side, there is an issue. Bystander coordination on a local level may lead to escalations on a higher level by pitting large groups against each other since they have different standards. The dynamics of agreements between large groups can lead to massive conflicts and wars. Most people naturally sympathize with their own group, the one they know best. Alliances are thereby formed. However, on a larger scale, these different groups or alliances are likely to come into conflict. The tendency towards agreement on a local level can polarize larger groups precisely because each group thinks it is in the right, and, more importantly,

feels that it is right.[61] One could try to minimize the warlike potential in humans, as Steven Pinker does, with calls for empathy.[62] But
we should not disregard the destructive potential of our species.
In a war, both sides will have stories and fictions at the ready to
arouse latent sympathy for their side. Today's nationalism, heightened by fiction, may be a recent phenomenon, but the tendency it
represents is an old one.[63]

In their defense, Kurzban and DeScioli might argue that each
side in a violent conflict will suppress extreme behavior so as to
not dissuade bystanders from joining their side. The mechanism
of bystander coordination would therefore lead to a lessening of
violence and, perhaps, more ambiguous cases in terms of moral
choices between sides. Still, this model does not offer clear incen-
tives for bystanders to intervene. After all, side-taking can be dangerous, whether one has chosen the winning or the losing side.
Inaction may be the more rational strategy from the individual
standpoint. Although the model does not directly address fiction
as a potential training ground for encouraging bystander cooperation, it seems a plausible extension of their argument and could be
used to inspire intervention by valorizing it.

This speculation about the dangers of side-taking helps to explain what I consider the stronger connection between empathy
and the emergence of fiction and its binary portrayals of characters. As I have argued, people resist empathetic identification for
various reasons. In addition to the mental effort it takes, the loss
of self is also a risk (see chapter 1). In this respect, fiction offers a
safe and finite space for experimenting with empathy, thereby limiting empathetic engagement; when the story ends, the audience or
reader or viewer can return, mentally and emotionally, to their own
selves.[64] Similarly, while actual side-taking (in debates, elections,
sport events, or civil wars) tricks us into empathy by bypassing

our empathy-blocking mechanisms, fiction mimics this effect and trains us about the pleasurable aspects of taking sides by offering stark, *aesthetic* (as described in the introduction) choices between characters. It also adds a pleasurable reward for empathizing by offering its audience the thrill of "going for a ride."[65]

Although moral distinctions between characters can be a powerful guide to side-taking, readers or audience members will not necessarily choose the same side. There is probably no antagonist, villain, or monster that won't find someone to take its side. Zombies, for example, became fashionable in contemporary culture so they could be more easily killed onscreen without attracting empathy. Several more recent zombie movies and television series—*Day of the Dead* (1985), *Shaun of the Dead* (2004), *Warm Bodies* (2013), and the series *iZombie* (2015–19)—have broken that mold and, just as with Mary Shelley's original Frankenstein monster, they present creatures with whom the viewer could identify. Even flesh-eating zombies are, therefore, potential recipients of empathy and side-taking.

To advance a different theory of fiction, let me offer an interesting case of side-taking with morally deleterious effects. In the nineteenth century, adultery fiction became a popular genre, beginning with Goethe's *Elective Affinities* and including Gustave Flaubert's *Madame Bovary*, Clarín's *La Regenta*, and Theodor Fontane's *Effi Briest*. I have written about these novels elsewhere and will here only briefly point to the resulting effect.[66] In these texts, the female protagonist gives in to an affair and usually does not initiate it. There are different motivations for the female protagonist to do so, including boredom; sometimes her reasoning is left unexplained. In general, the woman remains silent about her misery as a result of the affair, which ends badly for her (Fontane's *Adultera* is the rare exception to this) and sometimes for the man as well.

What is most peculiar about these novels is the reader's position to the text, both in terms of the novels' actual historical readerships and the implied reader. The novels often found a divided reception in terms of sympathy towards the female protagonist, even though in most cases, the author provides clear signs that these women have been abandoned, fallen prey to circumstances, or are at least naive. At the same time, they are not simply helpless victims without agency. Yet the harsh social verdicts they face at the novels' ends go beyond what even their detractors think they might deserve. The reader typically has observed the minute operations of trickery put in place by their seducers, witnessing instances of abuse and abandonment inflicted upon the central female character. The author may share moments when she reaches out for help without getting it. So which position do readers assume with relation to novel and its heroine?

Some take a position against the woman for her behavior. If these readers still derive enjoyment from the book, it is because they feel righteous (as William Flesch would describe it). Not a few readers will identify with the heroine. This identification may be blocked to some degree by the author withholding access to the thoughts or feelings of their protagonist; we often do not know, for example, whether they have really fallen in love with their seducer; their actions instead remain somewhat erratic. And even if readers do identify with the heroine, the narration (and sometimes the narrator) places the reader at a peculiar distance from the female protagonist: The implied reader is often the only witness who sees that the heroine is not evil or mean but, rather, was tricked—perhaps by her own emotions, perhaps by others. And since there is no character within the novel to speak up for her, the implied reader is the only possible candidate. (In Rainer Werner Fassbinder's film version of *Effi Briest*, the director felt compelled to give Effi the final word, an accusatory monologue aimed at the bourgeois society that had suppressed her.) By making the implied reader the heroine's advocate—a character strikingly absent from the narrative—the novel provides an emotionally rewarding role for the reader.

There is a catch, though. In these novels, recall: (1) The reader witnesses the injustice done to the heroine or the circumstances (mis) guiding her actions; (2) When the heroine is shunned or harshly punished for her decisions, no one speaks up for her; (3) This leads the implied reader to "jump in" to the narrative by imagining their advocacy for these women, as if the reader were a benevolent character in the novel. (4) This emotional involvement rewards the reader by making them feel righteous and positive about their advocacy.

But to sustain the reader's engagement through this advocacy, the heroine must continue to suffer; otherwise, there is no role for the reader in the text. That is, structurally, the implied reader needs to approve of and even wish for the heroine's ongoing punishment since it is this mechanism that provides a morally positive role for the audience. Or, as in *La Regenta* and especially in *Madame Bovary,* the reader-advocate can also get increasingly frustrated with the heroine for her naive complacency in her own suffering. This may lead the reader to embrace or tacitly wish to prolong her punishment, not for moral failings but for torturing the reader. Empathy's side-taking dynamic, in this case, leads to the observer endorsing a morally untenable position. (I will come back to this troubling dynamic in chapter 4.)

For now, let me just suggest that in the case of fiction, we are dealing with weird morality, namely a morality that is triggered by good intuitions about who is morally superior but that leads to effects that we cannot easily call morally or ethically correct. Fiction promotes side-taking and provides clues about which side to take. However, fiction also creates the expectation for a payback for this act of side-taking. This payback can be an emotional reward of feeling good for seeing one's side win or the other side being punished. And it can extend to specific expectations of the characters' performance, emotions, and fate that we would call abusive if they were real people.

The chapter has proposed a three-stage architecture of empathy comprising: (1) a tendency towards empathy that we called hyperempathy; (2) empathy-blocking mechanisms; and (3) means of bypassing the blocking devices to allow empathy. Given humanity's impressive ability to feel empathy and our tendency to use it, people need to learn to control and thus limit empathy in order to prevent self-loss and exploitation by others. There are probably many forms of empathy blocking available to us, and most of them are likely operating without rational oversight. How, then, do we allow empathy to operate?

The three-person model of empathy describes how an external observer witnessing a conflict tends to quickly take a side, sometimes arbitrarily, and begin to see the conflict from their chosen perspective. Seeing the situation from one perspective leads to agreement, empathy, and confirmation of the original decision to choose one side over the other. Even bad or morally dubious side-taking decisions can be supported and strengthened via empathy. This effect leads to a radicalization of differences in conflicts. Hence my argument that *empathy, left uncontrolled, tends to strengthen, rather than resolve, conflicts.*

This is not to say that empathy has no place in conflict resolution. Instead of contributing to the settlement of a dispute, I posit, empathy often becomes part of the problem, something else that must be overcome. This caveat leads me to take a careful look at what might seem to be the best justification for empathy—humanitarian aid—in the next chapter.

3

False Empathy, Filtered Empathy

Many of the people I talk to about my concerns with empathy acknowledge that empathy may indeed have dark sides. However, at some point in the conversation they almost inevitably suggest that empathy is ultimately good regardless, since we empathize with people in need and help them. This chapter addresses my serious doubts about this claim. While I am not against empathy, I believe that the connection between empathy and helping people in need is more complex and murkier than people acknowledge.

The chapter proceeds in two steps. First, I develop the general "scene of humanitarian empathy"; then I look at what has been perhaps the boldest political step in the cause of humanitarianism in the twenty-first century thus far: Europe's—and particularly Germany's—welcoming of North African and Middle Eastern refugees fleeing civil war. For the impatient readers, let me foreshadow one of my claims: I believe that in many cases of humanitarian empathy, people do not actually develop empathy with the suffering people in need of help but rather identify with the helpers, whether real or imaginary. I call this form of empathy *filtered empathy*. My goal here is not to dismiss the power of empathy but rather to evaluate its impact to improve the world.

Most people assume that empathizing with suffering people is a "natural" feeling that just needs the right cultural context to flourish. As a result, perhaps, empathy is widely believed to have played a major part in the development of humanitarianism (as Steven Pinker suggests).[1] In this chapter, I will explore these assumptions by attempting to explain the effect that suffering, pain, and victimhood have on observers. My investigation proceeds phenomenologically to unfold *the scene of humanitarian aid* and related scenes of victimization. I loosely define humanitarianism here as intervention on behalf of people in need on the basis of a shared humanity. Building on chapter 2, we will ask what triggers empathy in situations that involve suffering people.

At first glance, the logic of victim empathy in general and humanitarianism in particular seems quite straightforward: we see the suffering of another or the injustice they are enduring and we "share their feeling," "imagine to be them," or "feel for them."[2] And because of this emotional response, we step in to help. But I find this model both simplistic and highly problematic. The "humanitarian impulse," like the side-taking discussed in the previous chapter, contains within it a dark aspect of empathy that can have (and has had) negative theoretical and real-world consequences. There is a historic dimension to explain the rise of humanitarianism that we will discuss later. First, though, I will discuss the *scene of empathy* that leads many people to altruistic acts.[3]

This scene of empathy, as discussed by Martha Nussbaum and others, has a series of discernible components.[4] One is the survivor or victim, a figure whose suffering or misfortune is understood by the observer as being undeserved or, as in the case of punishment, disproportionate. (I use the word "victim" here in the broadest sense, without implication of an opposing perpetrator; one can be a "victim" of circumstance.) Few things elicit side-taking as powerfully as do suffering and mistreatment. In chapter 2, I discussed the three-person model of empathy and how people who witness a conflict tend to take a side. In this chapter, I examine the peculiar attraction victims might have for our side-taking by means of a phenomenological examination of the scene of empathy.

The first important marker of this scene is the possibility of improving the victim's situation or alleviating their suffering. There is some evidence that people are more prepared to feel empathy when the person they are observing has the possibility of getting better or is already on the path to recovery, instead of stagnating or having no hope of improvement.[5] Change and development are also a key part of the narrative in literature and film, drawing the reader or viewer in to find out whether conditions will improve.[6]

Positive change allows the empathetic observer to withdraw their empathy once the other no longer needs it. Recalling concerns about self-loss from chapter 1, we feel more empathy when we have an exit strategy, when the self-loss aspect of empathy is contained. If the situation seems hopeless, unsurprisingly, people intuitively feel and show less empathy. This applies to chronic illness, aging, and other permanent or inevitable conditions, as well as to suffering beyond our powers to relieve. It is possible to deliberately cultivate empathy for people in such situations, as hospice or aid workers admirably do, but the danger of resentment and frustration is clear: unending empathy can lead to permanent self-loss, which can in turn develop a number of negative feelings, such as a deadening of emotions or fantasies of punishing the suffering other.

This temporal dimension of the scene of empathy contains within it a second defining characteristic. The observer intuits that their empathy and the intervention it motivates can actually alter the course of the suffering they see. This confidence takes a variety of forms, ranging from the belief that hope alone will have an impact to fantasies of omnipotence. Here, then, is the second aspect of the scene of empathy: empathy is more probable if we do not simply assume that change comes on its own but rather see it as dependent on a specific engagement by the observer who intervenes or imagines doing so. It seems likely, I hypothesize, that the intervention leads most clearly to empathy if it can be imagined as part of a narrative that features some kind of turning point.[7]

These aspects of the scene of empathy so far may seem somewhat unsurprising. However, here is a more puzzling question: For whom does the observer actually feel empathy? With whom do we, as the empathizer, coexperience the situation or circumstance requiring intervention? Could it be that people tacitly assume that empathy occurs with the victim, while many people actually favor the perspective of the (real or imaginary) helper? If this assumption is correct, we need to ask what positive or negative implications such helper empathy (or identification) has.

Heroes, Helpers, and Humanitarianism (or Helpers as Heroes)

I posit that empathy is less likely to emerge in the absence of an intervening helper, whether real or imagined, and that we are more likely to have empathy with the victim when we identify with the one who intervenes to help them. Helper identification is the medium of humanitarian empathy. Put differently, in order to experience empathy, we place ourselves in the role of helper.

Before unfolding the implications of this thesis, it will help to more clearly describe the scene of empathy:

1. The catalyst of empathy in the context of humanitarian aid consists of the recognition of another person, who appears to the observer to suffer, to be threatened, to need help, or to be disadvantaged in some way. There is no requirement that the observed person is actually suffering or feeling threatened. The suffering, want, or danger only needs to exist in the mind of the observer.[8]

2. The situation being observed unfolds as a temporal event with compelling narrative elements. It does not matter what the real backstory is, simply that the observer has imagined or assumed one. Typically, this narrative would highlight the innocence of the victim and the unfairness or injustice of their negative situation.

3. The narrative allows for the possibility of a better future. Because the suffering of the victim is based on specific, time-limited circumstances that the observer has registered, intuited, or invented, there is (or appears to be) hope for positive change, whether wildly implausible or immediate and concrete.

4. The observer must believe that not only is positive change possible but that it will not come on its own. In order to for it to happen, a second person must intervene: a helper must effect change.

If one aspect of the scene is missing, humanitarian empathy is less likely to develop. This model also helps clarify what many people imply when they say they feel empathy or have pity with someone. Empathy in this sense is more than cognitively or emotionally understanding the suffering of other people. Rather, to empathize with the victim means to perceive and coexperience their (temporal) situation, one that contains a narratively cogent

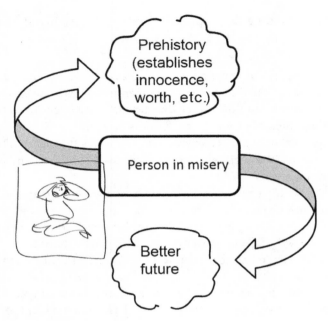

FIGURE 3.1
The narrative scene of empathy (with observer and helper)

backstory, an opportunity for intervention, and the possibility of improvement. The crux of my argument is that the empathizing observer assumes two perspectives in addition to their own—those of the victim and the helper—thus completing the mental scene of empathy.

While in the ultimate empathy fantasy the observer-helper is thanked for their intervention by the victim, one could also speculate about the need to imagine yet another perspective through which the intervention is seen and recognized as being good. This third perspective or person can be described as a second-order observer who offers the praise and gratitude that the observer, in their role as helper, deserves.

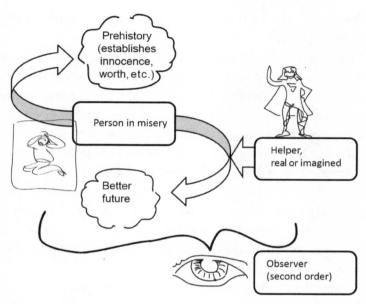

FIGURE 3.2
The narrative scene of empathy with observer and helper. The observer only arrives at empathy with the person in misery through the mediating figure of the helper.

At first glance, this scheme seems somewhat complicated, contradicting the feeling that empathy is straightforward and similar to other emotions: natural, intuitive, unreflective. The naive understanding of empathy works like this: one sees a suffering person, feels their suffering, perhaps copies their suffering in one's own mind, and for this reason is compelled to step out of one's own point of view and help. But there are numerous indications that empathy has a far more complex architecture (as discussed in chapters 1 and 2). The pleasure we find in stories with highly artistic scenarios speaks to this complexity; perhaps we celebrate the narrative arts because they can develop empathy-inspiring scenes with the most clarity.

An example will help us to clarify the structure. One of the most influential cinematic representations of the Holocaust is, undeniably, Steven Spielberg's *Schindler's List* (1993), a movie that received seven Academy Awards and was ranked eighth in the best one hundred American movies of all times by the American Film Institute in 2007. In the movie, we witness Nazi atrocities first in the Krakow ghetto and later in Auschwitz. We witness and experience most of the events through the character of the German industrialist Oskar Schindler (Liam Neeson), an alcoholic, a bohemian, an opportunist, and a war profiteer who discovers his calling to save Jewish lives. On the sideline, we also get glimpses of a couple of Jewish characters and their fate.

It seems that the huge critical and financial success of the movie is owed in large part to the trick of offering the perspective of the unlikely hero-helper to the audience. Despite its success, the movie was fiercely criticized. Among the issues raises by critics was the fact that the Nazi regime is personified by a psychopathic military officer instead of the seemingly harmless bureaucrats who made most of the decisions in Nazi Germany and who triggered Hannah Arendt's famous expression about the "banality of evil."[9] With its use of black-and-white film, the movie blurs the line between documentary and fiction and creates a realistic effect. The horror of the Shoah is experienced from a tourist's perspective when the camera moves at one point into what seems at first to be gas chambers, but then turns out to be actual shower rooms. And of course, a point of critique is the use of a non-Jewish protagonist to tell a Holocaust story. Indeed, the film ends with Schindler crying about his not having been able to save more Jews, before fleeing in a limousine. The overall effect, critics charge, is that a movie about genocide becomes a feel-good melodrama about the twelve hundred Jews Schindler saved rather than the more than six million Jews and others who were murdered. An emblematic critique has been to call the film "Holocaust Park."[10]

The fervor of the debate reflects how far our actual experiences of empathy can diverge from our expectations of how it should work. While we ethically should have empathy with the Jewish victims, it seems easier for many people to relate to a helper who is plagued with flaws. Perhaps everyday empathy requires an Oskar Schindler figure to help it unfold. The filmmakers may have recognized that the audience (even the Jewish viewers among them) would have less empathy with the victims than with the heroic savior. By identifying with Schindler, they coexperience how he discovers and expresses his empathy. Identification is a simple form of empathy in which someone places themselves in the role of another and thereby collapses the distance between the observer and the observed, allowing the observer to project their own feelings into the situation of the observed and turning the individual people into the variables.[11]

Identifying with the helper rather than the victim has several attractions. It allows the observer to experience how a difficult situation can be changed and to imaginatively share in the gratitude reserved for the savior figure. Further, identifying with someone who has (or seems to have) empathy also means experiencing their empathy. Finally, as an intermediary figure, the helper allows the observer to feel empathy without being exposed to the risk of self-loss. I term this kind of empathy—which is channeled through identification with a third figure (whether real, an imagined ideal, or even a fictional character)—*filtered* (or *indirect*) *empathy*.

Filtered empathy is, I argue, characteristic of support—whether financial or political—for humanitarian aid and the victims of humanitarian crises. Narrative forms around such events construct the space for possible identifiable heroes. The observer may develop an especially strong empathetic connection when a humanitarian hero is absent and must therefore be invented to fill this gap in the narrative. In a situation where improvement is possible but isn't forthcoming, hope takes the form of the savior who, since no one else is available, could be the observer himself.[12]

What could be wrong with this picture? Is this dynamic, in fact, a negative aspect of empathy, or is it simply a positive way of manipulating people into supporting causes deemed good or worthy? It seems likely that the mechanisms of filtered empathy may have led to such innovations as abolition, religious tolerance, human rights, and legal equality for all people since the eighteenth century. At the same time, there are both moral and historical grounds for arguing against the deployment of (filtered) empathy in support of humanitarian campaigns. The moral problem with the scene of empathy in such cases is that the empathy it creates is limited or weak. Once the complex structure of this scene (observer-helper-victim-appreciator) begins to unravel, the compassion for the victim that empathy precipitated and that impels one to do good disappears. Filtered empathy (as opposed to, for example, rational insight or some form of compassionate empathy) does not ultimately promote the well being of the victim as much as it does that of the observer. Indeed, we might apply the same criticism to such cases as did detractors of *Schindler's List*: We are identifying with the wrong figure! It is empathy with no staying power or resonance. The bar for achieving it is so low, which means that because it is so easy to create empathy for the victim, it is just as easy to cut it off.

This in turn leads to a deeper moral problem: Empathy not only makes the other into a victim but can also compel them into victimhood. When empathy remains bound to the entire scene, the other can only be understood, intellectually and emotionally, when they play the role of victim, even without knowing they are doing so. Filtered empathy does not "accompany" the other but instead only attaches to them when they become a victim, trapping them into that role, perhaps permanently, thus denying them agency. One can imagine situations in which this would be highly problematic: relief workers keeping people in dependency, for example, or teachers not training students to be self-sufficient.[13] This is a consequence of identifying with the helper-hero, for whom the suffering other is only useful for as long as they suffer, turn to the helper, and thereby confirm the helper's superiority. Should the victim fail to deliver to the helper what the helper requires, which could be recognition, explicit praise, or indirect approval by improving, the helper might slip into resentment.

I should add that the vast majority of the actual aid workers that I have met over the years avoid falling into this trap by effectively limiting or blocking empathy, achieved through maintaining a measure of cynicism. The dynamic of humanitarian empathy may affect people who support humanitarian causes more than those actually working on the front lines.

Humanitarian empathy, as described here, is astonishingly self-serving, given its orientation around the self of the observer. Identification-based empathy can even be seen as a kind of narcissism. (Here again we see how narcissism, rather than being the opposite of empathy, goes hand in hand with it). This does not mean that every form of empathy with those in need rehearses this dynamic. I have little doubt that our world needs more and not less compassion, or that empathy has a role to play in that. For example, people narrating their struggle and how they overcame it can elicit empathy for their prior suffering, thus allowing their audience to more richly experience what it means to suffer. Still, one should be aware that a lot of this compassion with people in need slides into the dynamics and pitfalls of helper identification that this chapter discusses.

Instead, it is my contention that empathy is not required as an impetus for humanitarian intervention—and that its deployment in such situations has a dark side. Indeed, I would argue that the impulse for humanitarian intervention is more often and more effectively rooted in morality and in the development of an imagined common interest with those outside of our family or tribe. Herein lies a historical argument about the development of humanitarianism as well, that I will very briefly sketch in the following.

Many recent commentators have stressed empathy's largely positive contribution to historic developments. Throughout history, one can identify key moments at which the humanitarian and empathetic impulses seem to coincide. The development of notions of hospitality, the emergence of Buddhism and Christianity, the Islamic golden age, and Western Enlightenment all come to mind. The academic discourse on empathy that began around 1900, as described in the previous chapter, could also be added to the list, given that it occurred at a time of increased humanitarian activities, exemplified by the rapid growth of the International Red Cross, founded in 1863; the Nobel Peace Price, first awarded in 1901; and actions inspired by the events of World War I.

The Enlightenment seems to be the most significant period for the rise of the modern humanitarian movements, including abolitionism, which embraced ethical and empathetic tendencies that were more inclusive than any previous such developments in the West. The Enlightenment expanded the motivation to help others—from the family and the group to a distant and often abstract Other whom the "helpers" might never meet. As described by Lynn Hunt, "Eighteenth-century readers, like people before them, empathized with those close to them and with those most obviously like them—their immediate families, their relatives, the people of their parish, in general their customary social equals. But eighteenth-century people had to learn to empathize across more broadly defined boundaries."[14] To explain how this expansion took hold, Hunt points to novels and literature as the core medium for mobilizing empathy. In fact, one can make the point that fiction writers not only invoke empathy in novels but also theorize it. A case in point would be the 1779 play *Nathan the Wise* by Gotthold Ephraim Lessing. The play imagines a world order in which Jews, Christians, and Muslims not only tolerate each other; they become a true world family by means of adoption, love, and marriage.

Thomas Lacquer likewise locates the origins of the humanitarian impulse in the same period but ascribes it to transformations in the legal regimes of Western European polities: "In the late eighteenth century, the ethical subject was democratized; more and more people came to believe it was their obligation to ameliorate and prevent wrongdoing to others. Through law, more and more people could be included in the 'circle of we.'"[15]

However, the historical proximity of the emergence of a more abstracted empathy and the rise of humanitarianism proves neither that empathy lies at the center of this historical development nor that empathy constitutes the best basis for humanitarianism today. (To be clear, my skepticism does not mean that I question the general goals of humanitarianism to promote our shared humanity. I strongly believe we need more equality, though not equalization. The two challenges of our age are, in my mind, real equality and an end of the destruction of the environment, including but not limited to the impact of global climate change. By real equality, I mean that the poorest person on earth and the richest can meet each other at eye-level in all social contexts. Put in economic terms, this would mean the income difference should not exceed a ratio of something like 1:12.[16] To me, our current global state of affairs seems to be utterly indefensible, radically unfair, and life negating.)

Modern humanitarianism (or the unleashing of what Martha Nussbaum calls "political emotions" on a global scale[17]) moved from the ingroup to the global community with the advent of the Enlightenment. What we now would call empathy was indeed a key concept of the Enlightenment (sympathy, pity, compassion). However, I am skeptical of the idea that humanitarianism unfolded directly out of this new concept of empathy. Contrary to the argument (as presented by Hunt and others) that empathy for the weak, suffering, and neglected was the main driving force behind this impulse, I would like to suggest an alternative that seems more likely to me. This alternative also involves empathy, but in the service of a different concept.

One of the central conceptions of the late eighteenth century is individuality. People were increasingly freed from those forces—confessional, occupational, familial, political—that had determined their lives from birth. A hierarchical determinism gave way to what the German sociologist Niklas Luhmann calls a "stratified functionality."[18] The historical shockwaves from this "saddle point," as the historian Reinhart Koselleck calls this period, are massive.[19] The new emphasis on the nuclear over the extended family had far-reaching implications as well, increasing social mobility and allowing greater choice over one's profession. Together, these other forces emphasized the individual. Around 1770, these developments culminated in new value being placed on the concept of "self."[20]

Empathy and compassion (as well as, to use the terminology of the time, sympathy, pity, and sentiment) were discovered at the end of the eighteenth century as the means by which the isolated individual could establish contact with others. As long as people were determined by their age, class, gender, race, religion, profession, and location, no complex mental operations were necessary for such connections. Everyone was simply part of an in-group of similar people. The new individual, however, was isolated and defined by difference and autonomy. The individual thus needed to embrace new social technologies to connect with other people who were considered utterly different. Empathy promised a solution to the dilemma of social connection that was increasingly considered unlikely. In short, the rise of empathy was due not to its global reach of expanding pity, but rather to its ability, through bridge building, to strengthen momentary feelings of similarity between people that were understood to be inherently different. It was this detachment of the individual from the in-group, I suggest, that led to the global reach of the new empathy.

Momentary feelings of similarity have a peculiar feature: they can emerge with members of the in-group or out-group alike. Since difference was considered the norm, and momentary similarity the exception, it now became fully feasible to establish short-lived empathy bridges with people from different classes, ethnic backgrounds, and far-flung places. In the dramas and novels of the age, characters are placed in extreme situations—and in these extreme situations all people would feel the same. The production of similarity effects as a condition of empathy is the goal of complex narrative and dramatic setups.[21]

In short, a novelty from around 1770 was the practice of tracing most human practices to the self. This would mean that it was empathy as similarity effect (driven by a rising individualism) rather than empathy as compassion that led to the rise of the human rights regime.[22] This might bring us back to the account offered by Laqueur, who describes the legal regimes of the new individualism. Empathy has its place in this narrative to be sure, but as a tool for the self and not for the sake of altruism. The new empathy is not so much a form of humanitarian compassion as it is an attitude of extending the self and finding it mirrored elsewhere.

This alternative historical explanation does not undermine Hunt's suggestions entirely. It is clear that empathy became valued around the end of the eighteenth century. David Hume, Adam Smith, Lessing, and others devoted substantial thought to the force by which one person relates to another. Hume referred to what we now would call empathy as "sympathy" and Lessing as *Mitleid* (pity). The new genre of the eighteenth century—the novel— offered audiences new forms of transportation, as did drama in the centuries before.[23] But empathy's global humanitarian effects are not as one-dimensional as they might appear. It might not be simply the victim stories of Richardson's novels but also the hero stories that made human rights palatable to the Western tongue. Empathy and human rights come with strings attached. This is certainly also true for the helper identification, in which the victim has to perform a service for the hero-helper.

Let me offer a quick recap: my suggestion is that a strong catalyst of empathy consists of scenes taken in by an observer that contain a "victim." The range of such scenes is broad and contains all cases in which an individual or a group appears to the eyes of the observer to be suffering, to be caught in an unhappy situation, or to need help, without a simple resolution in sight. This applies to famine, war, and to individual misfortunes. Another attribute of these scenes is a change over the course of time, noticed by the observer, that implies the possibility of improvement or at least a lessening of suffering.

The typical case that is the focus of this chapter is the one in which a possible intervention from a helper could alleviate the situation. In this case we have chosen the term humanitarian aid in its broadest sense, even if many cases fall outside of what is usually understood as humanitarian or development aid. Such scenes offer the observer an object of identification in the person of the helper or hero. "Identification" here means the shared identity of the observer with the observed: when I identify myself with someone, I put myself directly into their situation and imagine how I would feel in that situation. By means of this identification with the helper, empathy with the victim becomes easier since I adopt the helper's empathy and a filtered, or indirect, empathy becomes possible. It is filtered by the perspective of the helper and thereby limited to aspects fitting to victimhood, leaving out other aspects of the personality of the other. The intervening hero-helper comes to the aid of the victims, and the observer can coexperience the heroic acts. Thereby, something else happens. On the one hand, the observer becomes the hero-helper. On the other hand, the observer nevertheless retains a part of his outside perspective and thus can mentally praise, value, and lionize the hero-helper and make the helper's position desirable. That means that when we identify with the hero, we also praise ourselves for our empathy, or seek recognition from a third party. Consequently, the danger of filtered empathy is not simply shallowness but also resentment: if the victim does not play along, does not improve or praise the helper, people may grow impatient and actively hostile.

There is yet another way in which this form of filtered or indirect empathy is attractive: it partly avoids the danger of self-loss.

For it is not our own self that we lose, but rather that of the intervening helper, into whose position we temporarily place ourselves.

In the following section, I wish to analyze a highly remarkable case for helper identification, namely Germany's embrace of refugees since 2015. I will suggest that many Germans and other Europeans could suddenly embrace refugees because Angela Merkel served as a model of empathy for them and allowed them a form of filtered empathy by offering herself as target for identification. Curiously, however, the discussion of Angela Merkel also allows us to introduce a second imperfect form of empathy, which I call *false empathy*.[24] We will begin with the introduction of this second concept of false empathy before we bring back the notion of filtered empathy to understand the German situation.

Germany, World Champion of Empathy: Angela Merkel and the Refugees

The most courageous political act of the twenty-first century so far has, in my opinion, been the decision by Germany, Austria, and Sweden in September 2015 to open their borders to refugees fleeing the civil war in Syria and similar conflict regions. In that moment, it seemed that the three countries—and Europe as a whole—were finally addressing the biggest humanitarian crisis facing the continent since the wars in the former Yugoslavia two decades before. Not only did Merkel's pledge that all Syrians who arrived in Germany could apply for asylum there reverse Germany's own immigration policy, it made meaningless the European Union's rules, as codified in the Dublin Regulations, about dealing with asylum seekers. What led to this momentous decision?

Empathy, I will argue, played an outsized and ultimately corrosive role in the decision-making process.

There is no way to avoid talking about a single person here: Angela Merkel, who has been Germany's chancellor since 2005. No other political personality in Germany would have made—and stood by—this decision, although politicians of various stripes did stand in support of Merkel. There is no question that Merkel showed exceptional political courage and backbone. And other than Austria and Sweden, no other government in the world took such a risk—and indeed even Austria and Sweden both backpedaled shortly afterwards. Asylum and immigration are third-rail issues in many nations, as we see in Donald Trump's anti-immigrant rhetoric and policies, Great Britain's 2016 Brexit referendum, and the 2016 Austrian presidential elections. Indeed, Merkel herself has a mixed record on the issue of immigration and multiculturalism, going on record as late as 2010 as saying that Germany's experiment with multiculturalism had "utterly failed."[25]

This section examines the role empathy played both in Merkel's decision-making and in the political development since. Let me be clear: I fully support the decision to open the border and second the commitments involved. All rich countries should follow this example. My comments here are not an attempt to be clever in hindsight. Rather, I am critical of how the dynamics unfolded—and backfired.

How did Merkel's decision come about? Relevant, perhaps, to Merkel's decision is the particular resonance that the images of devastated Syrian cities and waves of refugees have for Germans, whose parents or grandparents may well have been similarly displaced by the devastation of the Second World War, which transformed several million Germans (as well as citizens of other nations) into "displaced persons" or DPs. My generation (I was born in West Germany in 1967) grew up in the shadows of these displacements, which came up in stories and conversations all the time. (It is worth pointing out that the semantic difference between "displaced persons" and "refugees" seem to favor the displaced: they are passive, blameless victims, while "refugees" have taken action, even though both are the consequences of similar political events.)

It is certainly also relevant to recall the Greek debt crisis of 2013, during which Merkel became the face of the arrogant authority of the European Union. Her inconsistent position towards Greece, which wavered between harsh and accommodating, made her the target of any number of hostile projections. In northern Europe, she was seen as too feminine, too weak; in southern Europe, she appeared as a caricature of Prussian coldness, as Bismark's heir, an emotionless dogmatist and a heartless woman. It may be, then, that Merkel found herself needing to either correct these (mis)perceptions or remake her political image.

Setting aside such speculations about her possible personal or political motivations, however, I want here to analyze a single incident that occurred shortly before the decision of the night of September 4, 2015. In the middle of July, Merkel made a now well-known public appearance with a group of schoolchildren. A Palestinian girl from Lebanon named Reem told the chancellor, speaking in German that was remarkably confident and complex for her age, that her family had been waiting for years for a decision on their residence permit but were now likely going to be deported. The chancellor tried to reply that Lebanon is not a war zone and that Germany could not take everyone from the camps there but did agree that four years of waiting is too long and that Germany could do better.

This seemed to be the end of the exchange, the chancellor turned again to the group as a whole. But then she stopped, and noticed that Reem was crying. Here is the transcript of what happened next:

> *The chancellor stops, looks at the girl, who is crying—and Merkel goes to her.*
>
> *Merkel:* Come, now. You did just great. [Och, komm. Du hast das doch prima gemacht.]
>
> *The chancellor comforts the crying girl.*
>
> *Moderator:* I do not think, Madame Chancellor, that it is a matter of doing great, but rather the painful situation she is in.
>
> *Merkel:* I know that it is a painful situation. And nevertheless, I want to comfort her, because I, because we all have no wish to put you in such a situation, and because it has been hard for you, and you have done a great job of showing many, many other people what kind of situations we can find ourselves in. All right?
>
> *The girl wipes the tears from her cheeks and is embraced by another girl.*[26]

What the transcript misses is first the warm and colloquial tone Merkel uses when she aims to comfort the girl, and then the scolding tone of the moderator who seems to gloat in his self-righteousness at having caught Merkel making an insensitive statement. A large-scale public debate started and Merkel was accused of being "cold-hearted" and "lacking empathy."[27] Obviously, the chancellor erred. She seems to have realized herself a moment later that the girl was probably not crying because of the stress of speaking to the chancellor but because her family was going to be deported. How did Merkel misjudge the situation? There are two possible interpretations, both involving empathy.

First, the chancellor's misfire could have been a projection of her own feelings. The worldview of a political figure is marked by anxiety about getting the wording of things just right and performing well. There is strong pressure not to say, or even imply, the wrong thing. The smallest misstatement will be seized upon by the press, even as they might ignore substantive policies. Fear of the gaffe is legitimate, as evidenced by the recent series of prominent politicians in Germany and the United States (to name only two countries) who have paid the price for ill-considered words or confused expressions when speaking off the cuff. Think of the US presidential bids derailed by single moment: Rick Perry's nervous debate performance in 2016 or Howard Dean's infamous scream in 2004. Germans will recall how the president of the Bundestag Philipp Jenninger was forced to resign after a 1988 speech describing Nazi propaganda techniques in which he did not read aloud the quotation marks and thus didn't clearly differentiate his own argument from the views he was describing. In this light, it would seem that Merkel has taken the pressure she feels to say everything correctly and placed it on the girl—doing just great—thereby failing to understand her. This would be a case of falsely projecting oneself (the politician fearing performance) into another (the young refugee).

Second, the chancellor could have recalled similar situations in her own experience when interpreting Reem's reaction. Surely she has seen young people collapse in front of the camera before, get stage fright, or break down in tears. In this light, she could have simply falsely applied a general schema or stereotype of young people to the particular situation of a single girl.

In both cases, Merkel's apparent lack of empathy missed the main point, namely that this girl faces deportation to a country of which she only remembers the camps. For the audience, the unusually maternal, friendly, warm tone of Merkel quickly turned into false praise—that is, praise for the wrong thing, a clear misunderstanding of the child. Paradoxically, it is a failure of empathy as a direct result of showing empathy. Merkel was empathizing with the girl but for the wrong reasons; this comes across as patronizing to viewers and paints Merkel as cold.

The moderator jumps in immediately. While he is correct to point out that the chancellor has likely misunderstood the child, he misjudges his tone and comes across as condescending and paternalistic. Merkel, in turn, displays irritation, becomes defensive, but then deftly turns things around. The moderator, it seems, allowed Merkel see her own answer from the outside, a perspective that according to the three-person model of empathy would cause even the chancellor to side with the Palestinian girl in their interaction.

The argument here is not that Merkel did anything wrong, or that her apparent lapse of empathy reflects a callousness on her part.[28] Nor do I want to paint the chancellor as emotionally distant, as the press and wide swaths of the public clearly did. Rather, my point in analyzing this episode is to explore to what extent it served as the catalyst for the chancellor's subsequent change of mind concerning Syrian refugees. In particular, I am struck by the fact that the chancellor explicitly used a phrase in talking with Reem that would take on great meaning in the later decision, one that would soon afterward become famously associated with her:

> Merkel: It is sometimes hard in politics. So, when you stand in front of me, you are a really appealing person. But you also know that there are thousands and thousands more in the Palestinian refugee camps in Lebanon. And if we say, "you can all come, and you, in Africa, you can all come, and you can all come." *That—there's no way we can do it.* [*Das, das können wir auch nicht schaffen*; emphasis mine]

A few months later, Merkel had dropped the negative from her assessment and the phrase "we can do it" (*wir schaffen das*) became the mantra of Merkel's refugee policy, becoming one of the most discussed—both criticized and praised—political statements in Germany since World War II.[29] What changed here? How did this happen?

It would be naive to propose a single cause for Merkel's change of position. She herself has not offered one so far. As chancellor, she has cultivated an approach based on careful consideration, restraint, and deliberate action. Nevertheless, there are in every life key scenes that lead to major decisions. If her dialogue with the schoolgirl Reem was, as I believe, just such a moment, then one likely interpretation emerges: *false empathy.*

There is hardly a stronger catalyst for empathy than a marked failure of empathy. By false empathy, I mean an inaccurate empathetic response, the erroneousness of which is observed from the outside and communicated to the empathetic person; this empathetic mistake then feeds back on the empathizer and leads to their revising and probably overemphasizing empathy, following the logic of the overcorrection bias.[30] External correction may thus lead to an overemphasized self-correction. When the weight of the correction rests on an intellectual understanding of a situation, the empathizer can make a simple intellectual correction (in the sense of the theory of mind model discussed in the introduction). In Merkel's case, however, the weight rests not on the intellectual aspect of her initial error but rather on her failure to emotionally participate in the fate of the girl. Her mistake was held up as evidence not just of failing to take the girl's side but also of an inability to empathize in general.[31]

False empathy arises from the tension between the theoretical readiness to empathize and the simultaneous sense that a specific act of empathy is inadequate. There are many situations that can alert the empathizer that their empathy is false; the most common of these is when a person with whom one believes one empathizes replies, "You don't understand me." This charge can also come from a third party, as in the case of Merkel and the moderator. The rebuke can take the form of a factual correction, a challenge, criticism, or an accusation.

Reactions to false or inadequate empathy also take various forms. False empathy can be the first step towards more accurate empathy and in this sense works as a corrective. It can also lead to (over)compensation as the (self-)accused tries to reverse the error, inspiring empathetic overreactions. And it can be frustrating, leading the empathizer to give up or react with aggression towards those with whom they thought they were empathizing.

What is striking about this moment with the German chancellor is that she opened herself to criticism and was punished for her false empathy at exactly that moment when she was showing an unusually warm and caring side. In such moments, criticism can be particularly powerful, prompting a need to prove one's ability to empathize. The words "come on now, you did just great" sound sarcastic in this context, as the chancellor herself will have recognized. While experienced, ambitious politicians may have a particularly thick skin when it comes to having their weaknesses pointed out, their drive for recognition is not to be underestimated. It is my belief that Merkel's episode of false empathy led to an emotional need to compensate; "no way we can do it" becomes, a few weeks later, "we can do it."

By itself, Merkel's reaction to the fallout from the television interview may not have been a decisive turning point. But her decision to open Germany's borders to refugees was made following widely discussed reports about and images of the conditions in the refugee camps on the Syrian border and the makeshift attempts by Syrians to enter Europe. The most influential of these was the powerful image of the body of a three-year-old boy, Aylan Kurdi, washed up on beach in Turkey. The photograph, taken by the Turkish photojournalist Nilüfer Demir on September 2, 2015, became the emblematic image of the refugee crisis. We can speculate about why the photograph moved so many Western viewers: It seemingly draws on iconography of the Western art tradition that centers on the concept of the threshold (from water to land, from Asia to Europe); the dead boy is wearing Western clothing in the colors red (shirt) and blue (pants), the colors of the Virgin Mary, and perhaps resonated as an image of arrival, of advent. Less ideologically, the way in which the boy is lying, with his face down and to one side, suggests that he could almost be sleeping or taking a quick rest. The ancient tradition of presenting death as the brother of sleep comes to mind. (Hypnos is a brother of Thanatos, and the visual arts often used this genealogy for presentations.[32]) Indeed, one finds oneself wishing against rationality that this boy would jump back up again. I for one cannot look at this picture without tears. (But does that mean I empathize with the boy? Not directly; I perceive the scene from the imaginary perspective of a person walking up to the boy touching him, hoping against the odds that he will wake up and spring to life. In my personal experience, it is a case of filtered empathy, as described above. Likewise, I can also imagine with horror the perspective of a close relative.)

As a head of state, Merkel would not (one hopes) have based such a consequential political decision on her emotional reaction to images like these. But was she able to resist the false empathy dynamic?

These speculations notwithstanding, I would like to suggest that false empathy, in one way or another, also became a collective phenomenon in Germany during the refugee crisis. To repeat: this does not mean a kind of phony or faked empathy, nor

FIGURE 3.3
The dead Syrian boy Aylan Kurdi. Mural in Frankfurt am Main, Germany, by Justus Becker and Oguz Sen at the Frankfurt Osthafen with damage.
Source: Wikimedia Commons.

disproportionate empathy. Rather, it means that overnight—literally, between September 4 and to 5, 2015—Angela Merkel gave the nation a rude awakening. She implicitly accused the leaders of the world of individually and collectively having failed to act empathetically, and she showed Germans (along with the citizens of the other nations of the world) how to put an appropriate and proportional empathy into action. So, Angela Merkel, who I believe was reacting to her own false empathy dynamic, became the one who through her decision-making accused everyone else (and herself) of false empathy. Her overcorrected false empathy in turn elevated her into the projected hero-helper of filtered empathy for millions of others. Her reaching out to the refugees allowed people to identify with her gesture and thus reach out to people in need.

And similar to Merkel, millions may also have felt the effect of overcorrection for not having felt the need to welcome refugees in need before. Merkel became a global icon and, in one case at least, was linked iconically to Mother Teresa.[33]

In the wake of Merkel's "we can do it" declaration, many in Germany and throughout the West found themselves shaken, reacting quite strongly, even hyperempathetically. Germans flocked by the thousands to the train stations all over Germany to greet the arriving refugees in the fall of 2015, many bringing gifts and offering various help. Arriving children in particular received huge attention. In Germany, as in other countries, the apparent opening of borders to refugees precipitated an enthusiastic culture of welcoming. In fact, the word *Willkommenskultur* (culture of welcoming) became the word of the year in Austria in 2015.

Empathy indeed played a core role in the rapid assent of this culture of welcoming. But this could also explain why it was short-lived and why, at least to some degree, it backfired. Both filtered empathy and false empathy can create a quick straw fire of enthusiasm, but this does not usually last.

False empathy is a powerful drug. The dynamic leads to intoxication and enthusiasm, as well as to deep emotions and heightened empathy. False empathy shakes one out of apathy, often quite quickly and strongly, but then dissipates and returns the false empathizer back into (moral or political) lethargy. In fact, like many strong sentiments, it is likely to motivate backswing dynamics. Indeed, Merkel herself announced a little more than a year after the invitation to Syrian refugees that she would no longer be using her famous "we can do it" slogan, in part because it had become tired and in part because it had "provoked" some people.[34]

The dark dynamics of filtered empathy can be seen in the progression of sentiments about refugees in Germany. I suggested above that the widespread reaction to the refugee crisis could be less about direct empathy than about identification with a helper figure such as Angela Merkel. When pressured to show empathy, one looks for models; imitating an empathizer is emotionally easier that empathizing directly with another. Identification is in this sense an empathy avoidance strategy. As I suggested in the previous section, the helper functions as a filter for our empathy. The victimized other is consequential only insofar as they burnish the image of the helper. Yet we still place high expectations on the person in need. As helper, we expect to be recognized for our (heroic) intervention. Recognition can take the form of direct acknowledgment of gratitude, but we also expect the target of empathy to show signs of improvement as a result of our help. For the refugees in Germany, the implicit price of received filtered empathy included their rapid integration into German society by, for example, learning the language, being cheerful, and rejecting economic stagnation or marked foreignness. These expectations were certainly set too high, given that so many refugees were dealing with displacement, loss of family members, various degrees of trauma, and a lack of community. Their failure to "Germanize" quickly enough resulted in a huge cultural backlash and sense of resentment towards them.

The record low showing of Merkel's Christian Democratic Union (CDU) party in Germany's 2017 election and state elections in 2018 is largely attributed to her refugee policy. Likewise, the astonishing rise of the far-right, anti-immigration party Alternative for Germany (Alternative für Deutschland) as the third strongest party in the Bundestag seems to be a direct effect of refugee politics. Alternative for Germany's success is even more remarkable given that it attracted a wide range of culturally conservative voters who might otherwise have identified with the CDU.[35] It seems likely that in casting their votes, they rebelled against Merkel's humanitarian impulse.[36] Public apathy towards the plight of refugees in Germany turned first to enthusiastic empathy and then to widespread antipathy.[37]

When identification with either leader figures like Merkel or lower-profile aid workers in refugee camps leads to good deeds (donations, volunteering, or even becoming an aid worker), it is a positive and praiseworthy dynamic. But this kind of empathy is often short-lived, strongly self-centered, and dependent on external recognition. It is a short path from either filtered empathy or false empathy back to indifference or even resentment towards those who need our help. Like Oskar Schindler, it is all too easy to shed a tear and then climb into our limousine.

4

Empathetic Sadism

In a public online forum, Just_that_random_guy published the following comment in December 2015:

> There was this quote made by "Bedelia" a doctor and psychologist character from the tv series *Hannibal*. "Extreme acts of cruelty require a high level of empathy". I believe this to be true. Whenever I look at someone and I start imagining sadistic thoughts, I am able to understand and feel what the person would go through and the kind of pain and fear the person would experience and that's what actually turns me on. The stronger and more intense the pain and suffering I imagine to inflict on the person, the higher the gratification I derive.

In this quotation, which I reproduced in the introduction, the pseudonymous author is not characterized by a complete inability to empathize but rather by the wish to heighten his empathy. He uses this heightened empathy to arouse himself. To arrive at this empathetic state, he must imagine the pain of the other person, and so he imagines that he is causing that pain. Empathy here becomes *the goal* of sadistic behavior; it is in the service of arousal or, perhaps, even is itself the arousal. In this chapter,

I will pursue this very construct to suggest that sadistic and violent behavior can be, and in fact frequently is, performed for the sake of exciting empathy. Empathy becomes a goal in itself that justifies any means.

Perhaps the most radical and discomforting form of this thesis can be found the figure of the *empathetic rapist*, which, I argue, describes Just_that_random_guy. The idea—at which we might rightly recoil—is that a rapist could commit his crime not because he (and in this case, I will forego gender-neutral language given that the overwhelming percentage of those who commit rape, whether against women or men, are men) lacks empathy but because he has it or wishes to feel it. His goal is to understand his victim, in the midst of his victim's torment, in order to connect to them empathetically. This thought contradicts the common conception of rapists as monsters without feeling. In no way does this excuse or lessen the horror of the act of rape. On the contrary, this would make the culprit more blameworthy, because an empathetic perpetrator understands the pain he is causing quite well. A rapist who coexperiences the pain of his victim is still a rapist. However, my analysis here is not a moral or legal investigation but a more complex understanding of the culprit and his motivation to the act.

At the end of the last chapter we introduced the idea that empathy in many cases is more focused on the self and less so on the person with whom one has empathy. Empathy can serve the well-being of the person with empathy, even when the other is suffering. I will now develop this thought with more precision and spell out its logical consequences. In the simplest sense, this means that empathy for empathy's sake is evoked and enjoyed even (or perhaps especially) when the other is suffering.

This dynamic—*empathetic sadism*—is, I will show, a common phenomenon.

The Paradox of the Tragic: Aesthetic Empathy

There are several paths that lead to this conclusion. One route takes us there through aesthetics, from which the modern concept of empathy is derived. Theodor Lipps used the German word *Einfühlung* at the center of his theory of aesthetic reception around 1900, as I discussed in chapter 2. His theory was built around the empathizer (literally the "in-feeler"), not the target of empathy, which could be an inanimate object. (This aspect was critical to Lipps's understanding of the concept.) Daniel C. Batson, who has classified eight different uses of the term empathy, describes this *Einfühlung* concept as centered on the observer: "Imaginatively projecting oneself into another's situation is the psychological state referred to as *Einfühlung* by Lipps (1903) and for which Titchener (1909) first coined the English word *empathy*. Both were intrigued by the process whereby a writer or painter imagines what it would be like to be some specific person or some inanimate object, such as a gnarled, dead tree on a windswept hillside."[1] (The dead tree expects nothing from the aesthetic empathizer.) Indeed, consider how landscape architects of the eighteenth century cultivated such sights in the name of the sublime or the picturesque (as developed by Uvedale Price in the 1790s), planting crippled trees in unfriendly landscapes precisely in order to awaken this contemplative aesthetic pleasure.

From the perspective of intellectual history, empathetic concern about someone else's well-being is a later, almost artificial expansion of the concept of empathy. Empathy's origin in aesthetics provides a possible explanation for why our own experience of empathy overtakes our interest in the well-being of the other. When does empathy become—possibly paradoxically—a self-absorbed mode of behavior? Or is it "naturally" a self-absorbed behavior that only serves prosocial aims in the context of specific cultural advances? To put it another way: When does empathy exclusively or primarily benefit the empathetic person? Is it appropriate to speak of empathy for empathy's sake?

In aesthetics, the moral or ethical question of the other's well-being does not come first in the pleasure of observing art. Nevertheless, it is no surprise that this question does arise in relationship to tragedies and the tragic. The paradox of tragedy is that the observer is left with a positive (or somehow positively marked) feeling as the direct result of the terrible fate of the tragic hero. How can we account for this discrepancy of feelings?

There is a rich history of addressing this paradox, of reinterpreting the apparent asocial nature of the aesthetic. Edmund Burke, the eighteenth-century theorist of the sublime and beautiful, famously found a prosocial root of the sublime feeling that the observer enjoys at the expense of the observed:

> I am convinced we have a degree of delight, and not a small one, in the real misfortunes and pains of others . . . If this passion would be simply painful, we would shun with the greatest care all persons and places that could excite such a passion . . .
>
> And as our Creator has designed we should be united by the bond of sympathy . . . it is absolutely necessary my life should be out of any immanent hazard before I can take a delight in the sufferings of others, real or imaginary . . .[2]

Burke's reasoning here is that pain binds people together because it is an experience we can all share. Sympathy—from the Greek *syn/sym* (with, together, jointly) and *páthos* (feeling, suffering)—is a shared suffering. Burke suggests that when we perceive the suffering of another, we are glad because this sharing of pain evokes a communality and a connection. Curiously, though, for Burke this bond of sympathy might not exist, or pass by unnoticed, without suffering or without someone to observe the suffering.

At this point it is necessary to ask whether Burke's metapathology is not born of wishful thinking. Of course, Burke is correct that the observation of the tragic is somehow bound up with a positive feeling; why else would this narrative form be so celebrated? But the question of the misfortune of the tragic hero remains: Do tragedies make us wish for others to suffer? Alternatively, is the positive feeling the result of a prosocial impulse, the wish for someone else's happiness? Or is there yet another explanation?

The differences between these possibilities are not trivial, and the line connecting them is by no means easy to draw. Most theorists of tragedy since the Enlightenment posit that tragedy makes us more moral people with prosocial feelings. The morally and pedagogically valuable moment of a tragedy consists of our pity, as both Burke and his contemporary Lessing (in the *Hamburg Dramaturgy*) argue in one form or another.[3]

But there are those who would argue that tragedy is only concerned with the feelings of the observer. In this case, the tragic would be a particularly strong drug for exciting emotions in individuals, one released by observing the suffering of another. But these feelings are only very loosely coupled, if it all, with concern for the other's actual (and not only imaginary) well-being. In this formulation, the audience's excitement is tragedy's final purpose, which has led some critics, like Jean-Jacques Rousseau in *Lettre a M. D'Alembert sur les spectacles* (1758), to reject tragedy entirely.

A closely related phenomenon is known in film studies as the "paradox of sad-film enjoyment," in which the profound emotional effect of a sad film is associated with aesthetic pleasure and quality.[4] In their level-headed, empirical studies, Winfried Menninghaus and his colleagues argue that the feeling of being moved (the rhetorical *movere*) stands in the center of aesthetic experience. Whether being moved in this way has prosocial effects remains an open question. While it is possible that being moved opens an individual up to others, it could also narcissistically serve only the well-being of the viewer.

Between these two poles—that the tragic teaches us empathy through the mechanism of pity or that it only offers individuals enjoyment through a heightened emotional state—there are a range of middle positions. I do not have the space here to do them justice. One might be tempted to stake out a "both . . . and" position and suggest that it depends on the disposition of the individual whether their enjoyment is narcissistic or not. While it is perhaps impossible to argue with this particular position, it doesn't help to answer the principal question of the extent to which the experience of viewing someone, real or fictional, suffer a tragic fate incites the viewer to a nonegocentric form of empathy.

A further approach to solving this problem has to do with the possibility that fiction (including tragedy) suspends the difference between the observer and the hero, between the self and the other, so that the difference between self-interest and empathy is not so easy to pin down. Suzanne Keen has worked through the implications of this argument.[5] Its logical conclusion would be to claim that fiction allows us to enjoy empathy without compassion or obligation to help. To put it another way, fiction allows a form of empathy in which self-loss is a positive experience.

I approach the question of empathy in tragedy from a different perspective: that we understand tragedy as an invitation to empathize paired with an exit strategy—the tragic ending. There is an unwritten contract of literature in general (and especially of tragedies) that promises us a strong dose of empathy *for a short time*. We are invited to empathize and promised that it will not last; there will be an end, the hero will experience their downfall. In tragedies, we coexperience the tragic hero's fate from the perspective of their ultimate failure or demise. It is the anticipation of this terrible conclusion that attracts the viewer and inspires or heightens empathy, rather than the events that lead to that climax.

Anticipation is central to the structure of narrative. When we engage with narrative thought by following the plot, we do so by weighing hypothetical situations and considering other possibilities than the one presented. (This, in a nutshell, is my argument in a previous book.[6]) We wonder what will happen (suspense), what has already happened before (mystery), or what could explain the current situation (suspicion). In a tragedy, the search for positive alternatives heightens our narrative thinking immensely. We hope that the tragic hero will make different decisions and thus avoid their inevitable fate. The tragic figure is exposed or open to the audience because so much depends on the narrative uncertainty of their certain future. Anticipation is the feeling that connects audience and hero.

Anticipation is also central in ways that are specific to empathy. Because of empathy's relationship to the phenomenon of self-loss, it follows that the observer prefers and will seek out catalysts for empathetic identification that control, soften, or *limit the timespan* of self-loss. Tragedy promises the observer that they can identify and share feelings with the hero without losing themselves for too long; the object of their identification is sure to meet their end, allowing the viewer to return to themself. Tragedy, then, offers quite the deal to the viewer: Not only can they experience a particularly profound and moving spectacle but they then get to exit the experience at the end. The tragic hero's catastrophic, self-made fate becomes an escape hatch for the empathizer, ending their empathetic identification. The final stage in the arc of empathy is performed by the tragic work of art itself. Tragedy (and, in fact, fiction more generally) allows for self-loss with a limited time span. No wonder so many critics in the eighteenth century, like Rousseau, described it as a drug.

Unsurprisingly, numerous theorists of tragedy have written about the boundaries between the viewer and the tragic hero. Audiences face the double task of coexperiencing the situation of the hero, while also preparing to leave them behind. Aristotle, for example, emphasizes that the tragic hero must be an average person like us, not too good and not too bad, but that they must have committed an error, a clear misstep (in Greek, *hamartia*), that explains their predicament. Because this *hamartia* is theirs and not ours, we in the audience can pull away from the hero, can wash our hands of them (from the Greek *catharsis*, meaning purification or washing).

Tragedy is so firmly established in our thought as a cultural artifact that we learn, and learn to appreciate, this return structure relatively early in life. Interestingly, tragic stories tend to be either disturbing or simply uninteresting for children, who expect stories to have a happy ending. Part of this expectation is no doubt due to the way that children's literature has developed in our time, with safe and morally satisfying conclusions. But this pattern is historical and relatively recent, not universal. Horror stories—for example, the moralizing terror of *Struwwelpeter*, the German basis for the figure of the bogeyman—have long found enthusiastic young readers. Perhaps children's distaste for tragedy is at least partly because self-loss is less of a threat to children. Children are already used to being part of a parent-child unit, and so the attraction of the "empathy return ticket" that the complex structure of tragedy offers disappears. Without this, all that is left of tragedy is watching someone be harshly punished for making a minor bad decision, often with little choice in the matter. Little wonder, then, that children much prefer to identify with triumphant heroes.

To put it differently, tragedy is mostly of interest to people who both know the pleasures of empathy and are already familiar with the experience of self-loss through empathy; they therefore seek the double structure of softened or time-limited empathy. The expectation of a tragic (or tragedy-like) ending makes empathy possible from the outset. One empathizes with someone *because* they are going to fail. According to the logic of narrative thinking, this creates the counterintuitive hope that they may triumph, despite knowing the generic conventions and anticipating the inevitable ending. (I would argue that during the 2016 US presidential campaign, there was a certain "lost cause" empathy that the most enthusiastic supporters of the Democratic candidate Bernie Sanders embraced because they privately saw their candidate's end coming.)

Empathetic identification often arises intuitively but that does not necessarily mean it does so naively or blindly. One does not simply develop empathy for another person or their situation; rather, one finds oneself involved in a complex process that includes anticipation about the other's future and thus an appraisal about the progression of one's feelings of empathy. (In a technical sense, we could say that first-order observations of the other and second-order observations of ourselves in the process of empathy are combined.) In the case of tragedy, this means that anticipating the hero's tragic end and the corresponding end of one's emotional identification with them is already a part of the empathy process from the beginning.

Returning to the question of whether empathy is an expression of care for the other or whether empathy is felt for its own sake, the evidence from studying tragedy suggests that the promise of empathy is to be found in empathy itself; the empathizer's self-interest is the focus of tragedy. Of course, this does not rule out the possibility that others might benefit from this empathetic impulse, that there might be an altruistic motive, or that concerns for the other's well-being may lead to benevolent actions. It is, however, also clear that a logical extension of empathy for empathy's sake explains how someone can actively cause another to suffer in order to feel empathy—*sadistic empathy*.

Sadistic Empathy: An Overview

This is the basic form of empathetic sadism: A person creates, encourages, wishes for, or tolerates a scenario in which someone else is placed in danger or made to suffer, precisely in order to feel empathy with that person, now cast in the role of the victim. In its most extreme version, the empathetic sadist tortures their victim in order to share their feelings and to understand their victim through their suffering.

Behind empathetic sadism lies a more general observed behavior, namely the attempt to control other people in order to understand them intellectually and emotionally. Sadism is a special case of this but a revealing one, because emotions of suffering are especially strong and can be provoked or inflicted by external forces. (Consider how in several European languages early grammarians used the verb "suffer" to describe the passive voice, including the German *leiden*.)

Let us turn now to empathetic sadism (also known as *empathetic cruelty*).[7] I do not want to limit my investigation by declaring in advance whether this is a perverse form of empathy—a "warped empathy" as it is sometimes called in popular science, that only some extreme people like Just_that_random_guy and others like him might feel—or instead a possibility given within the spectrum of normal empathy.[8] As will become clear later, I lean toward the latter.

Narrative patterns in fiction can help orient this discussion. This is not because sadistic empathy is itself a fantasy but because cultural artifacts like novels and films can reveal certain patterns of behavior more clearly than everyday life does and because they can also be powerful models of behavior that people tend to copy. Indeed, it is noteworthy that the words we use to describe the enjoyment of another's pain (sadism) or our own pain (masochism) both derive from the names of novelists: the Marquis de Sade (1740–1814) and Leopold von Sacher-Masoch (1836–95).

For instance, an overly familiar character in fairy tales is the wicked stepmother who makes the children in her care suffer. Take Cinderella's stepmother. Instead of simply saying that Cinderella is not allowed to go to the ball, she pours a great pile of lentils into the sooty fireplace and tells her charge that she may attend, but only if she gathers up each individual lentil in an impossibly short time. It is safe to assume that she relishes Cinderella's anguish.

Another related figure is the sadistic lover who punishes his prey for coyly resisting his advances. (Such characters are overwhelmingly male, though the more recent cultural trope of the "cougar," an older woman pursuing a younger man, indicates that this dynamic is not necessarily gendered.) Such characters are closely bound up with the modern history of the novel and populate, famously, Samuel Richardson's novels *Clarissa* and *Pamela*, or Dostoyevsky's *The Brothers Karamazov*, which introduces the figure of the rejected lover, known only as the "mysterious visitor," who murders his victim cruelly and only much later in life is weighted down by his guilt.[9]

Eighteenth-century German novels stage such empathetic sadists in high frequency. Consider, for example, Lord Derby's mistreatment of the titular heroine of the epistolary 1771 novel *Die Geschichte der Fräuleins von Sternheim* (*The Story of Miss von Sternheim*) by Sophie von La Roche or how, in Ludwig Tieck's 1795–96 *Lovell*, the protagonist William Lovell behaves towards Emilie Burton. Indeed, it almost seems as if German novels of the time that do not feature empathetically sadistic male characters are exceptions in the genre. And although Goethe's *Werther* or Friedrich Hölderlin's *Hyperion* do not depict outward sadism against the female characters in whom the male heroes are desperately in love, they do portray acts of masochism and self-destruction by the male protagonists, which then feed back on the female heroines in the form of accusations and seem intended to cause their suffering. Even Goethe's hopeless lover, Wilhelm Meister, belongs in this canon, insofar as he hurts every female character in his orbit but only notices doing so at the end when, like Faust, he is gripped by the voice of conscience.[10]

The procession of oppressed young women and their empathetic torturers in novels continues into the nineteenth century across the Western literary tradition, culminating in such works as Flaubert's *Madame Bovary* (1856), with its scornful narrator; Clarín's *La Regenta* (1884–85); and Fontane's *Effi Briest* (1895). A prominent American example is Nathaniel Hawthorne's *The Scarlet Letter* (1850), which has an ostensibly kind narrator relishing

the sight of the female protagonist being punished for sexual behavior, with stigma and the burden of a child.

Film has only popularized various empathetic-sadistic figura-
tions. One such character is the great manipulator, from the title
character in Fritz Lang's *Dr. Mabuse* series (1922–60) to masterful
serial killers such as Hannibal Lecter in Jonathan Demme's *The
Silence of the Lambs* (1991) and John Doe in David Fincher's *Se7en*
(1995); another is the amoral psychopath, as embodied (either of-
fensively or satirically) by Patrick Bateman (played by Christian
Bale) in Mary Harron's 2000 film adaptation of Brenton Easton
Ellis' 1991 novel, *American Psycho*.

In fact, *Silence of the Lambs* can be regarded as a movie about
empathy. To start, its competing serial killers, Dr. Lecter and Buffalo
Bill, each empathize with their opponents or victims in precisely
opposite ways.[11] At the center of the films is an ideal of mental san-
ity, which demands a healthy balance of self-awareness and igno-
rance. The extremes of too much or too little self-awareness are
presented as pathological: Buffalo Bill is running away from himself and from self-knowledge, wishing to hide himself in a cloak of
human skin; he is literally stepping into the skin of others in order
not to have to be himself. (As a German, I cannot help seeing this as
a horrible act of empathy since the German idiom for walking into
someone's shoes is "to slip into someone's skin.")

Hannibal Lecter, on the other hand, knows too much. He can
read other people like a book, but in doing so has lost all respect
for them, which enables him to incorporate them all too easily into
himself, to literally eat them and, so to speak, make them part of
himself. Both are sadistically empathetic monsters who torture
and kill others for or because of their empathy. Only the FBI agent,
Clarice Starling, represents a stable middle ground between these
two extremes. To solve the case, she needs to learn to open up and

confront the traumas of her past (the death of her father, hearing the screams of farm animals being slaughtered as a girl), thereby understanding her own motivations and those of others, but in the right proportions. (I would argue that, *contra* the logic of the film, it is mere anti-intellectualism to claim that too much self-knowledge causes one to lose one's respect for life.)

Even this cursory overview highlights some relevant markers of empathetic sadism in fictional narratives. The element of time, for example, plays an important role. The catalyst for empathetic sadism can, schematically speaking, be found in the past, present, or future. These different temporal dimensions may seem to be rather superficial distinctions but they will allow us in the following to consider different variants of empathetic sadism separately. I will explore each temporal frame in greater detail below but want to outline here how they each work as catalysts.

In cases of revenge, the catalyst lies in the *past*: Someone must be punished as retribution for prior acts. In tales of unrequited love, the suffering of the spurned (or blithely ignored) lover is blamed on the object of their affections, and her (or in rare cases his) future suffering at the hands of the sadist is therefore seen as justified and proportionate. Some readers may mentally complete this thought by judging such a vindictive lover to be "sick" or "disturbed." While this may be true, the inverse is not; it is not only sick or disturbed people who react in this way. In punishing their beloved and anticipating their future suffering, the lover experiences their own past suffering again.

The catalyst for sadistic empathy lies in the *future* when the situation of another is manipulated in such a way that one can hope to simulate and thus to understand that person's feelings. The crucial difference between past and future suffering here is that the empathetic observer is themself bringing about the situation meant to lead to understanding, as in fictions that follow the plots of emotional manipulators.

Most common are experiences of empathetic sadism in the *present*, which defines how psychopaths like the fictional Patrick Bateman gratify their impulsive, immediate need to feel empathy. I now want to explore each time frame more closely.

Past: Punishment as Empathetic Sadism

In this section, I will consider the case of punishment. Humans tend to punish past actions and they experience emotional satisfaction when they observe the pain of the punished. This is a clear case of sadistic empathy. Three questions will guide the discussion:

1. Why do we need punishment?
2. Why do punishers do the dirty work of punishing?
3. What prevents punishment from getting out of hand and being excessive?

The general answer to the first question is simple. Punishment of wrongdoers and freeloaders is needed to prevent harmful actions and to ensure that everyone participates in the wellbeing of the community. Without some form of punishment, it seems likely that few individuals would be motivated to do service for the community. (Punishment, to be sure, does not need to be physical or explicit; it includes stigmatization, exclusion, verbal condemnation, or negation of benefits.) Even if they would, the freeloaders and wrongdoers would fare better for getting more benefits for less effort. In the following discussion, the general benefit of some form of punishment for society is assumed; the precise calculation of its advantage or the social dynamics that would require it is less important.[12]

The second question—why people who do the punishing do the work of punishment—poses an interesting dilemma. On the one hand, punishers do important work of society (question 1), but on the other, they do this at a disadvantage to themselves. (Here and in the following, we will focus on the case of the self-motivated punisher, not the representative of a large institution, such as prison guards who act for the state. This focus on self-motivated punishers allows our discussion to come closer to considering evolutionary benefits.)

This dilemma finds its expression in an understanding of punishment as a form of altruism.[13] The punisher is doing something for the community, at the cost of his own work, inconvenience, and risk of possible harm. Punishment seeks to both correct and prevent acts that damage the commonweal—a thief steals an object and so undermines the general structure of property rights; someone dodging their bus or train fare indirectly raises the transit costs for everyone else; and so on. There are two sides to the effort of punishment: first, the individual act of stopping the perpetrator; second, the symbolic signaling that this particular act and acts of its kind will not be tolerated. It seems to be this symbolic aspect that explains why even the punishment of crimes long past or of a mistake not likely to be repeated needs to happen for the community.

In short, it seems structurally important and even necessary for the community that the punishment takes place. In fact, not punishing the culprit is sometimes a punishable offense as well. Someone who observes a crime or morally wrong act and does not intervene can be seen as, on a second order, guilty of that crime too. This need to punish bystanders who fail to intervene only gives a further negative impetus for punishing, and it still does not explain its positive stimulus.

So far, we would have to conclude that the punisher is committing the acts of punishment as a gift for society without particular benefit to themself. One could try to argue that the punisher gains social standing and therefore gets a reward. However, it seems to me that there is another motivation for the punisher that leads to an immediate reward. The solution of the dilemma lies in the fact that people take pleasure in punishing others. Punishing others provides an emotional reward. Anger and the chance to quench it through retribution seem to offer the necessary drive to punish. In this sense, the punisher is not acting altruistically but rather out of self-interest. Sadistic empathy, the pleasure of the pain of others who are punished, could have emerged in an evolutionary context as an impetus for punishing antisocial acts because it serves a function for the species as a whole. Seen this way, sadistic empathy makes sense, as it would have a selection advantage for the community.[14]

There is strong evidence for considering the emotional basis for punishment. Throughout history, individuals have taken pleasure and enjoyment in punishing others for past crimes (real or imagined). Regardless of their societal or juridical functions, it seems to be universally true that punishment and revenge are connected to affect and emotions as much as they are to abstract ideas of justice, human or divine, evidenced by physiological signs of anger and clear punishment-reward cycles in the brain, measurable by fMRI, and various seemingly irrational decisions when it comes to punishment and revenge.[15] As suggested already in the introduction, the pleasure at punishment seems to differ for men and women.[16]

Consider, for example, the experiment called "the dictator game," in which one participant is asked to divide a sum of money between himself and another participant. The other person's only choice is to accept or decline the allocation. If he accepts it, both receive the money and walk away with it. If not, neither does, and both leave the experiment empty handed. It looks like a win-win situation for both. Curiously, when the first participant divides the money patently unfairly, the offer tends to get rejected by the other participant. Rejecting the offer, even if it is a bad one, is an irrational choice, since the second participant has nothing to lose and can only gain. In short: the second participant is willing to pay a price for their revenge.[17] The emotional satisfaction of punishing the other is worth more to the second participant than financial gain.

This speaks to an emotional basis of punishment, which is not to say that punishment is irrational. On the contrary, it may be that in the standard case emotions are rational and from a cognitive point of view represent usually adequate processes and trigger appropriate actions. (Of course, just like reason, emotional responses can be wrong.) Seen in this light, punishment can be described as the institutionalization of rudimentary emotions in moral, juridical, and political practices. The emotions of empathetic sadism serve as the immediate reward for the punisher who acts, knowingly or not, in the service of the community as a whole. In this sense, punishment is less altruistic than it may seem.

At the same time, empathetic sadism also poses a threat to the community. Even in its mildest form—schadenfreude, or taking satisfaction in the misfortune of others—it is an antisocial emotional state. Here we come to our third question: What prevents punishment from becoming excessive? Could people relish the joy of punishment too much? Could punishment move from altruism to unchecked schadenfreude? The answer can be found in the scene of punishment, a highly stylized, ritualized, and discursively coded action. This will require some elaboration.

Whoever punishes must know that they are right. (Again, we are focusing on the self-motivated punisher here, not the representative of a large institution.) Even in the case of an impulsive act of revenge, the action is considered just by the person doing it. This feeling of appropriateness contains the assumption that the one being punished has deserved their punishment and *that one could legitimate the act before others*. In other words, it is a theatrical scene for oneself and for others (even if the audience is imaginary). The scene of punishment, then, is a triple scene that invokes: (1) the memory of the past wrongdoing; (2) the actual punishment; and (3) anticipation of public justification about why the punishment was appropriate. This scene is one that we may experience from all sides and perspectives, such as victim, accused, and accuser and which we can play out in our imagination in every combination. Our perspective can jump from one point of view to another, though it doesn't have to. As I aim to show, this theatrical element of punishment cannot be underestimated.

Consider the families of the victims of capital crimes in countries where the death penalty is still enforced—notably the United States—who often insist on being present for the execution.[18] What motivates these people? Michel Foucault considered this desire as a matter of a crude, premodern practice, which an enlightened Europe tried to do away with over two hundred years ago.[19] However, perhaps there is more to the scene of punishment than a historical aberration.

To better understand the possible positions from which to observe the scene of punishment, I want to look in detail at the execution of Timothy McVeigh, the Oklahoma City Bomber. The events surrounding his execution in 2001 were followed with great interest in the American press. The families of the dead and the survivors of the attack who attended the execution as witnesses were subjected to extensive interviews.

Survivors and family members had different options for viewing the execution. They could choose to watch McVeigh's death via lethal injection through a large glass window or observe a close-up of his face as he died through a closed-circuit television feed, either from within the federal prison in Terre Haute, Indiana, or broadcast to a location in Oklahoma City. McVeigh reportedly stared for a long time at the observers in the adjacent room and then into the camera. It was a matter of intense discussion whether McVeigh's gaze was "cold" or not. In any case, the witnesses to the execution felt that this gaze signaled that he understood that they were watching him die.

The press was not allowed in any of the observation rooms. The absence of journalists, the witnesses realized, would put their reactions under increased scrutiny afterwards. If we wish to take the empathizing positions to the logical extreme, it is possible to imagine in this network of first- and second-order observers all sorts of reactions, from forgiveness to satisfaction and from a mediating observation of the observers to identification with McVeigh. The reconstruction of McVeigh's emotional state during the execution was of critical importance to some of the observers. One survivor, for example, reported, "I am glad that I saw him that close up and everything 'cause that way I knew from his eyes and his expression what he was feeling."[20] This is a remarkable statement, given that most of the witnesses reported McVeigh had shown no emotion.[21] Were those who "knew" how McVeigh felt, then, projecting those emotions based on how they hoped he would feel or how they might feel in his situation? This seems more likely than the ability on the part of some witnesses to detect emotions that the majority didn't see.

Correspondingly, the experiences of those watching the execution varied enormously. One observer described having a spiritual experience, an encounter that allowed her to forgive McVeigh:

> ". . . all of a sudden he came to me . . . I started to think of him as Timothy McVeigh, the soul, and not Timothy McVeigh, the man, and I started praying for him that this is his last chance, this is his last breath, and I prayed for him it just like overtook me."[22]

This woman empathized not with McVeigh but with an imaginary figure (perhaps a version of herself) who was close to him and who witnessed his last moments, feeling her way into a better or more religious aspect of herself, a person capable of forgiving.

Many of the witnesses, in contrast, wished that McVeigh's death had been more painful and suggested that lethal injection seemed too easy: "I wanted him to do a little suffering"; "I wanted something severe"; "I don't think it was gruesome enough. It should have been more painful"; "I wanted him to be hurt"; "To me it was a letdown because it didn't last long enough. I wanted him to suffer. I wanted him to hurt, you know."[23] A common sentiment was to compare McVeigh to his victims, some of whom suffered longer, or to the ongoing pain of the survivors. These witnesses wanted a punishment that would bring him closer to his victims by emulating their suffering.

The scene of punishment evokes and repeats the scene of the original wrongdoing. It perpetuates the presence of the past, and its ritualization allows the original act of violation to be repeated, like a film. Empathy with the victim of the prior violation scripts how the subsequent punishment is observed. The initial act becomes the matrix for the second act (the punishment) as the violator has to suffer accordingly. The comparison of both acts (transgression, punishment) is supported by or even becomes possible because of the observer-camera position; the punishment and the crime look the same from the empathetic observer position, which places pain alongside pain. This perspective is not dependent on the metaphor of the modern film camera—for millennia, ritualized punishment and the theatrical space of the courtroom have forged a removed but empathetic observer position. The trick is to place the first and second scenes together, to obscure or forget the differences between them. The victim's suffering becomes a key element in the expectations of the repetition: the punishment of the violator.

The poetic justice of even the seemingly primitive logic of "an eye for an eye and a tooth for a tooth" reveals a complex cultural dynamic requiring (positive) empathy to be transferred from the victim to the culprit (negatively). To explain this cultural dynamic, I propose that the empathy or pity for the victim (including self-pity of the observer) leaves a remnant that is preserved and that seeks a new expression, which it finds in the form of punishment. The continued presence of the past is a requirement for this form of empathetic sadism.

And here we get to a possible answer to our third question: In the juxtaposition of the first and second scenes (crime and punishment) there lies a safeguard against the expansion of empathetic sadism beyond the scene of punishment. There might be an *emotional* basis for proportionality of the punishment (that might of course be complimented by a rational weighing of the appropriateness of the punishment). The enjoyment of the ensuing punishment is bound or limited by the experienced pain-empathy of the initial transgression. The formula of ethical or judicial proportionality, according to this theory, is an emotional mechanism for preventing the misuse of sadistic empathy. Not all the pain that another suffers should bring us pleasure; only pain that is inflicted in proportion to the suffering of the victim.

One can immediately see that such a cultural (or legal) restraint does not always work perfectly. Someone who knows how to present themself or others in the role of the victim can be given license to incite or inflict a punishment, whether or not it is just. Think, for example, of someone who presents themself as being mistreated by a specific group (or even by "society" in general) and inflicts pain on representatives of that group with pleasure. For example, it has been widely speculated that the two shooters in the 1999 Columbine High School massacre, both high school seniors, were acting in revenge for the frequent bullying to which they were subject. (The shooters' actual motives were likely much more complex.[24])

Schadenfreude may expose the limits of this proposed mechanism that curbs expressions of empathetic sadism because it allows the satisfied observer to compare their rival's earlier triumph with their later misfortune. Principles of proportionality or poetic justice do not temper the pleasure in another's failure, as we can always find reasons, logical or not, as to why an enemy deserved what they got. Punishment operates as a culturally sanctioned form of sadistic empathy; people are allowed to and in fact are encouraged to enjoy the suffering of the perpetrators.

Present: Empathetic Cruelty and Sadistic Empathy

Let's begin with an extreme case. The blogger who lurks in these pages, Just_that_random_guy, makes no reference to events in the past. "Whenever I look at someone and I start imagining sadistic thoughts, I am able to understand and feel what the person would go through . . . and that's what actually turns me on." He is aroused, he explains, for two reasons: because the other is suffering and feels pain; and because he understands and shares the feelings of the other.

The first catalyst for his arousal is called *empathetic cruelty*. Reacting with pleasure to the pain of others is an atypical reaction, and studies employing brain imaging show how in such cases the regions of the brain associated with pleasure and reward are integrated into the observation of pain.[25] This tendency is often associated with people who have psychopathic tendencies (I use the term "psychopath" as a composite of the twenty traits of the often-used Hare Psychopathy Checklist scale, but not as a technical medical term). The psychologist Alfred Heilbrun suggested in 1982:

> One way to interpret the results would be in terms of a sadistic . . . psychopathic model of violence in which inflicting pain or distress upon another is arousing and reinforcing (pleasurable). Such a model would assume that acts inflicting pain are more intentional than impulsive and that empathetic skills promote arousal and sadistic reinforcement (pleasure) by enhancing the psychopath's awareness of the pain and distress being experienced by the victim.[26]

For a while, the reasoning among many researchers of psychopathy was that psychopaths display no empathy. And indeed, a large number of brain imaging studies revealed little to no empathetic brain reactions.[27] However, more recently some studies have found close to normal empathetic brain reactions when participants with psychopathic traits *were asked to use empathy.*[28] These findings suggest that psychopaths do not lack the capacity for empathy but just do not routinely use it. This insight reverses the standard thinking about what actually characterizes sadists and psychopaths.

The second catalyst could be called *sadistic empathy-simulation*, or simply *sadistic empathy*, since its actual goal is not pain as such but rather to provoke an empathetic state. In both cases, sadism in the observer does not manifest from a lack of empathy or a failure to empathize but because of too much empathy, misuses of empathy, or a longing to empathize. Some new explanations for understanding psychopathy propose an abnormal processing of pain observation. The bases for these models are neuropsychological findings about the observation of pain in others. One's own feelings of pain and the observation of pain in others activate similar neural networks (matching the predictions of the perception action model).[29] This is also true for people with sadistic tendencies and for young people on the spectrum of aggressive conduct disorder (CD). There appears to be no such thing as a complete lack of empathetic brain reactions, at least with regard to the principal similarity of brain activities in processing pain. Instead, young people on this spectrum seem to have a heightened pain perception.[30]

How exactly to interpret these findings is as yet unclear.[31] Are the empathetic reactions to pain supplemented by pleasure simply because they are too strong a stimulus to the system? Pain and pleasure are neurologically close to each other; some people, perhaps people with a history of abuse, may have them mixed up. Can empathetic observation, like aesthetic processes, be enjoyed from a distance, so that the difference between imagined others and actual living others is elided in favor of the former?[32] Or is the observation of pain pleasurable because it enables an identification with the otherwise inaccessible other (as Just_that_random_guy describes), an extreme version of the sentiment, "I enjoy finally understanding you and sharing your feelings"? Perhaps it is indirectly pleasurable because it offers control over or sets limits on one's empathy?

Regardless of which of these possibilities come into play, we can assume that when the pain of the other has become associated with pleasure, one will seek out this pleasure. People with psychopathic tendencies can be skilled manipulators of others (manipulativeness and pathological lying are items on the Hare Psychopathy Checklist) and seem to possess a heightened theory of mind.[33] It should come as no surprise, therefore, that they can use these abilities in the service of that goal—to hurt others and coexperience their pain.

Of course, not all sadists are psychopaths, and I now want to explore the extent to which sadism is a part not only of everyday life but, in fact, of all human experience.

Future: Manipulative Empathy

When empathetic sadism is future oriented, either as mere anticipation or as an active manipulation of the situation of the other, it can be called *manipulative empathy*. This form differs from empathetic cruelty discussed above because it involves behaviors on the part of the empathizer intended to guide the other into a particular situation in which they will be emotionally predictable and it will be possible for the empathizer to coexperience their emotions. There can be pleasure in this manipulation: first, because it awakens feelings in the observer, and second, because it makes the other readable and provides the observer with the satisfaction of correctly predicting their feelings.

This formulation allows us to look past familiar definitions of sadism by identifying behaviors usually considered positive with this impulse. When, for example, one buys someone a present, they eagerly anticipate the recipient's surprise and pleasure at receiving the gift. The egocentric aspect of gift giving sits uncomfortably close to empathetic manipulation. Even in the smallest ways, it seems, people want to guide the other into an intelligible emotional situation, whether positive or negative.

The tendency to turn our attention to those situations in which we understand others better, share their feelings, and try to precipitate more of these situations is an aesthetic one. (The term "aesthetic" here refers to the sense of clarity and the exceptional state in which the mixed emotions give way to a unified image.) A wide spectrum of socially sanctioned behaviors falls under this pattern of manipulative empathy. In addition to gift giving, pedagogical forms of empathy (a teacher sharing in a student's moment of recognition, for example) or even conveying a piece of good (or bad) news can fall into this category. Negative but still commonplace forms of manipulative empathy include moralizing; teasing; criticizing; patronizing; testing; bullying; threatening; pressuring (as in employees or subordinates); blackmailing; giving false hope and disappointing; irony; sexism; all forms of coercion, including subtler forms of duress; and deliberate embarrassment.

None of these behaviors must necessarily be understood as sadistic empathy; still, one wonders what the motivation could be for the excessive criticism of another, if not to empathetically share their emotional response (embarrassment, self-loathing, etc.). Irony can be part of a deliberate conversational mode in which both parties understand the dialogue as a game. Along with teasing and other confrontational dialogic modes, irony brings multiple conversational partners to the same emotional state and makes them readable to one another. What all these behaviors share is an attempt to constrain the situation of the other, even in the absence of a precise understanding of them; it is simply ensuring *that* the other responds emotionally to the situation in a predictable manner. (It is interesting to note that these everyday forms of sadistic empathy take place in disguise. The boss or the teacher gives all appearances of wanting to help the other. The ironist is playing an intellectual game. The moralizer can point to the general good).

We should note here that shame plays a large role in manipulative empathy because a person who is ashamed is particularly readable. Shame can also have nearly unambiguous physical signs, such as blushing or tears. It occurs in public, in the presence of observers. The public nature of shame and embarrassment make them strong candidates for empathy. The German language, which has produced a variety of empathy-related terms—such as *Einfühlung* and *Schadenfreude*—includes the interesting notion *Fremdschämen*, which means feeling the shame of another. Shame and embarrassment are strong stimuli for voluntary or involuntary empathy because of their readability and public nature; they are especially well suited for sadistic and manipulative forms of empathy. And, similar to some other forms of empathy triggers, shame includes a *scene of empathy*.

Cinderella's stepmother belongs on the spectrum of manipulative empathy. She dumps the lentils into the fireplace because she believes that doing so will prevent Cinderella from going to the ball. Imagining how Cinderella will set herself to work sorting legumes from ashes—first the realization, then the disappointment setting over her that she will not make it in time, then the shame is having to perform such labor—makes her emotionally legible to her stepmother (and, not coincidentally, to the reader who pities her).

There is a remarkable range among the possible forms of manipulative empathy—and a correspondingly wide scope of possible moral evaluations. Consider Lisa Zunshine's description of a literary figure—which she names the "empathic (or sadistic) benefactor"—who leads others into trouble in order to help them out of it.[34] Such figures may want to empathize with the suffering, so that any improvement resulting from their intervention is only a kind of alibi for their pleasure. Or they may have their eyes set on an altruistic goal the whole time and therefore see suffering as a necessary, if unfortunate, step to get there. (One of Zunshine's examples is Jean-Jacques, the imaginary educator in Jean-Jacques Rousseau's *Emile*, who is clearly well-meaning but shows sadistic tendencies throughout.)

Akin to the sadistic benefactor is the figure wielding *advocative exploitative empathy*.[35] This advocate empathizes with the one suffering and takes their side in order to find pleasure and satisfaction in playing the role of advocate. Because the suffering of the other is necessary for the existence of their role, this can mean that the advocate wishes for positive change while at the same time prolonging the suffering. (The sadistic-empathetic advocate can also be seen as representing the reader of a literary text or the viewer of a film who, while rooting for a character's fortunes to improve, so enjoys this feeling of advocacy that they wish the character's suffering continues.[36])

These two figures suggest that sadistic empathy—above all, the future-oriented version—can include positive elements of genuine care, even if the impulse to help functions as a mask or pretext for secret, empathetic pleasure. Moreover, the sadistic empathizer might postpone the moment when they jump in to help. This should not be taken to mean that every helper actually cultivates sadistic empathy, nor that someone who chooses a care profession is acting objectionably. On the contrary, even someone with such motives can do a great deal of good—as long as they are able to avoid trapping those being helped into the role of victim.

Does this tendency toward manipulative empathy favor the hypothesis of this chapter: that we can become sadists *because* we want to understand or share the feelings of others? It is an indication but not yet convincing proof. One could object that the power of the observer is always bound up in the suffering of the other, so that sadism is really about power and not empathy at all. Or one could shift the emphasis away from *empathetic understanding* of the other and focus instead on how the pain of the other is transformed into pleasure in the observer.

However, in every form of sadistic empathy, from punishment to manipulation, there is an enjoyment of the other's negative emotions. While many academic and journalistic observers of this phenomenon use the concept of perversion to describe cases of empathetic cruelty, I have been arguing that there is another plausible interpretation of sadistic empathy—that the pleasure it leads to is derived instead from understanding and empathizing with the other. Their pain does not lead directly to pleasure; rather, it is the emotional transparency of the other as made possible by the pain that does so. In witnessing or even causing through manipulation the other's pain and suffering, the observer imagines the other's feelings and places themself in their position to share their feelings.

To further test this hypothesis, I want to return to the extreme case of the empathetic rapist. Popular literature has long ago accepted that rape is not about sexuality but rather dominance.[37] Because rapists were assumed to have a deficit of empathy, psychologists and criminologists have recommended empathy training as a form of rehabilitative treatment for those convicted of violent sexual crimes.[38] In recent years, however, the picture has grown more complicated. For example, a study by Yolanda Fernandez and W. L. Marshall has shown that in a group comprising twenty-seven male inmates convicted of rape and twenty-seven male inmates convicted of nonsexual crimes, the former group showed more empathy for women in general, as measured through the standard psychopathy survey and a specific "rapist empathy measure".[39] At the same time, they exhibited less empathy for specific victims, which can be understood in different ways: either as an underlying deficit or as a retroactive strategy for avoiding blame. At the very least, this research suggests that the view of rapists lacking empathy is simplistic.

Should rape, in some cases, be understood as an empathy crime? Do some perpetrators commit rape as a means to feel empathy and because they can relate to how it feels to be a victim? As I have shown in this book, certain forms of empathy have direct negative effects; some of empathy's dark sides can have devastating impacts on the lives of others. If we follow this line of reasoning, the situation looks as follows. By means of his (or in certain rare cases, her) act of violence, the empathetic rapist wants to feel empathy with the victim. When he understands the suffering of the victim, he can empathize. And since he himself has carried out all the actions, he is (or believes he is) in control of the feelings of the other. Even in the terrible suffering of the other, he can celebrate the pleasure of how intensely he understands the other and coexperiences his or her feelings. Clearly, empathy deficit does fit or explain this model, in that the act of rape becomes an extreme measure for stimulating empathy.

When we consider rape, we also need to consider the many ways rape is invisibilized, a tendency that may also be linked to empathy. There is, of course, the pernicious propensity to blame the actions of the rapist on the victim, because of how she was dressed, how she acted, or how immoderate she was.[40] Another way in which sexual violence has been minimized or downplayed—and one especially applicable to this inquiry—is in the narrative representation of rapes. In a familiar trope, the woman initially and often repeatedly resists the advances of her assailant (though he is usually depicted through a romantic lens) before giving in, an action frequently conflated with consent.

A classic version of this rape narrative is dramatized in the film, *Gone with the Wind* (1939). After a fight between Scarlett O'Hara and Rhett Butler, he takes firm hold of her head between his hands and says, raging with jealousy, that he must know what is going on in her head. Then, as she dramatically resists and the music swells, he drags her into the bedroom. There is no question about what happens next. The film cuts to a close up of her face: she wakes up, happy and content, to a sunny day. The victim's discovery of her own desire provides a happy ending that implicitly affirms, even justifies, the act of rape. Regardless of the variations in this pattern that legitimizes and aestheticizes a crime, it persists.[41]

In order to empirically determine how widespread this pattern is, the first step is to decide on an archive. One of my students suggested data mining the online collection of erotic stories Literotica.com, which allows users to find any kind of erotic and pornographic stories by type or interest. One of the largest collections, with over 22,000 stories out of 380,000 as of March 2018, fall under the heading "non-consent/reluctance" (rape fantasies), another 32,000 in the BDSM (also labeled as "power games") category. The story collection is huge, as is their diversity. The typical story seem to range from about five to eight print pages of a book of this kind, but some stories are broken down in chapters and can reach one hundred pages. Most texts reveal various features of typical fiction writing with a fully developed narrative plot; some meet the standards of published short prose in literary magazines.[42] According to a large corpus analysis, the overall patterns of all stories "tend to represent sexual intercourse as an asymmetric engagement between an agent and a patient, rather than as a joint collaborative activity."[43]

In the non-consent category, there seem to be more texts written from a female perspective, but also a fair part from a male perspective, and also some stories with frequent perspective switches. While the site maintains information about its authors using pseudonyms, they do not necessarily offer accurate information. In any case, the authors declare themselves to be both female and male. The site has several millions of monthly readers, according to the information provided. The stories in the nonconsent category tend to follow a couple of narrative patterns. In a random selection, I encountered several stories of blackmail (threatening to compromise employment or marriage or hurting someone else), slavery (contemporary, historic, or fantasy), abduction (at night, from the street, or in an unexplained manner with someone waking up in captivity), gang rape, stories of intruders, and stories in which a woman is hard-pressed for money or a job and agrees to some activity but things go further (a photo shoot leading to sexual exploitation). Some stories were presented as a form of revenge for teasing behavior. There are some, but few, stories of female exploitation of males or homosexual violence. It is noteworthy to point out that I did not find any stories of domestic violence.

The stories usually offer a fair amount of dialogue between the victim and perpetrator prior to and during the forced sex. The rape stories offer their readers the perspective of both the aggressor and the victim for a coexperience (when the text is written from a male perspective, there are frequent suggestions about what the female experiences; when it is written from a female perspective, readers can follow the male aggressors both by their actions and by their utterances.) There is a strong focus on the arch of the woman's initial resistance and her later enjoyment. This needs to be emphasized. Almost always the women or other victims at the end enjoy the rape. Sometimes they feel betrayed by their bodies, their desires, but they tend to ask or wish for more. Usually the male perpetrators reference their knowledge of the female victim's enjoyment. Sometimes the male perpetrators explicitly comment on the female desire at the end in a derogatory way (as if the women had initiated actions) and typically they establish some superiority ("I knew that this was what you needed").

Usually, the female is the in passive victim role. A few stories give some agency to the women as well. For example, one story begins with a blackmail framework in which a young teacher is blackmailed about some nude pictures of her from her high school time. In order to get the pictures back, she has to do what the anonymous blackmailer communicates to her via letters. One of her assignments is that she has to seduce a younger male intern.

Both my student and I estimate that the clear majority of the stories under the non-consent heading follows the pattern of refusal, resistance, rape, focus on the female experience with a turn to enjoyment, pleasure on the part of the victim, and, finally, some acknowledgment by the male about this turn to enjoyment and a confirmation of the male superiority.

We must be careful about making conclusions based on this archive. Obviously, it contains not police records or court transcripts but rather works of fantasy; it is also an archive of erotic tales only that do not include other kind of fiction, such as the novel or film *Gone with the Wind*. In addition, they not entirely written by volunteers; some are created by paid ghostwriters. (My student told me that she had written stories for the site to help pay for school.) That said, these stories are definitely written for readers who expect and enjoy such a narrative arc. It seems highly likely that the readers are both male and female. The enjoyment male and female readers experience might be similar or different. One reading experience focuses on the victim who is overwhelmed first by the aggressor, then by her own desires. This could correspond to the (male or female) reader's desire to cede control in these fantasies. Another reading experience could be the described pattern of control and empathy by means of manipulation: The reader as the aggressor controls, understands, and shares the feelings of the victim.

What does this pattern accomplish? In addition to trivializing (or sexualizing) sexual violence, it informs our understanding about how empathy's dark aspects operate. The empathetic rapist relates to the victims; he understands the victims' feelings after putting them in a situation of profound distress from which he (unlike most people) takes the pleasure of coexperience and manageable self-loss.[44] This transformation of extreme pain (in the other) into a positive feeling (in the empathetic rapist) is mirrored in the narrative pattern that depicts the victim moving from pain to pleasure, even gratitude. The empathetic rapist in these narratives therefore takes pleasure through the empathetic mechanism twice. First, he arouses empathy in himself by provoking suffering through which he can correctly anticipate, recognize, and therefore to some extent share the feelings of his victim. Then, he can see the victim repeat this very same turn from pain to pleasure, which not only legitimizes his actions but also relieves him from his empathy-work as the victim mirrors his emotions (first pain, then pleasure) and becomes emotionally accessible in the process.

It bears emphasizing that these are only speculations on a serious topic. My goal is not to excuse criminal behavior by suggesting that rape could in some cases be an empathy crime. On the contrary, I am attempting to better understand what incites it and, therefore, how it might be prevented. At the same time, empathy helps explain how these common narratives operate and why they can provide such satisfaction among readers or viewers. Moreover, their ubiquity feeds into a general rape culture or, at the very least, does little to discourage it.

Sadistic empathy can be described as *empathy for empathy's sake.* The empathetic response becomes its own goal, independent of any consideration for—or, indeed, detrimental to—the well-being of the other. Acts of sadistic empathy empower the observer-actor, since they control the other's feelings, dominate them, and share their emotional response. Unlike the stereotype of the unfeeling sadist, sadistic empathy involves more than issues of power; it is about understanding and sharing feelings. Active sympathy and care are absent, as are actions that put an end to the suffering being observed or inflicted. Some forms of cruelty and everyday oppression are characterized not by a lack of empathetic feeling; rather, empathy is not then translated into caring actions. One phase of empathy—a shared feeling—is enjoyed and clung to without being turned into prosocial behavior.

These thoughts reinforce a model of empathy operating at various phases and levels, which, consciously or not, can cross paths and block or arrest one another. In the final section of this chapter, I offer a speculative model for the psychological development of sadistic empathy.

Developmental Stages of Sadistic Empathy

Sadistic empathy can be described as the managing of one's own feelings through the mastery of the emotional state of the other. As with every other social feeling, sadistic empathy must also be an acquired trait, though there is little conclusive research about this process, since it cannot be observed neatly in the laboratory. Some people with psychopathic traits are often (but not exclusively) described as being the product of childhoods full of abuse and

neglect.[45] The origins of everyday sadistic empathy—from bullying to shaming others—are far more speculative in nature. The
literature on the phenomenon of sadism focuses on dominance
and control, which also likely seem to play a role in the formation
of the personality type.[46]

To approach this aspect, I want to indulge in a speculative line
of thinking—not only speculative but also anecdotal, coming as
it does from my own household and based on my observations of
my own and other children when they were in preschool. Three
siblings of different ages are playing, building fortresses from
pillows and starting pillow fights. Things heat up without quite
coming to a direct conflict. One of the children pins another on
the couch. The other child is not hurt but, try as they might, they
cannot get up. The pinned child can "give up," and the one on top
will, depending on their mood, either let pinned child go or decide to keep them there a little longer. Tears are rare; more often,
the pinned child gives a pleasant laugh. Nevertheless, they are
clearly in duress. In fact, the dominant child typically waits until
the pinned down child shows a sign of distress. The children play
this game time and again; it becomes practically ritualized. Where
is the fun in this activity? Several possibilities present themselves
as plausible.

For the youngest child, the pleasure may be simply in occasionally besting his older sister. He celebrates his strength. No empathy
framework is necessary to explain it, even though the uncompli-
cated dominance on display may obscure an understanding that
the child being pinned is suffering. The middle child, while she
just may enjoy pinning down her younger brother, also already
knows that she is stronger and so simply winning is not as fun. Instead, the middle child appears to enjoy controlling her younger
brother's feelings as well. She learns that she can not only win in a

physical conflict but also manipulate the emotional battle. She is, in effect, saying, "I can awake strong feelings in you!" and, looking at her own accomplishment, "I am so clever that I know how you will feel when I do this to you!" In fact, the older child often addresses her brother to share her insight by telling him, "That's mean, isn't it!" Typically, the middle child stops quickly when the younger one indicates he is in pain or when she has effectively manipulated his emotions. This, of course, is a (mild) form of sadistic empathy.

The oldest child can expect to easily win the physical contest and also knows she can correctly anticipate the feelings of her siblings. She is, therefore, usually not interested in the game. Nevertheless, she does play occasionally, and when she does, one thing stands out: She decides herself when to stop, regardless of when the younger child gives up or if they show signs of pain. The pinned child's appeals fall on deaf ears. One way to interpret her behavior is that she is learning to control and suppress her empathy mechanisms ("Of course, I see that you are in pain, but I don't care.") Part of her assertion of control is that she decides when the game is over and does not let her brother's or sister's complaints affect her decision. (Another interpretation would be the oldest child knows that her parent is watching and also wants to signal her dominance to the adults.) The oldest child internalizes the game of dominance and turns it into a form of self-dominance, and therefore self-affirmation. In this game, the children are learning (or applying their already acquired knowledge) that they can control and manipulate the emotional state of others by means of force.

My observations here cannot be considered evidence, but they do open up space to speculate about how the emotional understanding of others is linked to a certain degree of sadism, manipulation, or subjugation.[47]

1. A person traps the other and manipulates them.
2. The emotional reaction of the other is thereby made discernible to the manipulator.
3. The predictability of this response, combined with the suffering of the person under control, allow, simplify, and activate empathy.
4. The manipulator coexperiences the emotions (including the suffering) of the other
5. The manipulator blocks or suppresses the shared pain (selective blocking of empathy)
6. The manipulator takes pleasure out of stages 1–5 or from all of them in combination. (Note that stages 2–5 constitute forms of empathy.)

In offering this developmental model for sadistic empathy, I am keenly aware that it could also offer a model of how empathy in general is learned. The standard model for empathy formation, very simply, posits that a child experiences suffering and later finds themself in the position to recognize the suffering of another in a similar situation. But why should one acknowledge the suffering of someone else? What is the advantage of doing so? Indeed, such a recognition places limits and makes demands on one's own behavior. In contrast, the speculative model for the formation of sadistic empathy makes the advantage very clear: the appeal of joining empathy with sadism. The child finds pleasure in every step of the process and is quickly and repeatedly rewarded for their acts. Sadistic empathy, therefore, offers a decisive advantage over altruistic empathy as a learned behavior. Could it be, then, that acquiring the mechanisms for sadistic empathy provides the base model for learning how to empathize more generally?

I put these last thoughts forward without any irony. However, I do not propose to that we should declare sadistic empathy the developmental origin of empathy. On the contrary: We should understand that there are few control mechanisms in the development of empathy that can rule out such forms of sadistic empathy. While we certainly need empathy, we should not simply endorse the cultivation of empathy—in our legal system, in our society, among our children—and count on it resulting automatically in prosocial behavior. Rather, as I will argue in the final chapter, we as parents, policymakers, and a society need to build ethical checks on the seductive power of empathy, while nevertheless endorsing and supporting it.

5

Vampiristic Empathy

Helicopter Parents, Stalkers, Fans, and Living through Others

In many of the cases discussed so far, empathy arises spontaneously, without forethought, and operates for a finite amount of time. Someone enters into a situation in which they observe another person suffering and is overcome with empathy—they take a side, see things from the other's perspective, or coexperience the other's dilemma—and, after the situation is resolved (or when the cost of empathizing becomes too much to bear), the observer withdraws their emotional support and returns to themself. The dynamic differs in cases of sadistic empathy, in which the observer deliberately harms another person in order to understand them cognitively and emotionally. This dark aspect of empathy is, however, still primarily activated in specific, temporary circumstances. In contrast, there are long-term empathetic relationships that can last a lifetime. In this chapter, I will explore the negative, even damaging effects that emerge out of extended periods of empathetic engagement.

Empathy is, of course, a critical factor in healthy long-term relationships, too, making it easier for us to understand our family

members or romantic partners and anticipate their emotional
needs and reactions. Love without empathy would be a sad thing
for most people. This empathetic connection is readily established
because we observe the other closely and continuously while sharing similar experiences. This closeness also means that the border
between us and the other becomes more porous, making unhealthy emotional attachments possible.

The ability and opportunity to coexperience with another over
an extended period contains a danger: that we might try to *program* others according to our own wishes. When controlled and
manipulated in this way, the other becomes merely a means for us
to access an experience that we desire without paying any regard
to their welfare. The other is robbed of their own agency. I describe
the extreme cases that I address in this chapter—helicopter parenting, obsessive fandom, and stalking—as *vampiristic empathy*.

Some readers will question whether these phenomena are related to empathy, arguing that I am like the man with the prover-
bial hammer, to whom everything looks like a nail. I will posit that
these alarming behaviors cannot be adequately explained without
involving empathy. Rather than the metaphor of hammer and nail,
I prefer to think of my approach as hammer and chisel, with which
I will chip away at the problems posed by these behaviors to make
a sculpture that, like a work of art, may take us closer to reality
through its artifice.

Helicopter Parents, Stage Mothers, and Vampirism

For twenty-five years, researchers have been using the term "helicopter parents" to refer to parents who metaphorically (and sometimes literally) hover above their children, leaving them little room
to develop on their own or take responsibility for their actions.[1]

As a professor, I can tell my share of stories about helicopter parents who call me during office hours or come to the university as their children's representatives. I remember one case in particular when I had to explain to a parent that I could not discuss confidential information, such as grades, with the parent of a student who was legally an adult. The parent burst out into tears: "It is all my fault, it is all my fault. My daughter does not deserve to be punished for that." Parents may even hover over their adult children in the workplace; it seems to be common today that parents submit résumés on behalf of their children and university students suggest that their parents "would influence their career choices after graduation."[2]

The children who emerge from such an upbringing tend to learn later than their peers how to take care of themselves and are on average less successful and more likely to suffer from depression and anxiety.[3] The scientific literature remains divided on how exactly to describe the phenomenon. Popular psychology experts and self-help books unhelpfully claim that between 20 and 60 percent of American parents behave like helicopters.

Popular representations of helicopter parenting often attribute it to the emotional instability of the parents, who out of fear and uncertainty keep their children too close, thereby depriving them of taking (or never allowing them to develop) responsibility for their own lives. These parents, we are told, are incapable of letting go of their children because they are pathologically overprotective. I find this explanation unsatisfactory, or, at least, incomplete, and offer another—though not necessarily contradictory—explanation by looking at parental empathy.

Phenomenologically speaking, such parents carefully assess their children's situation and anticipate what their best course of action would be in order to encourage what they consider optimal decision-making. They are concerned with protecting their children and with wanting them to succeed. This dynamic comprises two levels of emotional empathy. First, there is a sharing of feelings ascribed to the child: happiness at success or frustration over failure, for example. Next, there are secondary emotions, which emerge from the disjunction between actual and desired states. Parents react with nervousness, fear, or the concern that their offspring might make the wrong decision. And if the child responds to their success or failure differently than the parent would, this becomes a stimulus for parents to teach their children the appropriate response since the child *ought* to care more about their successes.

What does this have to do with empathy? Clearly, the way parents coexperience their children's feelings and situations is one factor. Another component is one that plays a minor role in most forms of empathy—the prescriptive view of how children ought to act and what they should feel. For helicopter parents, empathetic intervention seems to center around those cases in which admonishment is possible: parents empathize to improve the performance of their children. (I should note that helicopter parenting appears on the one hand to be connected to such subsequent mental health issues as depression and a lack of independent problem-solving abilities in the children; on the other hand, it correlates with higher rates of academic achievement.[4] The negative psychological impacts are found to be strongest in students reporting to have "over-controlling parents."[5])

According to one model, helicopter parents function like an external Freudian super-ego. For Freud, the super-ego reflected a mixture of morality and parental and societal expectations—the inner voice of the conscience. However, the super-ego role played by the helicopter parent focuses on achievement and success in school, at sports, or in other activities, as well as professionally and socially, whether or not these goals have personal substance or meaning. The children of helicopter parents are likely to internalize both this pressure to succeed and their parents' fear of failure.

The stern, threatening, or possibly even gentle superego was, for Freud, the internalized voice of a powerful father figure. Helicopter parents will most likely not see themselves as authoritarian but instead as wanting to share feelings and experiences with their children and envision a positive future for them. I see in this relationship a kind of aspirational empathy at work. The parent wishes for instances of success, recognition, and victory in which they can take part. The seemingly healthy parental wish for a child to get good grades, for example, might be rationally explained in terms of wanting an easier entry into college and a career for them; at the same time, it can also be rooted in the parents' need for external validation of their parenting skills. This need can manifest itself in a wide range of behaviors. At the more benign end of the spectrum is the type of overbearing parental advocacy I routinely see as a professor. At the other end is "parental vampirism," in which parents seek to relive their own youth through their children, without regard for whether the parent's plan aligns with the child's ideas about themself.[6]

Underlying this dynamic is the phenomenon that I call vampiristic empathy, a concept that, so far at least, does not have a direct clinical correlate. An extreme form of emotional identification, vampiristic empathy is the process of sharing another's experience to the extent that the observer appropriates it over time, while neglecting the other's independent well-being. Put more precisely, vampiristic empathy is the process of coexperiencing another's situation while supplanting their objectives, goals, or desires with one's own. A benign expression of this dynamic would be living vicariously through someone else—this recalls a typical (and unproblematic) form of engagement with fiction.[7] It also includes attempts by the empathetic observer to attach their own aspirations to the life of another in order to allow for high levels of empathetic identification. In helicopter parenting, the selfish concern of the observer is masked by apparent concern for the other.

The most drastic instance of parental vampirism is found in the stereotypical figure of the stage mother, who aggressively grooms her child to become a model, actor, singer, dancer, or beauty pageant winner at any cost. Through her child's success on stage, the mother imagines herself there and basks in the reflected glory. Likewise, the abusive sports father who yells at and in some cases assaults other parents, children, and referees seems to be driven by a similar desire to see himself in his triumphant child. (As I discussed in the previous chapter, events on stage and in the arena are one of the clearest instances of ritualized empathy.)

A tragic real-life example comes from the life and death of Jon-Benét Patricia Ramsey (1990–96). The still-unsolved murder of the child beauty queen gave rise to rich speculation about the role her mother played in her life. The mother, Patsy Ramsey, herself a former Miss West Virginia, had pushed her daughter into a career of competing in child beauty pageants and was condemned in the court of public opinion for the hyper-feminizing and sexualizing of her daughter. Initially, the police department of Boulder, Colorado, even suspected her as having in a role in her daughter's death, though they subsequently declared that no immediate family members were involved after examining DNA evidence. In the popular media, Patsy was described as having a love-hate relationship with JonBenét as a result of her overidentification with, or excessive jealousy of, her daughter, and she was accused of unconsciously trying to relive her own childhood through her daughter. If this were true, she would indeed qualify as a vampiristic empathizer.

It is also possible that some of the reporting of the case applied especially sexist patterns to the mother's behavior under the guise of an impartial investigation. There is virtually no utterance or behavior by JonBenét's mother that has not been discussed as proof of her guilt, including her own meticulous appearance shortly after her daughter's body was found. It is as if the accusation that she had an unhealthy relationship with her daughter gives license to the media and others to have a similarly unhealthy relationship with her.

To balance this grim example, one could point to the 1993 HBO stage-mom satire, *The Positively True Adventures of the Alleged Texas Cheerleader-Murdering Mom*, in which the titular character played by Holly Hunter hires someone to have her daughter's cheerleading rival killed. Based on a true story in which the obsessive mother was herself denied a place as a cheerleader as a young woman, the movie thus presents the exaggerated figure of a murderous helicopter parent who wishes to relive her own youth through her daughter at all costs. A similar dynamic unfolds in *Buffy the Vampire Slayer*, season 1, episode 3.[8]

Despite these extreme examples, I want to repeat that across the whole spectrum of helicopter parenting, the driving emotions are positive ones—the wish for success and admiration. Punishment and negative pressure are more likely to be hidden secondary impulses, arising if the child is not successful and living up to the parental ideal.

The point at which legitimate concern for a child turns into vampiristic empathy is not easy to determine. Parents and other guardians have good reasons to worry about the well-being of their charges. Indeed, they frequently need to and should intervene on the child's behalf. But at some point, this intervention goes so far as to strip the child of agency, becoming an obsession for the parent. In theory, one could argue that the "healthy" participation of parents has been exceeded when the parental measures result in an undermining of the autonomy of the children and when the children are forced to conform to the ideals of the parents to their own detriment. In practice, however, the boundaries are far more fluid. Legitimate parental concern, intrusive helicopter parenting, and the harmful vampiristic empathy of stage mothers and sports dads go some distance hand in hand. Of course, parents should and do delight in their children's success. (Behaviors opposite to helicopter parenting—disinterest and parental neglect—are arguably more harmful to a child's long-term wellbeing and almost certainly more prevalent.) Their joy, however, has more than one motivation behind it: a shared happiness directed at the child; the self-centered relief at not having to worry; self-praise about one's parenting acumen; and the self-indulgent feeling that a child's success reflects on the parent. This emotional and cultural overlapping and ambiguity makes the phenomenon particularly interesting from the perspective of empathy research.

In the literature on stage parents and stage mothers, E. D. (Adie) Nelson has suggested about motherwork that "its dramaturgy may require that mothers engage in dreamwork on behalf of their children" to market their children as finished, competitive products.[9] Education in this framework serves as a site for a veiled parental vampirism, expressed through the narcissism of parents who want their "entry" to be the winning one.

One precondition for helicopter parenting is social and cultural. For more than two hundred years, philosophers and education theorists—including Jean-Jacques Rousseau, Karl Philipp Moritz, Immanuel Kant, Johann Heinrich Pestalozzi, and Maria

Montessori—have posited that the ideal upbringing comprises an education aimed at inculcating autonomy in children. This stands in stark contrast to modern cultural practices of pedagogy and parenting, as well as to our contemporary obsession with achievement, competition, celebrity, and fame.

Many of the fantasies of helicopter parents seem to be directed towards real or imaginary performances, whether literally on stage, on screen, on a fashion runway, or in a sporting venue; or more metaphorically on the social stage through public recognition, financial success, or conversation and gossip among family, neighbors, or the community. In all these cases, the child becomes an object on display.

In other words, these scenes—whether benign or vampiristic—overlap with typical scenes of empathy. The stage, in particular, is an especially rich incarnation of ritualized empathy. As I discussed in earlier chapters, we go into the theater to experience the events on stage and to feel our way into the characters and situations. The stage makes the work of empathy uncommonly easy; even people with low empathy can be emotionally captivated by the theater. Similarly, we routinely stage theater-like situations in our fantasies, either in order to feel empathy or to become the object of the empathetic identification ourselves. And so children too readily become the object of empathy when they are placed on a real or imaginary stage.

Because parents find themselves pulled between opposing expectations and practices, their healthy empathetic identification with their children can degrade into these vampiristic stage fantasies. As the child becomes a kind of stage for the parents to replay their own childhood triumphs or traumas, healthy parental concern and pride can transform into other, darker forms of empathy. When they were children, parents were simply actors on the stage;

as parents, they have the opportunity to be the stage director, to make everything the same but better—regardless of the roles that their children want to play or are even capable of playing, thereby limiting their children to prescribed scripts.

Stalkers, Fans, and Obsessive Empathy (Identification)

According to the US Bureau of Justice, "the term 'stalking' means engaging in a course of conduct directed at a specific person that would cause a reasonable person to fear for his or her safety or the safety of others or suffer substantial emotional distress."[10] While celebrity stalking gets the most attention, the vast majority of stalking victims know their tormentors and are statistically most likely to be divorced or separated from their stalkers. Among American college students, 25 percent of women say they have been pursued by a stalker at some point.[11] Among celebrities, and most of all among movie stars and popular musicians, the rate is likely appreciably higher. According to the Bureau of Justice, an estimated 3.4 million persons age eighteen or older were victims of stalking during a twelve-month period, which is around 1.4 percent of the US population. In 43 percent of the cases, stalking involved threats to the victims.[12]

At first glance, helicopter parents seem to have little in common with obsessive fans and stalkers. It seems rare for the stalker, follower, or fan to want to protect the object of their obsession or help guide them to success. To be sure, stalkers often seem to justify their actions as being in the best interests of their devotional object. In fiction, think of *Taxi Driver*'s Travis Bickle (Robert DeNiro), whose spree of violence was (in his own mind, at least) driven by his desire to save Jodi Foster's Iris from a life of prostitution.

The celebrities stalked by obsessive fans have, of course, already achieved tremendous success; but even the far greater number of stalking victims who are not famous are usually functioning adults with families and careers. Rather, the similarity between these phenomena can be found in the extreme way in which one person watches and tracks someone else: in short, it is obsessive observation. As in the case of helicopter parenting, there are ritualized stagings of observation that can create an imagined closeness. And like some helicopter parents, the fan or stalker sees in or projects onto the object of their obsession a perfection (whether real or not) that they lack in their own lives.

Is empathy at work in this behavior? As with helicopter parents, not every stalker is motivated by empathetic identification. Other explanations include negative intentions, such as revenge or rivalry, and "positive" ones, as in the (unwanted) pursuit of emotional intimacy.[13] Many of the most egregious stalkers suffer from psychosis. Only a few stalkers seem to be physically violent, even if they threaten violence, but their victims still suffer from their obsession and live in fear.[14]

While the vast majority of stalking victims are not famous, the phenomenon of celebrity stalkers throws the role played by the dark side of empathy into high relief. The dynamic at work in these cases, however, is undoubtedly similar to that among many of those who stalk ex-spouses or ex-partners, coworkers, or people who have spurned their unwanted advances. In fact, I will suggest below that stalkers draw from celebrity culture by glorifying their victims like celebrities.

The phenomenon of obsessive fandom is usually coupled with public performances. Even before the pervasive nature of contemporary celebrity, performers could make a great impact on the public, becoming stars of opera and theater, for example. I do not know to what degree stalking is rooted in human nature but it certainly seems to have been enabled and enhanced by media and cultural institutions like the stage and arena. At least since antiquity, athletes have attracted the kind of devotion that we might call obsessive fandom; the stereotype of the female stalker has existed since antiquity as well.[15] It was, however, the mass media that emerged in the late nineteenth and early twentieth centuries— newspapers, radio, and most significantly film—that transformed the nature of fame and fandom. The 1920s were the first intense period of celebrity adulation for Hollywood stars and such athletes as Babe Ruth and Jack Dempsey.

New communication methods also play a critical role in the increase in stalking. Thanks to the telephone and, now, mobile devices and text messaging, the stalker can quickly cross into their target's private sphere, imagining their actions to be normal use of communication media (although cyberstalking is a criminal offense in many jurisdictions). While some forms of cyberstalking and especially cyberbullying correlate with a lack of empathy, a desire for empathy can also motivate cyberstalkers.[16] The lines between following a friend on social media platforms like Facebook or Instagram, obsessively checking in on them, and stalking are not always clear, except from the perspective of the victim. In many cases of intensive social media following, a victim may feel fear, independently of what the stalking individual intends. Note again that the US Bureau of Justice's definition of stalking stresses the victim's perspective and not that of the stalker. For the follower/stalker, the mental act of stalking may be less clearly distinguished from caring and fandom. For the stalker, there is an instant gratification to slipping into someone else's life for a short time, even under the guise of either care or mere curiosity that hides the victim's fear.

The internet has increased the stalker's arsenal dramatically. Stalkers can now seek out information and opportunities to contact their targets via instant messaging, email, and social media; and through it they can post true or false information about their victim, subscribe them to various services, or steal their identity.[17] In general, the internet creates the impression of proximity and intimacy without placing any responsibilities on the internet user. The faceless anonymity of the internet user allows for a sphere of escapism that is ideal for coexperiencing another's situation at an intimate distance. Indeed, research shows that many adolescents use the internet to look for relationships while escaping face-to-face interactions.[18]

Stalking, the internet, and vampiristic empathy go hand in hand. In fact, following the logic of this book, we could suggest that our age's fascination with empathy is connected to our heightened engagement with media. From the novel to the internet, media have habituated us to participating in and sharing emotions without needing to directly react. This empathetic dynamic may not increase our humanity or humanitarian impulse, as Lynn Hunt suggests; rather, it fosters a relationship that is rich in self-focused narcissism and self-serving vampirism by the observer.[19]

Stalking reveals the self-focused, vampiristic tendency of empathy while also benefiting from the stage effect or celebrity effect of the media. What stalkers seek and apparently find in their victims may include not just the feeling of closeness and intimacy but also the sensation of being observed and, if their target is famous, in the spotlight. Through empathizing with their victims, the stalker wants to be seen as being as special, worthy of being observed themselves.

A particularly crude and unusually explosive example of stalker fandom is John Hinckley, Jr., who was released from psychiatric confinement in 2016, subject to numerous restrictions. Hinckley had become obsessed with *Taxi Driver* and Jodie Foster, following her to New Haven when she famously attended Yale University, enrolling in some courses at Yale, delivering letters to her dorm room, and calling her repeatedly—textbook examples of stalking behavior. Then, in an attempt to impress her, he wrote that he was going to shoot and kill the president. After stalking Jimmy Carter during the 1980 presidential election, he decided to assassinate Ronald Reagan instead after he became president. In 1981, he shot at Reagan outside the Hilton Hotel in Washington, D.C., seriously wounding him, a police officer, a Secret Service agent, and Reagan's press secretary, James Brady. Found not guilty by reason of insanity, Hinckley was committed to a psychiatric institution.

In Hinckley's actions, I see evidence of a glittering *observation fantasy* that involves both observing and being observed. The stalker fan anticipates, I posit, a quasi-magical moment in which observation from without transforms into a perception from within: the observer puts themself into the position of the observed. This differs from the empathetic coexperiencing that I have previously discussed. Rather than simply imagining themself in the other's situation, the stalker fan imagines being the other in a situation in which they are being observed and therefore—this is the key point—a worthy object of the observers' devotion.[20] Observer and observed are in this way blended into one, creating a novel feeling of heightened presence.[21]

While this dynamic closely follows my description of the identification mechanism of empathy in the previous chapter, the emphasis differs because the stalker fan not only hopes to (in the evocative German idiom) *schlüpfen in die Haut eines anderen* (slip into another's skin) but also imagines what it would be like to be the other in the state of being observed. (One could say that to elevate and idealize the observed reveals something central about the act of observation: to be observed implies that one is worthy of observation. Stalkers may seek exactly this kind of approval.) In the introduction, I described a phenomenon I called "glowing skin," in which the observer imagines themself (as I did when I was a child) standing on stage with a spotlight illuminating their presence. In this scenario, the stalker's gaze is also an imaginary spotlight that shines on both the object of their obsession and, through empathetic identification, themself.

To summarize, this is what stalker fans seek: to elevate their target through their adulation, while at the same time elevating themselves out of obscurity. And for elevating their hero in this way, the stalker demands a reward. This reward usually comprises sharing the other's experiences, not simply as an expansion of one's own experience—something most fans might seek, deriving pleasure and a sense of community through their fandom—but rather as an intensification of their own life emerging from their blending of the observer and observed positions, paired with a purification or aesthetic clarity of life from the observer position, as discussed in the introduction. The actual and naturally more complex experiences of the other remain inaccessible, of course.

In this respect, the stalker reveals another negative aspect of empathy. They want to put their image of the other in place of the original, which is a way of indirectly occupying that position themself. Sigmund Freud in *Totem and Taboo* saw this sort of identification at work in rituals of cannibalism through which the other was incorporated and eliminated. The more one wishes to be in the superior position of the other, the more acutely the actual other becomes an obstacle. This is at least one possible manifestation of the glowing skin phenomenon.

In films full of fast action and soaring emotions, when the dramatic stakes are high, or in tense sporting events, the imaginative presence of the observer is encouraged.[22] Observers can enjoy the feeling of heightened presence and pure excitement that the next moment will decide everything. Indeed, through a variety of cinematic techniques developed over a century, the film viewer is manipulated by the filmmakers to do so. Of course, the true other might not experience pure presence at all. They may fear failure or, as professionals, do a rational risk analysis of their next moves. But this real other is not of interest for the observer. The seductive gameplay of computer games may operate similarly, as the game player finds themself in a position of identification with their digital avatar.

The longing for intensity, presence, and aesthetic clarity becomes the motor of identification; inhabiting the glowing skin is the reward. But for some stalkers and obsessive fans, this reward is not enough. They also expect recognition from the targets of their obsession. This explains a variety of behaviors that aim to transform the observer-observed relationship into a two-way dynamic. Even ordinary fans get a charge when their heroes smile or wave at them. Various public fora, from sports and concert arenas to red carpet walks, are designed with these kinds of interactions in mind, ritualizing a certain invasiveness. But some fans want more; they want to be noticed individually; they want to be rewarded for their identification work by the person behind the persona. This can lead to unrealistic but harmless fantasies of love or friendship with the celebrity or manifest itself negatively as threatening behavior. In the latter cases, the stalker fan shows that they can break into the private sphere of the celebrity—even into their home—and have no qualms about doing so.

Identification thus turns into resentment, since the other does not respond to the emotional effort of the observer. The stalker fan can react as though they were the victim and their revenge, their reward, and their resentment are therefore justified in their own mind. The object of their obsession is punished for the imaginary relationship of identification between the obsessive fan and their image of that object.

Vampirism

The vampires we know from the cinema are pale, almost as if they spent too many daylight hours watching movies. They live vicariously through others and thus function as a reflection of the people starring at them on the screen. If we consider the longing faces of many cinematic vampires—for instance, Friedrich Wilhelm Murnau's 1922 *Nosferatu* and, especially, Werner Herzog's 1979 remake of the Murnau film with Klaus Kinski as Count Dracula—we can reason that what these vampires long for is the lives of others, since they have no lives of their own. Likewise, vampiristic empathy hides the emptiness of the empathizer and fills the void with the experiences of others who can be hollowed out in the process.

One possible motivation for these obsessive forms of empathetic identification is love, the hope of winning the affections of the other. In such cases, obsessive empathy remains focused on the other. Similarly, a longing for friendship, closeness, dialogue, or recognition might express itself in obsessive empathy.

But in the more extreme cases discussed above—helicopter parenting, stage mothering (or sports fathering), and stalking—the other often ceases to be a distinct and whole person. The dark empathizer wants some aspect of the other for themself; their interest in the other's well-being comes and goes as it serves this end. In the case of the helicopter parent, the obsessive focus on the well-being of the child hides a selfish desire for success. What the obsessive observer seeks is a coexperiencing that will result in heightened feelings of perfection, presence, success, or even the "glowing skin" of standing on stage for all to see.

What drives empathetic identification to the point of vampirism? Stanley Cavell offers an influential analysis of vampirism in his reading of the 1944 film *Gaslight*. He offers a portrait of "intellectual men as systematically plagiarizing women's thoughts, perhaps as a spur or supplement to their own originality, perhaps out of a distrust of their own originality. This suggests a route of motivation for men's wanting to know what women know, that it is a projection of their doubts about the worth of their own knowledge, of their intellectualization of their lives."[23] Cavell surmises that the basis of this vampiristic behavior is to be found in the doubt about one's original identity. The vampire wants to complete or compensate for their own inadequate originality, which could also be described as perfection or pure presence. This does not necessarily mean that the other (in Cavell's analysis, the woman) possesses originality, lives in a state of pure presence, or is perfect. They only appear to do so from the perspective of the obsessive empathizer. To be more precise, the observer's perspective overlays the qualities of originality, presence, or perfection onto the object of their obsession, imparting a "glowing skin" effect through their observation.

In cases of vampirism, empathy is not an end in itself as it was in episodes of sadistic empathy; rather it is a means to intensify or enrich one's own experience. As with sadistic empathizers, vampiristic empathizers have little regard for the other's well-being. But their pleasure comes not from anticipating and subsequently manipulating another's feelings—and not at all from causing pain, as is the case with sadists; instead, they find satisfaction from appropriating the (subordinated) experiences of the observed other. When these experiences are positive, the happiness of both observer and observed can coincide. Even in these situations, however, concern about the observed's well-being is more likely a side effect of the observer's own goals and not selfless care for the other.

Vampiristic empathy creates its own feedback loop. Under obsessive observation, the observed's life appears more present, more perfect, more original, or more intense. In comparison, the vampire's own life will appear dull, empty, and meaningless, full of doubt and failure. This emptying of the self feeds the vampire's emotional hunger.

This process returns us to Nietzsche's theory of how the "objective person" projects a strong self by thinning themself (see chapter 1). Like the fan, stalker, or the vampiristic empathizer, the "objective person" longs for strong and meaningful experiences in the lives of others for their own vicarious experience. As suggested, the "objective person" (the empathetic observer) will lionize the other, will endow them with an imaginary self, put the spotlight on them in the act of empathetic observation at the price of emptying himself or herself out. The stalker wants to coexperience the life of their hero, but the cost is making their own life appear pale. And as in the helicopter parent, this process of endowing the other with a self is paired with resentment and an ugly underbelly of demands on the other to live up to one's expectations. A radical literary representation of this dynamic can be found in Elfriede Jelinek's dark novel *The Piano Teacher*, in which the stalking heroine, who has had her life controlled by the regime of practicing her instrument, extends her controlling tendency on others and ends up mutilating and hating herself and the person she stalks, who might have a better life than she.

A Dark Culture of Empathy?

Is our media-obsessed culture moving toward vampiristic empathy? The answer, I fear, may be yes. Social media create spaces in which imaginary proximity, stage effects, and narcissism thrive. As I have been arguing, there are many cases in which empathy and narcissism go hand in hand. Vampiristic empathy in particular reveals how we can coexperience the life of others for selfish means. The problem of our age may not simply be that we are self-absorbed and driven by self-representations but that others are of interest for us less for who they are than as vehicles for our self-experience. Narcissism is not wholly unhealthy; it can help liberate us from self-negating dependencies and a culture of Stockholm syndrome. Self-focus that is masked by outward other-focus, however, too easily leads to the exploitation of others for our own gain, turning empathy into a weapon of suppression or domination that simultaneously hollows us out in the process.

Epilogue

EMPATHY BETWEEN MORALITY
AND AESTHETICS

I magine that there was a drug that could increase your ability to feel empathy. Would you take it? Would you give it to your children? Would you vote to have it added to your community's water supply? If, as various philosophers and political and spiritual leaders have suggested, the world suffers from an empathy deficiency, the question should be an easy one. I hope that here, at the conclusion of this book, you are discomforted by this thought experiment and the suggestion that such a drug would, without question, improve humanity. Empathy is not necessarily pernicious, but neither is it principally good. In summarizing the findings of this book, I will suggest that there is, in fact, no strong link between empathy and morality. Empathy is, rather, more deeply connected with two different domains: aesthetics and emotional development. Empathy intensifies our experiences and widens the scope of our perceptions. We feel more than we could without it, and it enables us to participate more fully in the lives of others, even fictional characters. This form of engagement can be described in terms of aesthetic experience and the deepening of our emotions and it provides strong reasons to teach and cherish empathy.

To begin with the question of morality, empathy can be used for both good and bad ends. As we have seen, an empathetic torturer is plausible, and a rapist may be driven by empathy rather than its absence. Empathy can, of course, motivate positive, prosocial actions. There is a parent's primal empathetic connection to their child. (I do not question that this form of empathy may have been a driving force of the evolution of empathy in mammals, and in humans in particular—perhaps even its main cause.[1]) Even parental concerns are not so straightforward, though. Helicopter parents, after all, want what's best for their children, though they may mistake that impulse with more selfish ends. People can also empathize for the sake of feeling empathy or in order to gain access to the feelings of another person, not to help or support them. In these cases, empathy becomes self-serving, independent of moral considerations.

Empathy plays a morally complex role in increasing polarization through side-taking. While empathy can attract support to the "right" side of a debate or conflict, it can also lead to whitewashing the beliefs or actions of the "wrong" side or it can help validate antisocial, even reprehensible moral views. Jesse Prinz teaches us to be careful not to expect ethically correct choices from empathy.[2] In addition, empathetic identification with one side or another may more often deepen conflicts than lessen them.

If empathy motivates someone who witnesses an injustice or a misfortune to intervene and try to relieve someone's physical or mental suffering, it obviously has a positive impact. My argument is not "against empathy" but rather that to consider this dynamic as the ur-form of empathy and its darker manifestations—false or filtered empathy, sadistic empathy, and empathetic vampirism— as deviations would be naive. Empathy resists being instrumentalized for "good" ends and refutes the logic that more empathy will necessarily make a person better. While there are numerous indications that empathy is associated with socially beneficial behavior, this is not a simple causal relationship; rather, it requires a complex network of cultural practices that positively channels self-interested experience.

Instead of broadly asking whether empathy is good or bad, I want to sharpen the inquiry and ask instead whether we should encourage and teach empathy. The best-intentioned attempts to inculcate a sense of empathy—as the school experiment in Northern Ireland (discussed in chapter 2) showed—can lead to the opposite results. Although those students were able to understand other perspectives and exhibit empathy for them, they also appeared to more sharply divide the world into "us" and "them." In light of this, then, should techniques for increasing one's ability to empathize be taught?

Absolutely, though not for reasons of moral improvement. Our understanding of empathy and its utility will become much more nuanced if we free ourselves from the mentality that increasing empathetic identification must have a moral dimension. I would suggest, instead, that one immediate and central advantage to empathy is that it can expand our perspective on the world. More specifically, empathy increases our aesthetic perception in three interrelated ways: first, by widening the scope of that which we experience; second, by providing us with more than one perspective of a situation, thereby multiplying our experience of the situation; and third, by intensifying that experience. To go into a little more detail:

1. Empathy allows us to live in more than one world. Through empathy we can imagine the experiences of others and actually co-experience them emotionally, participating in their emotional and cognitive reactions to the world around them. Closely linked

to this idea is our aptitude for narrative, which transports us as a reader or audience member into new, otherwise inaccessible worlds. (The psychological literature, as previously discussed, makes a distinction between transportation and empathy, since narrative situations do not necessarily require us to slide into the skin of another but only into an imaginary situation, in which the self and the other are more or less distinct.)

2. Empathy can multiply how we experience a particular situation by opening up different points, allowing us to move back and forth between perspectives—ours and those of others viewing the same situation from other points of view. A variety of aesthetically significant situations belong in this category. In classical theories of tragedy and drama, the moment of recognition (*anagnorisis*) is of particular importance. This is the moment when characters are unexpectedly brought together by an unexpected discovery: Electra recognizing her exiled brother, Orestes, at their father's grave in Aeschylus's *The Libation Bearers*, for example. Many of these scenes of recognition are particularly moving or powerful precisely because the audience already knows the hidden identities. It is not the element of surprise that moves the audience, therefore, but rather the play of perspectives. When Odysseus reveals his identity to Penelope's suitors in book 22 of *The Odyssey*, our empathetic identification oscillates between the characters. When we share Odysseus's perspective in particular, we imagine not only how he feels about finally lifting the secret of his identity to the suitors but also how, bow in hand, he is seen by them, and we experience the strong feelings of the suitors, who know they are about to die. This phenomenon—what I called in the introduction "glowing skin," when an experience is heightened by the awareness of being observed—is enabled by empathy.

Although *anagnorisis* is a literary effect, it may reveal a common, everyday experience in which we similarly see events unfold from multiple perspectives; we act and we reflect on how we are seen by others in those situations. Even in such mundane

interactions as when we go shopping and have a cursory back-
and-forth of empathetic alignment with the salesperson, our
perceptions of human actions or expressions (even our own)
are heightened, deepened, or complicated by empathetically
taking on more than one perspective. Empathy's ability to multiply our perceptions is an essential aspect of our social lives.
3. Empathy also enables an aesthetic intensification of a moment,
a feeling of importance, of pure presence. Such moments have a
unique temporal structure. When we are intensely absorbed in
a specific moment, we may imagine and experience the future
and the past of this moment and consider alternative versions of
the events it comprises, including counterfactual versions, as if
mentally looping back and forth within the moment and making it a knot of temporal developments. Consider a person immediately before a decisive action. In the empathetic weighing
of this moment, the possible future outcomes and the present
moment are already intermingled; it becomes a prolonged, multi-
dimensional event. This temporal looping effect is the point
at which empathy and aesthetic experience come together.[3] In
Against Empathy, Paul Bloom critiques empathy for producing
spotlighted visions of reality that exclude larger contexts. The
intensification of the moment is the positive side of this effect.

I contend that people who are less able to empathize have a
more impoverished view of the world than those with a strong
empathetic ability and, for this reason, teaching people how to empathize more effectively has value. One indirect result of an education that promotes aesthetic empathy may be an increase in more
altruistic forms of empathy and a more intense appreciation of
others, though I would maintain that such an outcome should not
be its purpose.

In addition to empathy's aesthetic effects, its role in increasing our overall emotional awareness bears emphasizing. Emotions

signal how we should act and help us adjust our behavior when necessary.[4] Empathy helps us recognize our own emotions more clearly. Many of our emotions are not easily accessible to us unless we learn to identify them in others. This training, I suggest, makes it possible for us to discover them by coexperiencing them through the emotional lives of others or being exposed to them through works of art.

This is a vast topic full of questions that go beyond what I can discuss here. Suffice it to say, for example, it is naive to assume that we automatically recognize in others the feelings and impressions we ourselves have experienced, even when we do register strong emotions in others. There is a deep divide between inside and outside perspectives. From the outside, the feelings of others may be less intense while also being clearer and more perceptible to the observer than they may be to the person experiencing them, since people are often not clear about their own feelings. Another question is whether empathy can communicate *new* or *unfamiliar* feelings. Regardless, empathy plays a major role in teaching us emotions by bringing us closer to the emotions, thoughts, and feelings of others, adding to the diversity of our emotional lives. With practice, we can better understand emotions and their different intensities and progressions. An empathetic training model would prepare us to recognize the range of emotions within us or let new feelings in—without being overwhelmed by them.

In teaching, learning, or promoting greater empathy, we should not be distracted by the prospect of some short-term moral benefit. Rather, the reward for embracing empathy is the enrichment and intensification of our aesthetic perception of the world around us and the emotional experiences within ourselves and others. Aesthetically attuned people are not morally superior nor are they more altruistic; emotionally aware individuals not more ethical. If we are vigilant about the darker aspects of our thoughts and behavior that empathy can access, using this powerful element of our humanity to heighten our aesthetic and emotional awareness of the world around us will lead to a richer life. When we free ourselves from the overly optimistic view that empathy should make us morally good, we can still cherish how empathy widens the scope of our experiences dramatically and enables a rich and complex coexperiencing of our joint world.

Notes

Introduction

1. "Do Sexually Sadistic Serial Killers Really Lack Empathy," r/serial killers, October 29, 2015, https://www.reddit.com/r/serialkillers/comments/3qoey8/do_sexually_sadistic_serial_killers_really_lack.

2. Stephanie Preston and Frans de Waal have proposed the separation between the self and the other as a necessary condition for empathy, since this separation protects one from emotional overlap or contamination. See Stephanie D. Preston and Frans de Waal, "Empathy: Its Ultimate and Proximate Bases," *Behavioral Brain Science* 25, no. 1 (2002): 1–20. This idea has become widely accepted in standard literature; see Jean Decety and C. Daniel Batson, "Empathy and Morality: Integrating Social and Neuroscience Approaches," in *The Moral Brain: Essays on the Evolutionary and Neuroscientific Aspects of Morality*, ed. Jan Verplaetse (Dordrecht: Springer 2009), 109–27; and Claus Lamm, Markus Rütgen, and Isabella C. Wagner, "Imaging Empathy and Prosocial Emotions," in *Neuroscience Letters* (June 2017): 1–5.

3. We will return over the course of this book to questions concerning narrative and fiction. See on that topic Suzanne Keen, *Empathy and the Novel* (Oxford: Oxford University Press, 2007); Jonathan Gottschall, *The Storytelling Animal: How Stories Make Us Human* (Boston: Houghton Mifflin Harcourt, 2012); Brian Boyd, *On the Origin of Stories* (Cambridge, MA.: Harvard University Press, 2009).

4. Jerome Bruner, *Making Stories: Law, Literature, Life* (Cambridge, MA: Harvard University Press, 2003).

5. Paul Bloom, *Against Empathy* (New York: Harper Collins, 2016); Jesse Prinz, "Against Empathy," *Southern Journal of Philosophy* 49, no. 1 (2011): 214–33.

6. Goldie is concerned with the mistakes deriving from perspective-taking, including the case of what happens when we imagine meeting ourselves. Peter

Goldie, "Anti-Empathy," in *Empathy: Philosophical and Psychological Perspectives*, ed. Amy Coplan and Peter Goldie (Oxford: Oxford University Press 2011), 302–17.

7. Toni M. Massaro, "Empathy, Legal Storytelling, and the Rule of Law: New Words, Old Wounds?" *Michigan Law Review* 87, no. 8 (1989): 2099–2127; Wilhelm Worringer, *Abstraction and Empathy: A Contribution to the Psychology of Style* (New York: International Universities Press, 1953).

8. See Michael Tomasello, *The Cultural Origins of Human Cognition*, (Cambridge, MA: Harvard University Press, 2001). The same could be said of language. It is an interesting thought experiment: how would we think and feel if we had no language? These questions bring us closer to considering how nonlinguistic animals think but they tell us nothing about "us," since an "us" without language is someone quite different. We simply cannot imagine how we would think and act without language.

9. Autism is not a central object of inquiry for this book. For more on how people with autism exhibit lower levels of empathy and self-awareness, see Michael V. Lombardo, Jennifer L Barnes, Sally J. Wheelwright, and Simon Baron-Cohen, "Self-Referential Cognition and Empathy in Autism," *PLoS One* 2, no. 9 (2007): e883.

10. Nina Strohminger and Shaun Nichols, "The Essential Moral Self," *Cognition* 131 (2014): 159–71.

11. Hartmut Rosa, *Resonanz* (Berlin: Suhrkamp 2016.)

12. Steven Pinker, *The Better Angels of Our Nature: The Decline of Violence in History and its Causes* (London: Penguin, 2011).

13. See Simone G. Shamay-Tsoory, Judith Aharon-Peretz, and Daniella Perry, "Two Systems for Empathy: A Double Dissociation between Emotional and Cognitive Empathy in Inferior Frontal Gyrus versus Ventromedial Prefrontal Lesions," *Brain* 132, no. 3 (2009): 617–27. See also my discussion later in this introduction ("Four Approaches to Empathy Research").

14. Barack Obama, Commencement Speech. Northwestern University, June 19, 2006. http://www.northwestern.edu/newscenter/stories/2006/06/barack.html.

15. See Sara H. Konrath, Edward H. O'Brien, and Courtney Hsing, "Changes in Dispositional Empathy in American College Students over Time: A Meta-Analysis," *Personality and Social Psychology Review* (2010): 180–98. We will return in more detail to these and similar findings in chapter one.

16. Jean Decety and Claus Lamm, "Human Empathy through the Lens of Social Neuroscience," *Scientific World Journal* 6 (2006): 1146–63; also Frederique de Vignemont and Tania Singer, "The Empathic Brain: How, When and Why?" *Trends in Cognitive Sciences* 10, no. 10 (2006): 435–41.

17. Cf. Goldie, "Anti-Empathy"; Daniel C. Batson, "These Things Called Empathy: Eight Related but Distinct Phenomena," *The Social Neuroscience of Empathy*, ed. Jean Decety (Cambridge, MA: MIT Press, 2009), 3–15.

18. See Philip J. Mazzocco et al., "This Story is Not for Everyone: Transportability and Narrative Persuasion," *Social Psychological and Personality Science* (2010): 361–68; Blakey Vermeule, *Why Do We Care about Literary Characters?* (Baltimore: Johns Hopkins University Press, 2011).

19. The simulation of similarity by means of extreme dramatic situations recalls an important German enlightenment conception of sympathy in the theater. See Gotthold Ephraim Lessing, *Hamburg Dramaturgy* (New York: Dover, 1962).

20. On the history of the concept of self-interest, see Kelly Rogers, ed., *Self-Interest: An Anthology of Philosophical Perspectives from Antiquity to the Present* (London: Routledge, 2014).

21. See Ezequiel Gleichgerrcht and Jean Decety, "Empathy in Clinical Practice: How Individual Dispositions, Gender, and Experience Moderate Empathic Concern, Burnout, and Emotional Distress in Physicians," *PLoS One* 8, no. 4 (2013): e61526.

22. See, for example, Colin Allen and Fritz Breithaupt, "Why We Should Fear Emotionally Manipulative Robots: Artificial Intelligence Is Learning How to Exploit Human Psychology for Profit," *Zócalo Inquiry*, July 17, 2017, http://www.zocalopublicsquare.org/2017/07/17/fear-emotionally-manipulative-robots/ideas/nexus/.

23. For the argument that empathy and theory of mind have provided a selection advantage, see Robin Dunbar, *Grooming, Gossip and the Evolution of Language* (Cambridge, MA: Harvard University Press, 1997).

24. Robin Dunbar has suggested that group size, empathy-like skills, and brain size are evolutionarily linked. See Robin Dunbar, "Neocortex Size as a Constraint on Group Size in Primates," *Journal of Human Evolution* 22 (1992): 469–93.

25. Capuchin monkeys seem to be especially prosocial. See Jennifer L. Barnes, et al., "Helping Behaviour and Regard for Others in Capuchin Monkeys (Cebus apella)," *Biology Letters* 4, no. 6 (2008): 638–40.

26. See Inbal Ben-Ami Bartal, Jean Decety, and Peggy Mason, "Empathy and Pro-Social Behavior in Rats," *Science* 334, no. 6061 (2011): 1427–30. And, for a critical perspective, see Alan Silberberg et al., "Desire for Social Contact, not Empathy, May Explain "Rescue" Behavior in Rats," *Animal Cognition* 17, no. 3 (2014): 609–18.

27. See Colin Allen and Marc Bekoff, *Species of Mind: The Philosophy and Biology of Cognitive Ethology* (Cambridge, MA: MIT Press 1999).

28. Michael Tomasello, *The Origins of Human Communication* (Cambridge, MA: MIT Press, 2010).

29. See Frans de Waal, "Empathy in Primates and Other Mammals," in *Empathy: From Bench to Bedside*, ed. Jean Decety (Cambridge, MA: MIT Press, 2012), 87–106; David G. Premack and Guy Woodruff, "Does the Chimpanzee Have a Theory of Mind?" *Behavioral and Brain Sciences* 1, no. 4 (1978): 515–26.

30. A. Gopnik and Janet W. Aslington, "Children's Understanding of Representational Change and its Relation to the Understanding of False Belief and the Appearance-Reality Distinction," *Child Development* 59 (1988): 26–37.

31. Ágnes Melinda Kovács, Ernő Téglás and Ansgar Denis Endress, "The Social Sense: Susceptibility to Others' Beliefs in Human Infants and Adults," *Science* 330 (2010): 1830–34; Andrew Meltzoff, "Understanding the Intentions of Others: Re-Enactment of Intended Acts by 18-Month-Old Children," *Developmental Psychology* 31 (1995): 838–50.

32. Josep Call and Michael Tomasello, "Does the Chimpanzee Have a Theory of Mind? 30 Years Later," *Trends in Cognitive Sciences* 12, no. 5 (2008): 187–92.

33. Peter Carruthers, "Simulation and Self-Knowledge: A Defence of Theory-Theory," in Peter Carruthers and Peter K. Smith, eds., *Theories of Theories of Mind* (Cambridge: Cambridge University Press 1996), 22–38.

34. Simon Baron-Cohen, Alan M. Leslie, and Uta Frith, "Does the Autistic Child Have a 'Theory of Mind'?" *Cognition* 21, no. 1 (1985): 37–46.

35. Vilayanur S. Ramachandran and Lindsay M. Oberman, "Broken Mirrors: A Theory of Autism," *Scientific American* 295, no. 5 (2006): 62–69. Critically, see Ilan Dinstein et al., "Normal Movement Selectivity in Autism," *Neuron* 66, no. 3 (2010): 461–69.

36. Michele Tine and Joan Lucariello, "Unique Theory of Mind Differentiation in Children with Autism and Asperger Syndrome," *Autism Research and Treatment* (2012): 1–11.

37. David Comer Kidd and Emanuele Castano, "Reading Literary Fiction Improves Theory of Mind," *Science* 342, no. 6156 (2013): 377–80. See also Matthijs Bal and Martijn Veltkamp, "How Does Fiction Reading Influence Empathy? An Experimental Investigation on the Role of Emotional Transportation," *PloS One* 8, no. 1 (2013): e55341.

38. About the competitive advantage of theory of mind, see Nils Bubandt and Rane Willerslev, "The Dark Side of Empathy: Mimesis, Deception, and the Magic of Alterity," *Comparative Studies in Society and History* 57, no. 1 (2015): 5–34.

39. Studies of psychopaths/sociopaths and bullies have found either equal or higher levels of theory of mind in comparison to average or people around them. See, for example, Jon Sutton, Peter K. Smith, and John Swettenham, "Social Cognition and Bullying: Social Inadequacy or Skilled Manipulation?" *British Journal of Developmental Psychology* 17, no. 3 (1999): 435–50.

40. Wendell Wallach and Colin Allen, *Moral Machines. Teaching Robots Right from Wrong* (Oxford: Oxford University Press, 2008).

41. Decety and Lamm, "Human Empathy," and de Vignemont and Singer, "The Empathic Brain."

42. See Jean Decety and Claus Lamm, "The Role of the Right Temporoparietal Junction in Social Interaction: How Low-Level Computational Processes Contribute to Meta-Cognition," *Neuroscientist* (2007): 580–93.

43. For an overview, see Jean Decety, "Human Empathy," *Japanese Journal of Neuropsychology* 22 (2006): 11–33.

44. Wolfgang Prinz, "Modes of Linkage between Perception and Action," in *Cognition and Motor Processes*, ed. Wolfgang Prinz (Berlin: Springer 1984), 185–93.

45. For an overview, see Decety, "Human Empathy."

46. Gregory Hickok, *The Myth of Mirror Neurons: The Real Neuroscience of Communication and Cognition* (New York: W. W. Norton, 2014).

47. Tania Singer et al., "Empathic Neural Responses are Modulated by the Perceived Fairness of Others," *Nature* 439, no. 7075 (2006): 466–69.

48. See Jean Decety and Thierry Chaminade, "Neural Correlates of Feeling Sympathy," *Neuropsychologia* 41, no. 2 (2003): 127–38.

49. See Simone G. Shamay-Tsoory, Judith Aharon-Peretz, and Daniella Perry, "Two Systems for Empathy: A Double Dissociation between Emotional and Cognitive Empathy in Inferior Frontal Gyrus versus Ventromedial Prefrontal Lesions," *Brain* 132, no. 3 (2009): 617–27.

50. M. F. Glasser et al., "A Multi-Modal Parcellation of Human Cerebral Cortex," *Nature* 18933 (2016): 171–78.

51. Vera Nünning, "Cognitive Science and the Value of Literature for Life," in *Values of Literature*, ed. Hanna Meretoja, Saija Isomaa, Pirjo Lyytikäinen, and Kristina Malmio (Leiden: Brill, 2015), 93–116.

52. Nancy Eisenberg and Randy Lennon, "Sex Differences in Empathy and Related Capacities," *Psychological Bulletin* 94, no. 1 (1983): 100–131.

53. For phenomenological investigations, see also Dan Zahavi and Søren Overgaard, "Empathy without Isomorphism: A Phenomenological Account," in Decety, *Empathy*, 3–20.

54. See de Waal, "Empathy in Primates and Other Mammals," 87, 86.

55. Daniel Batson, a social psychologist and expert on empathy, provides a helpful overview of the different uses of the term empathy. He distinguishes a total of eight concepts of empathy and emphasizes that they are differentiated primarily in terms of two questions: How do we know what the other is thinking or feeling? And, what moves someone to the point of behaving altruistically for someone else? See Batson, "These Things Called Empathy."

56. Abigail A. Marsh, "Empathy and Compassion: A Cognitive Neuroscience Perspective," in Decety, *Empathy*, 191–205; Gordon G. Gallup and Steven M. Platek, "Cognitive Empathy Presupposes Self-Awareness: Evidence from Phylogeny, Ontogeny, Neuropsychology, and Mental Illness," *Behavioral and Brain Sciences* 25, no. 1 (2002): 36–37.

57. There is a large debate concerning the role of self-control that cannot be adequately represented here. While there seem to be correlations between empathy and self-control, the causalities are simply not well understood. The majority of studies sees some positive connection; see, for example, June P. Tangney,

Roy F. Baumeister, and Angie Luzio Boone, "High Self-Control Predicts Good Adjustment, Less Pathology, Better Grades, and Interpersonal Success," *Journal of Personality* 72, no. 2 (2004): 271–324; Nancy Eisenberg et al., "Contemporaneous and Longitudinal Prediction of Children's Social Functioning from Regulation and Emotionality," *Child Development* 68, no. 4 (1997): 642–64; but for a more skeptical view see also Joshua M. Ackerman, Noah J. Goldstein, Jenessa R. Shapiro, and John A. Bargh, "You Wear Me Out: The Vicarious Depletion of Self-Control," *Psychological Science* 20, no. 3 (2009): 326–32.

58. In addition to Batson, "These Things Called Empathy, "see also Susanne Leiberg and Silke Anders, "The Multiple Facets of Empathy: A Survey of Theory and Evidence," *Progress in Brain Research* 156 (2006): 419–40.

1. Self-Loss

1. Arthur Schopenhauer, "Zur Ethik," in *Arthur Schopenhauers Sämtliche Werke*, 2nd ed., ed. Julius Frauenstädt (Leipzig: Brockhaus, 1919), 6:219, paragraph 211.

2. Friedrich Nietzsche, *Beyond Good and Evil*, trans. Walter Kaufmann (New York: Random House, 1966), 126–28.

3. Paul Bloom, *Against Empathy*.

4. This objective man is close to the scientific self in the nineteenth century as described by Lorraine J. Daston and Peter Galison in *Objectivity* (New York: Zone Books, 2007).

5. It is well known that Nietzsche was fond of technical machines. See Friedrich A. Kittler, *Discourse Networks 1800/1900* (Palo Alto, CA: Stanford University Press, 1992). During the age of Nietzsche, attempts were made to capture ghosts with cameras. See Bernd Stiegler, *Spuren, Elfen und andere Erscheinungen. Conan Doyle und die Photographie*, (Frankfurt: Fischer, 2014).

6. See Peter Carruthers, "How We Know Our Own Minds: The Relationship between Mindreading and Metacognition," *Behavioral and Brain Sciences* 32, no. 2 (2009): 121–38; Gallup and Platek, "Cognitive Empathy Presupposes Self-Awareness."

7. See also Peter J. Burgard, ed., *Nietzsche and the Feminine* (Charlottesville: University of Virginia Press, 1994).

8. Nietzsche, in fact, suggests that the actual behavior we call compassion or pity (in German, *Mitleid*) serves selfish means: it helps us feel superior to the other, to feel good about ourselves for helping, to reject human weakness that threatens us, etc. ("An accident which happens to another offends us: it would make us aware of our impotence, and perhaps of our cowardice, if we did not go to assist him. Or it brings with it in itself a diminution of our honour in the eyes of others or in our own eyes. Or an accident and suffering incurred by another constitutes a signpost to some danger to us; and it can have a painful effect upon

us simply as a token of human vulnerability and fragility in general. We repel this kind of pain and offence and requite it through an act of compassion; it may contain subtle self-defence or even a piece of revenge . . . how coarsely does language assault with its one word so polyphonous a being!" *Daybreak. Thoughts on the Prejudice of Morality*, trans. Reginald John Hollingdale. [Cambridge: Cambridge University Press, 1997], 133). Hence, it turns out that our com-passion, *Mit-Leid*, produces a *Leid* (suffering) that is actually quite different from that of the other. Nietzsche's ambition in *Daybreak* is to correct against the sanctioning of *Mitleid* as good and self-focus as evil; rebuffing Christianity and its culture of weakness and suffering.

One of the few cases of a positive *Mitleid* in Nietzsche stands out as exceptional: "*Our* pity is a higher and more farsighted pity: we see how *man* makes himself smaller, how *you* make him smaller" (Nietzsche, *Beyond Good and Evil*, 153; emphasis in original). We may ask who this "we" is. This "we" even seems to be capable of a higher form of *Mitleid*, which observes the effects of the *Mitleid* of others: the higher *Mitleid* overcomes the usual, weakening effects of *Mitleid*. It is a second-order *Mitleid* deriving from the Nietzschean I or we: "*Your* pity is for the 'creature in man,' for what must be formed, broken . . . and *our* pity . . . when it resists your pity as the worst of all pamperings and weaknesses? Thus it is pity *versus* pity" (Nietzsche, *Beyond Good and Evil*, 154; emphasis in original).

9. Friedrich Nietzsche, *On the Genealogy of Morals*, trans. Walter Kaufmann (New York: Random House, 1967), 36.

10. Nietzsche, *Genealogy*, 40.

11. The founder of Roots of Empathy, Mary Gordon, describes how learning to recognize one's own emotions and those of others will lead to empathy: Children "will learn how an understanding of temperament and gaining insights into their own emotions and those of others leads to empathy and builds rich human relationships." Mary Gordon, *Roots of Empathy: Changing the World Child by Child* (New York: The Experiment, 2005), 5.

12. Barack Obama, Commencement Speech. Northwestern University, June 19, 2006. http://www.northwestern.edu/newscenter/stories/2006/06/barack.html.

13. See for example the animated documentary "Seeking Refuge" (2012, director: Andy Glynne) produced for the BBC that presents the fate of five refugee children in Great Britain.

14. Konrath, O'Brien, and Hsing, "Dispositional Empathy."

15. Konrath, O'Brien, and Hsing, "Dispositional Empathy," 181. For the higher scores of females, see also Sara H. Konrath, "Critical Synthesis Package: Interpersonal Reactivity Index (IRI)," *MedEdPORTAL* 9 (2013): 9596, https://doi.org/10.15766/mep_2374-8265.9596.

16. See again Singer et al., "Empathic Neural Responses are Modulated by the Perceived Fairness of Others"; Eisenberg and Lennon, "Sex Differences in Empathy and Related Capacities."

17. Pamela Paul, "From Students, Less Kindness for Strangers?" *New York Times*, June 25, 2010.

18. Keith O'Brien, "The Empathy Deficit," *Boston Globe*, October 17, 2010.

19. Konrath, O'Brien, and Hsing, "Dispositional Empathy," 183.

20. Lynn Hunt, *Inventing Human Rights* (New York: W. W. Norton, 2008).

21. For a more complete discussion of empathy and Stockholm syndrome, see my *Kulturen der Empathie* (Frankfurt: Suhrkamp, 2009).

22. Sigmund Freud, *Massenpsychologie und Ich-Analyse*, Frankfurt: Fischer, 2005 [1921].

23. Ernst Kantorowicz, *The King's Two Bodies: A Study in Medieval Political Theology* (Princeton: Princeton University Press, 1957).

24. Melissa Ann Birkett, "Self-Compassion and Empathy across Cultures: Comparison of Young Adults in China and the United States," *International Journal of Research Studies in Psychology* 3, no. 1 (2013): 25–34.

25. Evidence exists for the positive impact of siblings for empathy, especially on younger siblings. See Corinna Jenkins Tucker et al., "Older Siblings as Socializers of Younger Siblings' Empathy," *Journal of Early Adolescence* 19, no. 2 (1999): 176–98.

26. Stephen F. Myler cites the one-child policy and overpopulation. See "Chinese Cultural Lack of Empathy in Development—Counselling Practice," http://www.academia.edu/3620724/Chinese_Lack_of_Empathy_in_Develop ment (accessed January 15, 2015).

27. Sara Konrath also identifies economic prosperity as a negative factor for empathy. Konrath, O'Brien, Hsing, "Dispositional Empathy."

2. Painting in Black and White

Epigraph: Hannah Arendt, *Eichmann in Jerusalem: A Report on the Banality of Evil* (New York: Penguin, 2006), 106.

1. Gustav Ahoda, "Theodor Lipps and the Shift from 'Sympathy' to 'Empathy,'" *Journal of the History of the Behavioral Sciences* 41 (2005): 151–63.

2. See Malika Maskarinec, *The Forces of Form in German Modernism* (Evanston: Northwestern University Press, 2018).

3. Worringer, *Abstraction and Empathy*, 14.

4. Again, I should emphasize that we do not know whether mirror neurons play a central role—or indeed any role—in human empathy. Still, it seems that there are neurons in the brain that "fire" in response to specific perceptual triggers associated with empathy-related situations. It is possible that these neurons thereby stimulate empathy-related processes, see David Freedberg and Vittorio Gallese, "Motion, Emotion and Empathy in Esthetic Experience," *Trends in Cognitive Sciences* 11, no. 5 (2007): 197–203.

5. See Christiane Voss, "Einfühlung als empistemische und ästhetische Kategorie bei Hume und Lipps," in *Einfühlung. Zu Geschichte und Gegenwart eines ästhetischen Konzepts*, ed. Robin Curtis and Gertrud Koch (Munich: Fink, 2009), 31–47.

6. See Batson, "These Things Called Empathy."

7. Preston and de Waal, "Empathy"; Mazzocco et al., "This Story is Not for Everyone."

8. Rolf Reber, *Critical Feelings: How to Use Feelings Strategically*, Oxford: Oxford University Press, 2016.

9. See Elizabeth A. Shirtcliff et al., "Neurobiology of Empathy and Callousness: Implications for the Development of Antisocial Behavior," *Behavioral Sciences & The Law* 2 (2009): 137–71.

10. Marco Iacoboni, "Imitation, Empathy, and Mirror Neurons," *Annual Review of Psychology* 60 (2009): 653–70.

11. Vittorio Gallese, "The 'Shared Manifold' Hypothesis: From Mirror Neurons to Empathy," *Journal of Consciousness Studies* 8, nos. 5–6 (2001): 33–50. Gregory Hickok argues against the inflated claims about mirror neurons. Hickok, *The Myth of Mirror Neurons*.

12. Jody Lynee Madeira, "Lashing Reason to the Mast: Understanding Judicial Constraints on Emotion in Personal Injury Litigation," *UC Davis Law Review* 137 (2006); Gleichgerrcht and Decety, "Empathy in Clinical Practice."

13. For further suggestions and approaches see Aleida Assmann and Ines Detmers, eds., *Empathy and its Limits* (New York: Palgrave, 2016).

14. See Jonathan Haidt, *The Righteous Mind: Why Good People are Divided by Politics and Religion* (New York: Vintage, 2002).

15. See Antoine Bechara et al., "Deciding Advantageously Before Knowing the Advantageous Strategy," *Science* 275, no. 5304 (1997): 1293–95.

16. Xiuyan Guo et al., "Empathic Neural Responses to Others' Pain Depend on Monetary Reward," *Social Cognitive and Affective Neuroscience* (2011): nsr034.

17. Dennis Krebs, "Empathy and Altruism," *Journal of Personality and Social Psychology* 32, no. 6 (1975): 1134. Claus Lamm, Andrew N. Meltzoff, and Jean Decety, "How Do We Empathize with Someone Who Is Not Like Us? A Functional Magnetic Resonance Imaging Study," *Journal of Cognitive Neuroscience* 22, no. 2 (2010): 362–76.

18. See Mira A. Preis and Birgit Kroener-Herwig, "Empathy for Pain: The Effects of Prior Experience and Sex," *European Journal of Pain* 16, no. 9 (2012): 1311–19; Michael E. Robinson and Emily A. Wise, "Prior Pain Experience: Influence on the Observation of Experimental Pain in Men and Women," *The Journal of Pain* 5, no. 5 (2004): 264–69; Yawei Cheng et al., "Expertise Modulates the Perception of Pain in Others," *Current Biology* 17 (2007): 1708–13; Jakob Eklund, Teresi Andersson-Sraberg, and Eric M. Hansen, "I've Also Experienced Loss and

Fear: Effects of Prior Similar Experience on Empathy," *Scandinavian Journal of Psychology* 50, no. 1 (2009): 65–69; Lisbet Goubert et al., "Facing Other in Pain: The Effects of Empathy," *Pain* 118, no. 3 (2005): 285–88.

19. Mira A. Preis et al., "The Effects of Prior Pain Experience on Neural Correlates of Empathy for Pain: An fMRI Study," *Pain* 154, no. 3 (2013): 411–18.

20. Preston and de Waal, "Empathy"

21. Elaine Hatfield, John T. Cacioppo, and Richard L. Rapson, *Emotional Contagion* (Cambridge: Cambridge University Press, 1994).

22. Gallese, "The 'Shared Manifold' Hypothesis."

23. Hatfield, Cacioppo, and Rapson, *Emotional Contagion*, 5. See also Hillary Anger Elfenbein, "The Many Faces of Emotional Contagion: An Affective Process Theory of Affective Linkage," *Organizational Psychology Review* (2014): 177–90.

24. On the different neural reactions to observations of acute and chronic pain, see Miiamaaria V. Saarela et al., "The Compassionate Brain: Humans Detect Intensity of Pain from Another's Face," *Cerebral Cortex* 17, no. 1 (2007): 230–37.

25. The return to the self can be described as part of the contract between the work and the recipient. See Keen, *Empathy and the Novel*.

26. See Fritz Breithaupt, "Blocking Empathy: A Three-Person Model of Empathy," *Emotion Review* 4, no. 1 (2012): 84–91.

27. See Alicia P. Melis, Felix Warneken, and Brian Hare, "Collaboration and Helping in Chimpanzees," in *The Mind of the Chimpanzee: Ecological and Experimental Perspectives,* ed. Elizabeth V. Lonsdorf, Stephen R. Ross, and Tetsuro Matsuzawa (Chicago: University of Chicago Press, 2010), 278–393; Frans de Waal, *Chimpanzee Politics* (Baltimore: Johns Hopkins University Press, 1998).

28. Daniel C. Batson et al., "Immorality from Empathy-Induced Altruism: When Compassion and Justice Conflict," *Journal of Personality and Social Psychology* 68, no. 6 (1995): 1042–54. See also Adam D. Galinsky and Gillian Ku, "The Effects of Perspective-Taking on Prejudice: The Moderating Role of Self-Evaluation," *Personality and Social Psychology Bulletin* 30, no. 5 (2004): 594–604.

29. Alexander Todorov, Manish Pakrashi and Nikolaas N. Oosterhof, "Evaluating Faces on Trustworthiness after Minimal Time Exposure," *Social Cognition* 27, no. 6 (2009): 813–33. See Stephen Porter, Leanne ten Brinke and Chantal Gustaw, "Dangerous Decisions: The Impact of First Impressions of Trustworthiness on the Evaluation of Legal Evidence and Defendant Culpability," *Psychology, Crime & Law* 16 no. 6 (2010): 477–91.

30. The term "tendency" is meant here in the sense of Gertrude Elizabeth Margaret Anscome, *Intention* (Cambridge, MA: Harvard University Press: 1957).

31. See Breithaupt, "Blocking Empathy."

32. For more on these distinctions, see the introduction, as well as Batson, "These Things Called Empathy," and Leiberg and Anders, "The Multiple Facets of Empathy."

33. Or at least these quick intuitive judgments match our learned forms of behavior, as Antonio Damasio argues. See Damasio, *Descartes' Error: Emotion, Reason, and the Human Brain* (New York: Penguin, 2005).

34. See Gerd Gigerenzer and Peter M. Todd, *Simple Heuristics That Make Us Smart* (Oxford: Oxford University Press, 1999).

35. See Robert Kurzban, Peter DeScioli, and Erin O'Brien, "Audience Effects on Moralistic Punishment," *Evolution and Human Behavior* 28, no. 2 (2007): 75–84.

36. For the range of positions, see Gallese, "Shared Manifold," and Tania Singer and Anita Tusche, "Understanding Others: Brain Mechanisms of Theory of Mind and Empathy," in *Neuroeconomics: Decision Making and the Brain*, 2nd ed., ed. P. W. Glimcher and E. Fehr (London: Academic Press, 2014) 513–32.

37. See Lamm, Meltzoff, and Decety, "How Do We Empathize."

38. Kurzban, DeScioli and O'Brien, "Audience Effects."

39. Singer, "Understanding Others."

40. See Philip L. Jackson et al., "Empathy Examined through the Neural Mechanisms Involved in Imagining How I Feel versus How You Feel Pain," *Neuropsychologia* 44, no. 5 (2006): 752–61.

41. See Trump's tweets of February 17, 2017, and June 15, 2017, @realDonald Trump.

42. I thank Peter Gilgen for reminding me of this episode.

43. See Martin Kolmar and Fritz Breihaupt, "Postfaktische Autoritäten," *Kursbuch* (March 2017): 17–28.

44. Fritz Breithaupt, "The Birth of Narrative from the Spirit of the Excuse. A Speculation," *Poetics Today* 32 (Spring 2011): 107–28.

45. See Meg Miller, "The Story Behind "I'm With Her," *FastCompany*, April 11, 2017, https://www.fastcompany.com/90109190/the-story-behind-im-with-her.

46. This difference corresponds roughly to the distinction between empathy and sympathy, with empathy meaning to feel like someone while sympathy means to feel for someone (or literally "with" someone). See Douglas Chismar, "Empathy and Sympathy. The Important Difference," *Journal of Value Inquiry* 22 (1988): 257–66.

47. Clark McCauley and Sophia Moskalenko, "Mechanisms of Political Radicalization: Pathways toward Terrorism," *Terrorism and Political Violence* 20, no. 3 (2008): 415–33.

48. This can involve social media such as Facebook or websites that directly promote terrorism (see Martin Rudner, "'Electronic Jihad': The Internet as Al Qaeda's Catalyst for Global Terror," *Studies in Conflict & Terrorism* 40, no. 1

(2017): 10–23), but mainstream media, with their tendency to polarize and seeking out conflicts, certainly play their part as well.

49. Gord McIntyre, "Terror on Your Doorstep: A Third of B.C.ers Believe Radicals Are Living in Their Block," *Province*, November 22, 2014, https://theprovince.com/news/b.c./terror-on-your-doorstep-a-third-of-bcers-believe-radicals-are-living-on-their-block/wcm/da516a54-8bd7-4046-a1cf-8605083572d5.

50. Keith C. Barton and Alan W. McCully, "Trying to 'See Things Differently:' Northern Ireland Students' Struggle to Understand Alternative Historical Perspectives," *Theory & Research in Social Education* 40, no. 4 (2012): 377.

51. Barton and McCully, "See Things Differently," 379.

52. See Keith C. Barton and Alan W. McCully, "You Can Form Your Own Point of View: Internally Persuasive Discourse in Northern Ireland Students' Encounters with History," *Teachers College Record* 112, no. 1 (2010): 142–81.

53. For a critical account of the events and proceedings of the Truth and Reconciliation Commission, see Richard A. Wilson, *The Politics of Truth and Reconciliation in South Africa: Legitimizing the Post-Apartheid State* (New York: Cambridge University Press, 2001). On the basis of numerous interviews, Wilson argues that the commission's work was inadequate and inconsistent and ultimately unsuccessful at putting to rest the desire for revenge.

54. For this discussion, see, for example, Keen, *Empathy and the Novel*, and Boyd, *On the Origin of Stories*.

55. Gottschall, *The Storytelling Animal*.

56. William Flesch, *Comeuppance: Costly Signaling, Altruistic Punishment, and Other Biological Components of Fiction* (Cambridge, MA: Harvard University Press, 2007).

57. Gottschall, *The Storytelling Animal*.

58. Peter DeScioli and Robert Kurzban, "Mysteries of Morality," *Cognition* 112, no. 2 (2009): 281–99; and Kurzban, DeScioli, and O'Brien, "Audience Effects."

59. Haidt, *The Righteous Mind*.

60. See Todorov, Pakrashi, and Oosterhof, "Evaluating Faces."

61. See Joshua Green, *Moral Tribes: Emotion, Reason, and the Gap Between Us and Them* (New York: Penguin, 2014.)

62. Pinker, *The Better Angels*.

63. For how nationalism belongs in this discussion, see Benedict Anderson, *Imagined Communities: Reflections on the Origin and Spread of Nationalism* (New York: Verso, 2016).

64. For this return structure of fiction, see above and Breithaupt, *Kulturen der Empathie*.

65. See Vermeule, *Why Do We Care about Literary Characters?*

66. See Fritz Breithaupt, "Empathic Sadism. How Readers Get Implicated," in *The Oxford Handbook for Cognitive Literary Studies*, ed. Lisa Zunshine

(Oxford: Oxford University Press, 2015), 440–62; and Fritz Breithaupt, *Culturas de la Empatía* (Buenos Aires: Katz Editores, 2011).

3. False Empathy, Filtered Empathy

1. Pinker, *The Better Angels of Our Nature.*

2. To be sure, each of these notions would be a different form of empathy or sympathy. See Batson, "These Things Called Empathy." However, as will soon become clear, the differences can be ignored for the context of this chapter.

3. See Daniel C. Batson, "The Empathy-Altruism Hypothesis: Issues and Implications," in *Empathy: From Bench to Bedside*, ed. Jean Decety (Cambridge, MA: MIT Press, 2012): 41–54.

4. Martha Nussbaum, *From Disgust to Humanity: Sexual Orientation and Constitutional Law*, Oxford: Oxford University Press, 2010.

5. See chapter 2.

6. For a list of literary triggers or catalysts of empathy, see Keen, *Empathy and the Novel*. See also the work by Amy Coplan, for example Coplan, "Catching Characters' Emotions: Emotional Contagion Responses to Narrative Fiction Film." *Film Studies* 8, no. 1 (2006): 26–38.

7. See Andrew Hamilton and Fritz Breithaupt, "These Things Called Event: Toward a Unified Theory of Events," *Sprache und Datenverarbeitung* 37 (2013): 65–87. See Bruner, *Making Stories.*

8. See Vermeule, *Why Do We Care about Literary Characters?*

9. Arendt, *Eichmann and Jerusalem.*

10. For these and other critical points of view, see Yosefa Loshitzky, ed., *Spielberg's Holocaust: Critical Perspectives on Schindler's List* (Bloomington: Indiana University Press, 1997).

11. According to Batson's scheme, this is a case of his fourth concept of empathy, intuiting or projecting oneself into the situation of another. See Batson, "These Things Called Empathy."

12. Related forms of identification and creation of perspectives have been studied in the context of narratology under the notion of focalization. See Gérard Genette, *Narrative Discourse. An Essay in Method* (Oxford: Blackwell, 1980); and James Phelan, "Why Narrators Can Be Focalizers—and Why It Matters," in *New Perspectives on Narrative Perspective*, ed. Willie van Peer and Seymour Chatma (Albany: SUNY Press, 2001), 51–64. For an overview of negative perspectives see Breithaupt, "Empathic Sadism."

13. In the psychological literature, the effects of abusive helping and the codependence of helper and helped are well known under the label of so-called Helper Syndrome, famously coined by Wolfgang Schmidbauer in *Hilflose Helfer. Über die seelische Problematik der helfenden Berufe* (Reinbek: Rowohlt Verlag, 1977). While the concept has moved into English, the original text has not. In English see,

for example, Mathias Burisch, "A Longitudinal Study of Burnout: The Relative Importance of Dispositions and Experiences," *Work & Stress* 16, no. 1 (2002): 1–17.

14. Hunt, *Inventing Human Rights*, 38.

15. Thomas W. Laqueur, "Mourning, Pity, and the Work of Narrative in the Making of 'Humanity,'" in *Humanitarianism and Suffering: The Mobilization of Empathy*, ed. Richard D. Brown (Cambridge: Cambridge University Press, 2009), 38.

16. The ratio of 1:12 corresponds to the number presented in Switzerland in a referendum, the so-called 1:12 Initiative. The referendum proposed 1:12 as the highest ratio between the best-paid and lowest-paid worker that would be allowable within a company. The referendum was defeated 35% to 65% in 2013.

17. Martha Nussbaum, *Political Emotions* (Cambridge, MA: Harvard University Press, 2015).

18. Niklas Luhmann, *Social Structure and Semantics* (Palo Alto, CA: Stanford University Press, 2003).

19. Reinhart Koselleck, *Futures Past* (New York: Columbia University Press, 2004).

20. Dror Wahrmann, *The Making of the Modern Self: Identity and Culture in Eighteenth-Century England* (New Haven: Yale University Press, 2006).

21. For a discussion of this dynamic in the eighteenth century, see Breithaupt, *Kulturen der Empathie*, 54–65.

22. A second, alternative explanation, which partially contradicts the first, comes in the form of a displacement of the understanding of morals and ethics. Until the end of the eighteenth century the leading conception of morality was based on scruples and conscience, often with religious overtones. But starting around 1800 the "inner voice" begins to disappear (although not entirely) and is replaced by conceptions of universal moral judgment. This transition can be explained by Enlightenment philosophy, but it could also be that the inner voice of romanticism becomes increasingly suspect, revealed as the voice of the newly discovered or invented unconscious. The universal perspective of moral judgment promises a higher point of view from which all humans are equal. Indeed, equality is championed in the French Revolution—and not pity or empathy. This higher point of view requires no deep insight into the thoughts and feelings of others. Astonishingly little empathy is required.

23. Keen, *Empathy and the Novel*.

24. The term "false empathy" is used in legal contexts to denote a problematic argument that claims to approximate what it would be like to be a different person. For example, a white person can quickly imagine how it would be like to be a black person and then falsely claim to argue on the basis of a deep understanding. See Richard Delgado, "Rodrigo's Eleventh Chronicle: Empathy and False Empathy," *California Law Review* 84, no. 1 (1996): 61–100.

25. "Merkel Says German Multicultural Society Has Failed," BBC News, October 17, 2010.

26. Translated by the author from the transcript published in German as "Was Merkel und das Mädchen wirklich gesprochen haben," *Die Welt*, July 16, 2015.

27. "#merkelstreichelt und Asyl für Reem: NDR unterschlug entscheidende 3,5 Minuten," *Nordbayrischer Kurier*, July 19, 2015, https://www.nordbayeris cher-kurier.de/inhalt.das-netz-tobte-aber-nach-drei-tagen-stellt-sich-der-sachverhalt-um-das-fluechtlingsmaedchen-und-die-kanzlerin-etwas-anders-dar-merkelstrei chelt-und-asyl-fuer-reem-ndr-unterschlug-entscheidende-3-5-minuten.7f69a 70a-55af-4a2f-a397-4e3d1823e706.html.

28. According to the arguments by Paul Bloom that we introduced earlier, we would have to say that politicians need to resist empathy and the "spotlight vision" that favors the one over the many. Of course the image of the Lebanese girl is appealing; however, as the chancellor, Merkel has to consider higher principles of fairness and sustainability. There is no civil war in Lebanon, but there is in Syria. Merkel acts motherly to the girl, but resists motherly political actions. See Boom, *Against Empathy*.

29. This phrase from Merkel's speech of September 11, 2015, is a common theme and refrain in her speeches until October 21, 2015. See "Merkel bekräftigt 'Wir schaffen das!'" *Frankfurter Allgemeine Zeitung*, October 21, 2015, http:// www.faz.net/aktuell/politik/merkel-bekraeftigt-wir-schaffen-das-13869117. html. Compare Alexander Marguier, "Die Sprücheklopferin: Angela Merkels 'Wir schaffen das,'" *Cicero*, September 16, 2015, http://www.cicero.de/berliner-republik/ angela-merkels-wir-schaffen-das-die-spruecheklopferin/59847; and Tilman Borsche, "Auf wen bezieht sich das Wort 'wir' in Merkels Satz 'Wir schaffen das'?" *Philoso-phie Magazin* 2 (2016): 55.

30. See, in general, Duane T. Wegener and Richard E. Petty. "Flexible Correction Processes in Social Judgment: The Role of Naive Theories in Corrections for Perceived Bias," *Journal of Personality and Social Psychology* 68, no. 1 (1995): 36–51. In an empathy-related context, see Wendy Berry Mendes and Katrina Koslov. "Brittle Smiles: Positive Biases toward Stigmatized and Outgroup Targets," *Journal of Experimental Psychology: General* 142, no. 3 (2013): 923–34; and Tatiana Lau, Carey K. Morewedge, and Mina Cikara, "Overcorrection for Social-Categorization Information Moderates Impact Bias in Affective Forecasting," *Psychological Science* 27, no. 10 (2016): 1340–51.

31. "#merkelstreichelt und Asyl für Reem."

32. In fact, Lessing, whom we introduced in this chapter, devoted a book to this topic (*Wie die Alten den Tod gebildet*, 1769) that rests on an implicit argument of empathy. It is because of this similarity that we can still imagine the dead. Herder, Goethe, and many other writers reacted to Lessing's suggestions.

33. *Der Spiegel* depicted her as Mother Teresa on its cover in September 2015.

34. Emmet Livingston, "Merkel drops the 'we can do it' slogan," *Politico*, September 17, 2016, https://www.politico.eu/article/angela-merkel-drops-the-we-can-do-it-slogan-catchphrase-migration-refugees/

35. See Holger Lengfeld, "Die 'Alternative für Deutschland': eine Partei für Modernisierungsverlierer?" *KZfSS Kölner Zeitschrift für Soziologie und Sozialpsychologie* 69, no. 2 (2017): 209–32.

36. As a personal anecdote, I could add that I may have played a minor role in the rise of the Alternative for Germany. Its key founder, Bernd Lucke, spent a sabbatical year as a guest professor at my university in 2011–12 in Bloomington. At that time, we had a series of conversations about all kind of things, especially politics. I was astonished at the crass opinions of this otherwise reasonable economics professor and mistook them for harmless counterfactual speculations. He suggested that Germany should leave the European Union and reintroduce its old currency, the Mark. In response, I resorted to a technique called "active listening" that refrains from articulating objections. This has the effect of encouraging the speaker to fully develop their thoughts, including their doubts. In this case, my strategy seems to have miserably failed. Instead of articulating my severe doubts, if anything I seem to have encouraged him more. He returned to Germany in summer 2012 with draft proposals for the new party, which he cofounded in September 2012. See Fritz Breithaupt, "Zu viel Mitgefühl ist gefährlich," *Der Sonntag*, May 5, 2017, http://www.haz.de/Sonntag/Gastkommentar/Zu-viel-Mitgefuehl-ist-gefaehrlich. Lucke was later ousted from the party when the more right-wing faction of the party took over.

37. To be sure, Germany continues to have open borders. Independent from public sentiments, the administrative processes of finding safe homes for refugees continue. The public schools have reacted strongly to adapt to the influx of newcomers.

4. Empathetic Sadism

1. Batson, "These Things Called Empathy," 6.

2. Edmund Burke, *A Philosophical Inquiry into the Origins of our Ideas of the Sublime and Beautiful*, ed. James Boulton (South Bend: Notre Dame University Press, 1958), 45–48.

3. In the current context, we will not be able to do justice to the complex thought Lessing has about empathy. Lessing views empathy as the exception. Usually, he says, we all are in different situations experiencing our own idiosyncratic feelings. However, he describes tragedies as powerful machines that allow empathy by creating similarity between people: in the extreme situations of tragedies, we would all feel the same. For a full discussion, see Breithaupt, *Kulturen der Empathie*.

4. See Julian Hanich et al., "Why We Like to Watch Sad Films: The Pleasure of being Moved in Aesthetic Experiences," *Psychology of Aesthetics, Creativity and the Arts* 8 (2014): 130–43.

5. Keen, *Empathy and the Novel.*

6. See Fritz Breithaupt, *Kultur der Ausrede* (Berlin: Suhrkamp, 2012); Breithaupt, "The Birth of Narrative."

7. The term "empathetic cruelty" is derived from Allan Young, "Empathic Cruelty and the Origins of the Social Brain," in *Critical Neuroscience: A Handbook of the Social and Cultural Context of Neuroscience* (New York: Wiley-Blackwell, 2016)

8. Liane Leedom, "Sadism and Warped Empathy in Sociopaths," *Lovefraud. com*, November 13, 2008, https://lovefraud.com/sadism-and-warped-empathy-in-sociopaths/.

9. Fyodor Dostoevsky, *The Brothers Karamazov*, trans. Richard Pevear and Larissa Volokhonsky (New York: Farrar, Strauss and Giroux, 1990), 301–12.

10. See Jane K. Brown, *Goethe's Allegories of Identity* (Philadelphia: University of Pennsylvania Press, 2014).

11. Carl Plantina argues that the audience can empathize with everyone, including Buffalo Bill. See Carl Plantinga, "Facing Others: Close-ups of Faces in Narrative Films and in Silence of the Lambs," in *The Oxford Handbook of Cognitive Literary Studies*, ed. Lisa Zunshine (Oxford: Oxford University Press, 2015), 291–311.

12. For some interesting new ideas, see DeScioli and Kurzban, "Mysteries of Morality."

13. For an overview about altruistic punishment, see Flesch, *Comeuppance.*

14. Young, "Empathic Cruelty."

15. Dominique J. F. De Quervain et al., "The Neural Basis of Altruistic Punishment," *Science* 305, no. 5688 (2004): 1254–59.

16. Singer et al., "Empathic Neural Responses."

17. See Flesch, *Comeuppance.*

18. For this and the following, see Jody Lyneé Madeira, *Killing McVeigh: The Death Penalty and the Myth of Closure* (New York: NYU Press, 2012).

19. Of course, Michel Foucault has argued that the transition was never complete and includes the shameful hiding of the body of the criminal. See Michel Foucault, *Discipline and Punish* (New York City: Pantheon, 1977).

20. Madeira, *McVeigh*, 232.

21. Madeira, *McVeigh*, 237.

22. Madeira, *McVeigh*, 237.

23. Madeira, *McVeigh*, 254–55.

24. See Dave Cullen, "The Depressive and the Psychopath: At Last We Know Why the Columbine Killers Did It," *Slate*, April 20, 2004, http://www.slate.com/

articles/news_and_politics/assessment/2004/04/the_depressive_and_the_psy
chopath.html.

25. See Jean Decety et al., "Atypical Empathic Responses in Adolescents with Aggressive Conduct Disorder: A Functional MRI Investigation," *Biological Psychology* 80, no. 2 (2009): 203–11.

26. Alfred B. Heilbrun, "Cognitive Models of Criminal Violence Based Upon Intelligence and Psychopathy Levels," *Journal of Consulting and Clinical Psychology* 50, no. 4 (1982): 546–57.

27. See Carolyn Zahn-Waxler et al., "Psychophysiological Correlates of Empathy and Prosocial Behaviors in Preschool Children with Behavior Problems," *Development and Psychopathology* 7, no. 1 (1995): 27–48; James R. Blair, "Responding to the Emotions of Others: Dissociating Forms of Empathy through the Study of Typical and Psychiatric Populations," *Consciousness and Cognition* 14, no. 4 (2005): 698–718; Susan E. Holt, J. Reid Meloy, and Stephen Strack, "Sadism and Psychopathy in Violent and Sexually Violent Offenders," *Journal of the American Academy of Psychiatry and the Law* 27 (1999): 23–32; Kent A. Kiehl and Morris B. Hoffman, "The Criminal Psychopath: History, Neuroscience, Treatment, and Economics," *Jurimetrics: The Journal of Law, Science, and Technology* 51, no. 4 (2011): 355–97.

28. Harma Meffert et al., "Reduced Spontaneous but Relatively Normal Deliberate Vicarious Representations in Psychopathy," *Brain* 136, no. 8 (2013): 2550–62.

29. See Philip L. Jackson, Pierre Rainville, and Jean Decety, "To What Extent Do We Share the Pain of Others? Insight from Neural Bases of Pain Empathy," *Pain* 125 (2006): 1–2, 5–9.

30. Decety et al., "Atypical Empathic Responses in Adolescents."

31. See also Young, "Empathic Cruelty."

32. See Frédérique de Vignemont and Pierre Jacob, "What Is It Like to Feel Another's Pain?" *Philosophy of Science* 79 (2012): 295–316.

33. C. L. Harenski et al., "Aberrant Neural Processing or Moral Violations in Criminal Psychopaths," *Journal of Abnormal Psychology* 21 (2010): 1–12.

34. Lisa Zunshine, *Getting Inside Your Head: What Cognitive Science Can Tell Us about Popular Culture* (Baltimore: Johns Hopkins University Press, 2015), 45–53.

35. Breithaupt, "Empathic Sadism," 440–62.

36. See William Flesch, "Readings and Bargainings," in *The Oxford Handbook for Cognitive Literary Studies*, ed. Lisa Zunshine (Oxford: Oxford University Press, 2015), 369–86.

37. See Kimberly A. Lonsway and Louise F. Fitzgerald, "Rape Myths in Review," *Psychology of Women Quarterly* 18, no. 2 (1994): 133–64.

38. William D. Pithers, "Empathy Definition, Enhancement, and Relevance to the Treatment of Sexual Abuse," *Journal of Interpersonal Violence* 14, no. 3 (1999): 257–84.

39. Yolanda M. Fernandez and W. L. Marshall, "Victim Empathy, Social Self-Esteem, and Psychology in Rapists," *Sexual Abuse: A Journal of Research and Treatment* 15, no. 1 (2003): 11–26.

40. Marnie E. Rice, "Empathy for the Victim and Sexual Arousal among Rapists and Nonrapists," *Journal of Interpersonal Violence* 9, no. 4 (1994): 434–49; David Lisak and Carol Ivan, "Deficits in Intimacy and Empathy in Sexually Aggressive Men," *Journal of Interpersonal Violence* 10, no. 3 (1995): 296–308; W. L. Marshall and Heather Moulden, "Hostility toward Women and Victim Empathy in Rapists," *Sexual Abuse: A Journal of Research and Treatment* 13, no. 4 (2001): 249–55.

41. See Lynn A. Higgins and Brenda R. Silver, *Rape and Representation* (New York: Columbia University Press, 1991).

42. See Susanna Paasonen, "Good Amateurs: Erotica Writing and Notions of Quality," in *Porn.com: Making Sense of Online Pornography*, ed. Feona Attwood (New York: Peter Lang, 2010), 138–54.

43. Alon Lischinsky, "Doing the Naughty or Having It Done to You? Agent Roles in Erotic Writing," *Porn Studies* (2017): 1.

44. See also Emy M. Koopman, Michelle Hilscher, and Gerald C. Cupchik, "Reader Responses to Literary Depiction of Rape," *Psychology of Aesthetics, Creativity, and the Arts* 6, no. 1 (2012): 66.

45. For an overview see Norman G. Poythress, Jennifer L. Skeem, and Scott O. Lilienfeld, "Associations among Early Abuse, Dissociation, and Psychopathy in an Offender Sample," *Journal of Abnormal Psychology* 115, no. 2 (2006): 288–97.

46. The status of a separate diagnosis of sadistic personality disorder is disputed. While the 1987 edition of the Diagnostic and Statistical Manual of Mental Disorders from the American Psychiatric Association included it, later editions removed it. Characteristics of sadism and sadistic personality disorder is the focus on control and dominance: "Unlike antisocial or other disorders relating to violence or illegal behavior, sadistic personality disorder was distinguishable in that their actions were meant primarily to gain pleasure or achieve dominance and control, rather than primarily for profit or due to the need to cope with stressors." Roger J. R. Levesque, "Sadistic Personality Disorder," in *Encyclopedia of Adolescence*, ed. Levesque (New York: Springer Science & Business Media, 2011), 2445.

47. See also Fritz Breithaupt, "Empathy for Empathy's Sake: Aesthetics and Empathic Sadism," *Empathy and its Limits*, ed. Aledia Assmann and Ines Detmers (New York: Palgrave, 2016), 151–65.

5. Vampiristic Empathy

1. Forster Cline and Jim Fay, *Parenting with Love and Logic: Teaching Children Responsibility* (Carol Stream, IL: Tyndale House, 2014).

2. See Noam Scheiber, "When Helicopter Parents Hover Even at Work," *New York Times*, June 21, 2017, https://www.nytimes.com/2017/06/21/business/ millennial-work-parent-lavar-lonzo-ball.html.

3. Holly H. Schiffrin et al., "Helping or Hovering? The Effects of Helicopter Parenting on College Student' Well-Being," *Journal of Child and Family Studies* 23, no. 3 (2014): 548–57.

4. Terri LeMoyne and Tom Buchanan, "Does 'Hovering' Matter? Helicopter Parenting and Its Effect on Well-Being," *Sociological Spectrum* 31, no. 4 (2011): 399–418; Rick Shoup, Robert M. Gonyea, and George D. Kuh, "Helicopter Parents: Examining the Impact of Highly Involved Parents on Student Engagement and Educational Outcomes," paper presented at the 49th Annual Forum of the Association for Institutional Research, Atlanta, GA, June, 2009, http://cpr.indi ana.edu/uploads/AIR%202009%20Impact%20of%20Helicopter%20Parents. pdf.

5. Schiffrin et al., "Helping or Hovering?"

6. I should note my researcher's folly here. I felt reasonably sure that the phrase "parental vampirism" was original, and especially so in regard to schooling. However, Mahinder Kingra, the very involved editor and secret coauthor of this book, found the notion used in a similar way in an anonymous article in 1901, "The Education of Parents," *School Journal* 62 (May 25, 1901): 570. In that article, the case of a mother is described who will not leave her thirty-year-old daughter alone. The article suggests that the mother uses the disguise of "parental affection" for mere "selfishness."

7. See again Vermeule, *Why Do We Care about Literary Characters?*

8. I thank Julia Cook for this reference.

9. E. D. (Adie) Nelson, "The Things That Dreams Are Made On: Dreamwork and the Socialization of 'Stage Mothers,'" *Qualitative Sociology* 24, no. 4 (2001): 439–58.

10. "Stalking," The United States Department of Justice, https://www.justice. gov/ovw/stalking (accessed October 29, 2018).

11. Beth Bjerregaard, "An Empirical Study of Stalking Victimization," *Violence and Victims* 15, no. 4 (2000): 389–406.

12. Katrina Baum, Shannan Catalano, and Michael Rand, *Stalking Victimization in the United States*, Bureau of Justice Statistics, January 2009, NCJ 224527.

13. On the different kinds of stalkers, see Paul E. Mullen, Michele Pathé, and Rosemary Purcell, *Stalkers and Their Victims* (Cambridge: Cambridge University Press, 2000); Troy E. McEwan, Paul E. Mullen, and Rachel MacKenzie, "A Study of the Predictors of Persistence in Stalking Situations," *Law and Human Behavior* 33, no. 2 (2009): 149–58.

14. Bjerregaard, "An Empirical Study of Stalking Victimization."

15. See Orit Kamir, *Every Breath You Take: Stalking Narratives and the Law* (Ann Arbor: University of Michigan Press, 2001).

16. Gayle Brewer and Jade Kerslake, "Cyberbullying, Self-Esteem, Empathy and Loneliness," *Computers in Human Behavior* 48 (2015): 255–60.

17. Jerry Finn, "A Survey of Online Harassment at a University Campus," *Journal of Interpersonal Violence* 19, no. 4 (2004): 468–83.

18. Emma Louise Anderson, Eloisa Steen, and Vasileios Stavropoulos, "Internet Use and Problematic Internet Use: A Systematic Review of Longitudinal Research Trends in Adolescence and Emergent Adulthood," *International Journal of Adolescence and Youth* 22, no. 4 (2017): 430–54.

19. Lynn Hunt, *Inventing Human Rights: A History*.

20. In Batson's taxonomy, this would be either empathy form number 3 or 5; see Batson, "These Things Called Empathy."

21. For a more complete discussion of the stage effect, see Fritz Breithaupt, "Empathy and Aesthetics," *Zeitschrift für Ästhetik und Allgemeine Kunstwissenschaft* 63, no. 1 (2018): 45–60.

22. See Hans-Ulrich Gumbrecht, *In Praise of Athletic Beauty* (Cambridge, MA: Harvard University Press, 2006).

23. Stanley Cavell, *Cities of Words: Pedagogical Letters on a Register of Moral Life* (Cambridge, MA: Belknap Press, 2004), 111.

Epilogue

1. For an overview, see Jean Decety and Jason M. Cowell. "Empathy and its Relationship to Moral Behavior," in *The Wiley Blackwell Handbook of Forensic Neuroscience*, ed. Anthony R. Beech et al. (Hoboken: John Wiley & Sons, 2018), 145–69.

2. Prinz, "Against Empathy."

3. For these considerations, see Breithaupt, "Empathy and Aesthetics."

4. For emotions as such signals to oneself, see Reber, *Critical Feelings*.

Bibliography

Ackerman, Joshua M., Noah J. Goldstein, Jenessa R. Shapiro, and John A. Bargh. "You Wear Me Out: The Vicarious Depletion of Self-Control." *Psychological Science* 20, no. 3 (2009): 326–32.

Ahoda, Gustav. "Theodor Lipps and the Shift from 'Sympathy' to 'Empathy.'" *Journal of the History of the Behavioral Sciences* 41 (2005): 151–63.

Allen, Colin, and Marc Bekoff. *Species of Mind: The Philosophy and Biology of Cognitive Ethology.* Cambridge, MA: MIT Press, 1999.

Anderson, Benedict. *Imagined Communities: Reflections on the Origin and Spread of Nationalism.* New York: Verso, 2016.

Anderson, Emma Louise, Eloisa Steen, and Vasileios Stavropoulos. "Internet Use and Problematic Internet Use: A Systematic Review of Longitudinal Research Trends in Adolescence and Emergent Adulthood." *International Journal of Adolescence and Youth* 22, no. 4 (2017): 430–54.

Anscome, Gertrude Elizabeth Margaret. *Intention.* Cambridge, MA: Harvard University Press, 1957.

Arendt, Hannah. *Eichmann in Jerusalem: A Report on the Banality of Evil.* New York: Penguin, 2006.

Assmann, Aleida, and Ines Detmers, eds. *Empathy and Its Limits.* New York: Palgrave, 2016.

Bal, Matthijs, and Martijn Veltkamp. "How Does Fiction Reading Influence Empathy? An Experimental Investigation on the Role of Emotional Transportation." *PloS One* 8, no. 1 (2013): e55341.

Barnes, Jennifer L., Tyler Hill, Melanie Langer, Margaret Martinez, and Laurie R Santos. "Helping Behaviour and Regard for Others in Capuchin Monkeys (Cebus apella)." *Biology Letters* 4, no. 6 (2008): 638–40.

Baron-Cohen, Simon, Alan M. Leslie, and Uta Frith. "Does the Autistic Child Have a 'Theory of Mind'?" *Cognition* 21, no. 1 (1985): 37–46.

Bartal, Inbal Ben-Ami, Jean Decety, and Peggy Mason. "Empathy and Pro-Social Behavior in Rats." *Science* 334, no. 6061 (2011): 1427–30.

Barton, Keith C., and Alan W. McCully. "Trying to 'See Things Differently:' Northern Ireland Students' Struggle to Understand Alternative Historical Perspectives." *Theory & Research in Social Education* 40, no. 4 (2012): 377.

Barton, Keith C., and Alan W. McCully. "You Can Form Your Own Point of View: Internally Persuasive Discourse in Northern Ireland Students' Encounters with History." *Teachers College Record* 112, no. 1 (2010): 142–81.

Batson, Daniel C. "The Empathy-Altruism Hypothesis: Issues and Implications." In *Empathy: From Bench to Bedside*, edited by Jean Decety, 41–54. Cambridge, MA: MIT Press, 2012.

Batson, Daniel C. "These Things Called Empathy: Eight Related but Distinct Phenomena." In *The Social Neuroscience of Empathy*, edited by Jean Decety, 3–15. Cambridge, MA: MIT Press, 2009.

Batson, Daniel C., Tricia R. Klein, Lori Highberger, and Laura L. Shaw. "Immorality from Empathy-Induced Altruism: When Compassion and Justice Conflict." *Journal of Personality and Social Psychology* 68, no. 6 (1995): 1042–54.

Baum, Katrina, Shannan Catalano, and Michael Rand. *Stalking Victimization in the United States*. Bureau of Justice Statistics, January 2009, NCJ 224527.

Bechara, Antoine, Hanna Damasio, Daniel Tranel, and Antonio R. Damasio. "Deciding Advantageously Before Knowing the Advantageous Strategy." *Science* 275, no. 5304 (1997): 1293–95.

Birkett, Melissa Ann. "Self-Compassion and Empathy across Cultures: Comparison of Young Adults in China and the United States." *International Journal of Research Studies in Psychology* 3, no. 1 (2013): 25–34.

Bjerregaard, Beth. "An Empirical Study of Stalking Victimization." *Violence and Victims* 15, no. 4 (2000): 389–406.

Blair, James R. "Responding to the Emotions of Others: Dissociating Forms of Empathy through the Study of Typical and Psychiatric Populations." *Consciousness and Cognition* 14, no. 4 (2005): 698–718.

Bloom, Paul. *Against Empathy*. New York: Harper Collins, 2016.

Borsche, Tilman. "Auf wen bezieht sich das Wort 'wir' in Merkels Satz 'Wir schaffen das'?" *Philosophie Magazin* 2 (2016): 55.

Boyd, Brian. *On the Origin of Stories*. Cambridge, MA: Harvard University Press, 2009.

Breithaupt, Fritz. "The Birth of Narrative from the Spirit of the Excuse. A Speculation." *Poetics Today* 32 (Spring 2011): 107–28.

Breithaupt, Fritz. "Blocking Empathy: A Three-Person Model of Empathy." *Emotion Review* 4, no. 1 (2012): 84–91.

Breithaupt, Fritz. *Culturas de la Empatía*. Buenos Aires: Katz Editores, 2011.

Breithaupt, Fritz. "Empathic Sadism: How Readers Get Implicated." In *The Oxford Handbook for Cognitive Literary Studies*, edited by Lisa Zunshine, 440–62. Oxford: Oxford University Press, 2015.

Breithaupt, Fritz. "Empathy and Aesthetics." *Zeitschrift für Ästhetik und Allgemeine Kunstwissenschaft* 63, no. 1 (2018): 45–60.

Breithaupt, Fritz. "Empathy for Empathy's Sake: Aesthetics and Empathic Sadism." In *Empathy and its Limits*, edited by Aledia Assmann and Ines Detmers, 151–65. New York: Palgrave, 2016.

Breithaupt, Fritz. *Kultur der Ausrede*. Berlin: Suhrkamp, 2012.

Breithaupt, Fritz. *Kulturen der Empathie*. Frankfurt: Suhrkamp, 2009.

Brewer, Gayle, and Jade Kerslake. "Cyberbullying, Self-Esteem, Empathy and Loneliness." *Computers in Human Behavior* 48 (2015): 255–60.

Brown, Jane K. *Goethe's Allegories of Identity*. Philadelphia: University of Pennsylvania Press, 2014.

Bruner, Jerome. *Making Stories: Law, Literature, Life*. Cambridge, MA: Harvard University Press, 2003.

Bubandt, Nils, and Rane Willerslev. "The Dark Side of Empathy: Mimesis, Deception, and the Magic of Alterity." *Comparative Studies in Society and History* 57, no. 1 (2015): 5–34.

Burgard, Peter J., ed. *Nietzsche and the Feminine*. Charlottesville: University of Virginia Press, 1994.

Burisch, Mathias. "A Longitudinal Study of Burnout: The Relative Importance of Dispositions and Experiences." In *Work & Stress* 16, no. 1 (2002): 1–17.

Burke, Edmund. *A Philosophical Inquiry into the Origins of our Ideas of the Sublime and Beautiful*. Edited by James Boulton. South Bend: Notre Dame University Press, 1958.

Call, Josep, and Michael Tomasello. "Does the Chimpanzee Have a Theory of Mind? 30 Years Later." *Trends in Cognitive Sciences* 12, no. 5 (2008): 187–92.

Carruthers, Peter. "How We Know Our Own Minds: The Relationship between Mindreading and Metacognition." *Behavioral and Brain Sciences* 32, no. 2 (2009): 121–38.

Carruthers, Peter. "Simulation and Self-Knowledge: A Defence of Theory-Theory." In *Theories of Theories of Mind*, edited by Peter Carruthers and Peter K. Smith, 22–38. Cambridge: Cambridge University Press, 1996.

Cavell, Stanley. *Cities of Words: Pedagogical Letters on a Register of Moral Life*. Cambridge, MA: Belknap Press, 2004.

Cheng, Yawei, Ching-Po Lin, Ho-Ling Liu, Yuan-Yu Hsu, Kun-Eng Lim, Daisy Hung, and Jean Decety. "Expertise Modulates the Perception of Pain in Others." *Current Biology* 17 (2007): 1708–13.

Chismar, Douglas. "Empathy and Sympathy. The Important Difference." *Journal of Value Inquiry* 22 (1988): 257–66.

Cline, Forster, and Jim Fay. *Parenting with Love and Logic: Teaching Children Responsibility.* Carol Stream, IL: Tyndale House, 2014.

Coplan, Amy. "Catching Characters' Emotions: Emotional Contagion Responses to Narrative Fiction Film." *Film Studies* 8, no. 1 (2006): 26–38.

Damasio, Antonio R. *Descartes' Error: Emotion, Reason, and the Human Brain.* New York: Penguin, 2005.

Daston, Lorraine J., and Peter Galison. *Objectivity.* New York: Zone Books, 2007.

Decety, Jean. "Human Empathy." *Japanese Journal of Neuropsychology* 22 (2006): 11–33.

Decety, Jean. "The Neural Pathways, Development, and Functions of Empathy." *Current Opinion in Behavioral Sciences* 3 (2015): 1–6.

Decety, Jean, and C. Daniel Batson. "Empathy and Morality: Integrating Social and Neuroscience Approaches." In *The Moral Brain: Essays on the Evolutionary and Neuroscientific Aspects of Morality*, edited by Jan Verplaetse, 109–27. Dordrecht: Springer, 2009.

Decety, Jean, and Thierry Chaminade. "Neural Correlates of Feeling Sympathy." *Neuropsychologia* 41, no. 2 (2003): 127–38.

Decety, Jean, and Jason M. Cowell. "Empathy and its Relationship to Moral Behavior." In *The Wiley Blackwell Handbook of Forensic Neuroscience*, edited by Anthony R. Beech, Adam J. Carter, Ruth E. Mann, and Pia Rotshtein, 145–69. Hoboken: John Wiley & Sons, 2018.

Decety, Jean, and Jason M. Cowell. "Friends or Foes: Is Empathy Necessary for Moral Behavior?" *Perspectives on Psychological Science* 9, no. 5 (2014): 525–37.

Decety, Jean, and Claus Lamm. "Human Empathy through the Lens of Social Neuroscience." *Scientific World Journal* 6 (2006): 1146–63.

Decety, Jean, and Claus Lamm. "The Role of the Right Temporoparietal Junction in Social Interaction: How Low-Level Computational Processes Contribute to Meta-Cognition." *Neuroscientist* (2007): 580–93.

Decety, Jean, Kalina J. Michalska, Yuko Akitsuki, and Benjamin B. Lahey. "Atypical Empathic Responses in Adolescents with Aggressive Conduct Disorder: A Functional MRI Investigation." *Biological Psychology* 80, no. 2 (2009): 203–11.

Delgado, Richard. "Rodrigo's Eleventh Chronicle: Empathy and False Empathy." *California Law Review* 84, no. 1 (1996): 61–100.

DeScioli, Peter, and Robert Kurzban. "Mysteries of Morality." *Cognition* 112, no. 2 (2009): 281–99.

De Vignemont, Frederique, and Tania Singer. "The Empathic Brain: How, When and Why?" *Trends in Cognitive Sciences* 10, no. 10 (2006): 435–41.

Dinstein, Ilan, Cibu Thomas, Kate Humphreys, Nancy Minshew, Marlene Behrmann, and David J. Heeger. "Normal Movement Selectivity in Autism." *Neuron* 66, no. 3 (2010): 461–69.

Dostoevsky, Fyodor. *The Brothers Karamazov*. Translated by Richard Pevear and Larissa Volokhonsky. New York: Farrar, Strauss and Giroux, 1990.

Dunbar, Robin. *Grooming, Gossip and the Evolution of Language*. Cambridge, MA: Harvard University Press, 1997.

Dunbar, Robin. "Neocortex Size as a Constraint on Group Size in Primates." *Journal of Human Evolution* 22 (1992): 469–93.

"The Education of Parents." *School Journal* 62 (May 25, 1901): 570.

Eisenberg, Nancy, Richard A. Fabes, Stephanie A. Shepard, Bridget C. Murphy, Ivanna K. Guthrie, Sarah Jones, Jo Friedman, Rick Poulin, and Pat Maszk. "Contemporaneous and Longitudinal Prediction of Children's Social Functioning from Regulation and Emotionality." *Child Development* 68, no. 4 (1997): 642–64.

Eisenberg, Nancy, and Randy Lennon. "Sex Differences in Empathy and Related Capacities." *Psychological Bulletin* 94, no. 1 (1983): 100–131.

Eklund, Jakob, Teresi Andersson-Sraberg, and Eric M. Hansen. "I've Also Experienced Loss and Fear: Effects of Prior Similar Experience on Empathy." *Scandinavian Journal of Psychology* 50, no. 1 (2009): 65–69.

Elfenbein, Hillary Anger. "The Many Faces of Emotional Contagion: An Affective Process Theory of Affective Linkage." *Organizational Psychology Review* (2014): 177–90.

Fernandez, Yolanda M., and W. L. Marshall. "Victim Empathy, Social Self-Esteem, and Psychology in Rapists." *Sexual Abuse: A Journal of Research and Treatment* 15, no. 1 (2003): 11–26.

Finn, Jerry. "A Survey of Online Harassment at a University Campus." *Journal of Interpersonal Violence* 19, no. 4 (2004): 468–83.

Flesch, William. *Comeuppance: Costly Signaling, Altruistic Punishment, and Other Biological Components of Fiction*. Cambridge, MA: Harvard University Press, 2007.

Flesch, William. "Readings and Bargainings." In *The Oxford Handbook for Cognitive Literary Studies*, edited by Lisa Zunshine, 369–86. Oxford: Oxford University Press, 2015.

Foucault, Michel. *Discipline and Punish*. New York City: Pantheon, 1977.

Freedberg, David, and Vittorio Gallese. "Motion, Emotion and Empathy in Esthetic Experience." *Trends in Cognitive Sciences* 11, no. 5 (2007): 197–203.

Freud, Sigmund. *Massenpsychologie und Ich-Analyse*, Frankfurt: Fischer, 2005 [1921].

Galinsky, Adam D., and Gillian Ku. "The Effects of Perspective-Taking on Prejudice: The Moderating Role of Self-Evaluation." *Personality and Social Psychology Bulletin* 30, no. 5 (2004): 594–604.

Gallese, Vittorio. "The 'Shared Manifold' Hypothesis: From Mirror Neurons to Empathy." *Journal of Consciousness Studies* 8, nos. 5–6 (2001): 33–50.

Gallup, Gordon G., and Steven M. Platek. "Cognitive Empathy Presupposes Self-Awareness: Evidence from Phylogeny, Ontogeny, Neuropsychology, and Mental Illness." *Behavioral and Brain Sciences* 25, no. 1 (2002): 36–37.

Genette, Gérard. *Narrative Discourse. An Essay in Method.* Oxford: Blackwell, 1980.

Gigerenzer, Gerd, and Peter M. Todd. *Simple Heuristics That Make Us Smart.* Oxford: Oxford University Press, 1999.

Glasser, Matthew F., et al. "A Multi-Modal Parcellation of Human Cerebral Cortex." *Nature* 18933 (2016): 171–78.

Gleichgerrcht, Ezequiel, and Jean Decety. "Empathy in Clinical Practice: How Individual Dispositions, Gender, and Experience Moderate Empathic Concern, Burnout, and Emotional Distress in Physicians." *PLoS One* 8, no. 4 (2013): e61526.

Goldie, Peter. "Anti-Empathy." In *Empathy: Philosophical and Psychological Perspectives*, edited by Amy Coplan and Peter Goldie, 302–17. Oxford: Oxford University Press, 2011.

Gopnik, A., and Janet W. Aslington. "Children's Understanding of Representational Change and its Relation to the Understanding of False Belief and the Appearance-Reality Distinction." *Child Development* 59 (1988): 26–37.

Gordon, Mary, *Roots of Empathy: Changing the World Child by Child.* New York: The Experiment, 2005.

Gottschall, Jonathan. *The Storytelling Animal: How Stories Make Us Human.* Boston: Houghton Mifflin Harcourt, 2012.

Goubert, Lisbet, K. D. Craig, Tine Vervoort, S. Morley, M. J. L. Sullivan, A. C. de C. Williams, A. Cano, and G. Crombez. "Facing Other in Pain: The Effects of Empathy." *Pain* 118, no. 3 (2005): 285–88.

Green, Joshua. *Moral Tribes: Emotion, Reason, and the Gap Between Us and Them.* New York: Penguin, 2014.

Gumbrecht, Hans-Ulrich. *In Praise of Athletic Beauty.* Cambridge, MA: Harvard University Press, 2006.

Guo, Xiuyan, Li Zheng, Wei Zhang, Lei Zhu, Jian-qi Li, Qianfeng Wang, Zoltan Dienes, and Zhiliang Yang. "Empathic Neural Responses to Others' Pain Depend on Monetary Reward." *Social Cognitive and Affective Neuroscience* (2011), nsr034.

Haidt, Jonathan. *The Righteous Mind: Why Good People Are Divided by Politics and Religion.* New York: Vintage, 2012.

Hamilton, Andrew, and Fritz Breithaupt. "These Things Called Event: Toward a Unified Theory of Events." *Sprache und Datenverarbeitung* 37 (2013): 65–87.

Hanich, Julian, Valentin Wagner, Mira Shah, Thomas Jacobsen, and Winfried Menninghaus. "Why We Like to Watch Sad Films: The Pleasure of being Moved in Aesthetic Experiences." *Psychology of Aesthetics, Creativity and the Arts* 8 (2014): 130–43.

Harenski, Carla. L., Keith Harenski, Matthew S. Shane, and Kent A. Kiehl. "Aberrant Neural Processing or Moral Violations in Criminal Psychopaths." *Journal of Abnormal Psychology* 21 (2010): 1–12.

Hatfield, Elaine, John T. Cacioppo, and Richard L. Rapson. *Emotional Contagion.* Cambridge: Cambridge University Press, 1994.

Heilbrun, Alfred B. "Cognitive Models of Criminal Violence Based Upon Intelligence and Psychopathy Levels." *Journal of Consulting and Clinical Psychology* 50, no. 4 (1982): 546–57.

Hickok, Gregory. *The Myth of Mirror Neurons.* New York: W. W. Norton, 2014.

Higgins, Lynn A., and Brenda R. Silver. *Rape and Representation.* New York: Columbia University Press, 1991.

Holt, Susan E., J. Reid Meloy, and Stephen Strack. "Sadism and Psychopathy in Violent and Sexually Violent Offenders." *Journal of the American Academy of Psychiatry and the Law* 27 (1999): 23–32.

Hunt, Lynn. *Inventing Human Rights.* New York: W. W. Norton, 2008.

Iacoboni, Marco. "Imitation, Empathy, and Mirror Neurons." *Annual Review of Psychology* 60 (2009): 653–70.

Jackson, Philip L., Eric Brunet-Gouet, Andrew N. Meltzoff, and Jean Decety. "Empathy Examined through the Neural Mechanisms Involved in Imagining How I Feel versus How You Feel Pain." *Neuropsychologia* 44, no. 5 (2006): 752–61.

Jackson, Philip L., Pierre Rainville, and Jean Decety. "To What Extent Do We Share the Pain of Others? Insight from Neural Bases of Pain Empathy." In *Pain* 125 (2006): 5–9.

Kamir, Orit. *Every Breath You Take: Stalking Narratives and the Law.* Ann Arbor: University of Michigan Press, 2001.

Kantorowicz, Ernst. *The King's Two Bodies: A Study in Medieval Political Theology.* Princeton: Princeton University Press, 1957.

Keen, Suzanne. *Empathy and the Novel.* Oxford: Oxford University Press, 2007.

Kidd, David Comer, and Emanuele Castano. "Reading Literary Fiction Improves Theory of Mind." *Science* 342, no. 6156 (2013): 377–80.

Kiehl, Kent A., and Morris B. Hoffman. "The Criminal Psychopath: History, Neuroscience, Treatment, and Economics." *Jurimetrics: The Journal of Law, Science, and Technology* 51, no. 4 (2011): 355–97.

Kittler, Friedrich A. *Discourse Networks 1800/1900.* Palo Alto, CA: Stanford University Press, 1992.

Kolmar, Martin, and Fritz Breihaupt. "Postfaktische Autoritäten." *Kursbuch* (March 2017): 17–28.

Konrath, Sara H. "Critical Synthesis Package: Interpersonal Reactivity Index (IRI)." *MedEdPORTAL* 9, no. 9596 (2013). https://doi.org/10.15766/mep_2374-8265.9596.

Konrath, Sara H., Edward H. O'Brien, and Courtney Hsing. "Changes in Dispositional Empathy in American College Students over Time: A Meta-Analysis." *Personality and Social Psychology Review* (2010): 180–98.

Koopman, Emy M., Michelle Hilscher, and Gerald C. Cupchik. "Reader Responses to Literary Depiction of Rape." *Psychology of Aesthetics, Creativity, and the Arts* 6, no. 1 (2012): 66–73.

Koselleck, Reinhart. *Futures Past.* New York: Columbia University Press, 2004.

Kovács, Ágnes Melinda, Ernő Téglás, and Ansgar Denis Endress. "The Social Sense: Susceptibility to Others' Beliefs in Human Infants and Adults." *Science* 330 (2010): 1830–34.

Krebs, Dennis. "Empathy and Altruism." *Journal of Personality and Social Psychology* 32, no. 6 (1975): 1134–42.

Kurzban, Robert, Peter DeScioli, and Erin O'Brien. "Audience Effects on Moralistic Punishment." *Evolution and Human Behavior* 28, no. 2 (2007): 75–84.

Lamm, Claus, Andrew N. Meltzoff, and Jean Decety. "How Do We Empathize with Someone Who Is Not Like Us? A Functional Magnetic Resonance Imaging Study." *Journal of Cognitive Neuroscience* 22, no. 2 (2010): 362–76.

Lamm, Claus, Markus Rütgen, and Isabella C. Wagner. "Imaging Empathy and Prosocial Emotions." In *Neuroscience Letters* (June 2017) 1–5.

Laqueur, Thomas W. "Mourning, Pity, and the Work of Narrative in the Making of 'Humanity.'" In *Humanitarianism and Suffering: The Mobilization of Empathy*, edited by Richard D. Brown, 31–57. Cambridge: Cambridge University Press, 2009.

Lau, Tatiana, Carey K. Morewedge, and Mina Cikara. "Overcorrection for Social-Categorization Information Moderates Impact Bias in Affective Forecasting." *Psychological Science* 27, no. 10 (2016): 1340–51.

Leiberg, Susanne, and Silke Anders. "The Multiple Facets of Empathy: A Survey of Theory and Evidence." *Progress in Brain Research* 156 (2006): 419–40.

LeMoyne, Terri, and Tom Buchanan. "Does 'Hovering' Matter? Helicopter Parenting and Its Effect on Well-Being." *Sociological Spectrum* 31, no. 4 (2011): 399–418.

Lengfeld, Holger. "Die 'Alternative für Deutschland': eine Partei für Modernisierungsverlierer?" In *KZfSS Kölner Zeitschrift für Soziologie und Sozialpsychologie* 69, no. 2 (2017): 209–32.

Lessing, Gotthold Ephraim. *Hamburg Dramaturgy.* New York: Dover, 1962.

Levesque, Roger J. R. "Sadistic Personality Disorder." In *Encyclopedia of Adolescence*, edited by Roger J. R Levesque, 2445. New York: Springer Science & Business Media, 2011.

Lisak, David, and Carol Ivan. "Deficits in Intimacy and Empathy in Sexually Aggressive Men." *Journal of Interpersonal Violence* 10, no. 3 (1995): 296–308.

Lischinsky, Alon. "Doing the Naughty or Having It Done to You? Agent Roles in Erotic Writing." *Porn Studies* (2017): 1–19.

Lombardo, Michael V., Jennifer L. Barnes, Sally J. Wheelwright, and Simon Baron-Cohen. "Self-Referential Cognition and Empathy in Autism." *PLoS One* 2, no. 9 (2007): e883.

Lonsway, Kimberly A., and Louise F. Fitzgerald. "Rape Myths in Review." *Psychology of Women Quarterly* 18, no. 2 (1994): 133–64.

Loshitzky, Yosefa. *Spielberg's Holocaust: Critical Perspectives on Schindler's List.* Bloomington: Indiana University Press, 1997.

Luhmann, Niklas. *Social Structure and Semantics.* Palo Alto, CA: Stanford University Press, 2003.

Madeira, Jody Lyneé. *Killing McVeigh: The Death Penalty and the Myth of Closure.* New York: NYU Press, 2012.

Madeira, Jody Lyneé. "Lashing Reason to the Mast: Understanding Judicial Constraints on Emotion in Personal Injury Litigation." *UC Davis Law Review* 137 (2006).

Marsh, Abigail A. "Empathy and Compassion: A Cognitive Neuroscience Perspective." In *Empathy*, edited by Jean Decety, 191–205. Cambridge, MA: MIT Press, 2012.

Marshall, W. L., and Heather Moulden. "Hostility toward Women and Victim Empathy in Rapists." *Sexual Abuse: A Journal of Research and Treatment* 13, no. 4 (2001): 249–55.

Maskarinec, Malika, *The Forces of Form in German Modernism.* Evanston: Northwestern University Press, 2018.

Massaro, Toni M. "Empathy, Legal Storytelling, and the Rule of Law: New Words, Old Wounds?" *Michigan Law Review* 87, no. 8 (1989): 2099–2127.

Mazzocco, Philip J., Melanie C. Green, Jo A. Sasota, and Norman W. Jones. "This Story is Not for Everyone: Transportability and Narrative Persuasion." *Social Psychological and Personality Science* (2010): 361–68.

McCauley, Clark, and Sophia Moskalenko. "Mechanisms of Political Radicalization: Pathways toward Terrorism." *Terrorism and Political Violence* 20, no. 3 (2008): 415–33.

McEwan, Troy E., Paul E. Mullen, and Rachel MacKenzie. "A Study of the Predictors of Persistence in Stalking Situations." *Law and Human Behavior* 33, no. 2 (2009): 149–58.

Meffert, Harma, Valeria Gazzola, Johan A. Den Boer, Arnold A. J. Bartels, and Christian Keysers. "Reduced Spontaneous but Relatively Normal Deliberate Vicarious Representations in Psychopathy." *Brain* 136, no. 8 (2013): 2550–62.

Melis, Alicia P., Felix Warneken, and Brian Hare. "Collaboration and Helping in Chimpanzees." In *The Mind of the Chimpanzee: Ecological and Experimental Perspectives*, edited by Elizabeth V. Lonsdorf, Stephen R. Ross, and Tetsuro Matsuzawa, 278–93. Chicago: University of Chicago Press, 2010.

Meltzoff, Andrew. "Understanding the Intentions of Others: Re-Enactment of Intended Acts by 18-Month-Old Children." *Developmental Psychology* 31 (1995): 838–50.

Mendes, Wendy Berry, and Katrina Koslov. "Brittle Smiles: Positive Biases toward Stigmatized and Outgroup Targets." *Journal of Experimental Psychology: General* 142, no. 3 (2013): 923–34.

Mullen, Paul E., Michele Pathé, and Rosemary Purcell. *Stalkers and Their Victims*. Cambridge: Cambridge University Press, 2000.

Myler, Stephen F. "Chinese Cultural Lack of Empathy in Development— Counselling Practice." http://www.academia.edu/3620724/Chinese_Lack_of_Empathy_in_Development (accessed January 15, 2015).

Nelson, E. D. (Edie). "The Things That Dreams Are Made On: Dreamwork and the Socialization of 'Stage Mothers.'" *Qualitative Sociology* 24, no. 4 (2001): 439–58.

Nietzsche, Friedrich. *Beyond Good and Evil*. Translated by Walter Kaufman. New York: Random House, 1966.

Nietzsche, Friedrich. *Daybreak. Thoughts on the Prejudice of Morality*. Translated by R. J. Hollingdale. Cambridge: Cambridge University Press, 1997.

Nietzsche, Friedrich. *On the Genealogy of Morals*. Translated by Walter Kaufmann. New York: Random House, 1967.

Nünning, Vera. "Cognitive Science and the Value of Literature for Life." In *Values of Literature*, edited by Hanna Meretoja, Saija Isomaa, Pirjo Lyytikäinen, and Kristina Malmio, 93–116. Leiden: Brill, 2015.

Nussbaum, Martha C. *From Disgust to Humanity: Sexual Orientation and Constitutional Law*, Oxford: Oxford University Press, 2010.

Nussbaum, Martha C. *Political Emotions*. Cambridge, MA: Harvard University Press, 2015.

Obama, Barack. Commencement Speech. Northwestern University, June 19, 2006, http://www.northwestern.edu/newscenter/stories/2006/06/barack.html.

Paasonen, Susanna. "Good Amateurs: Erotica Writing and Notions of Quality." In *Porn.com: Making Sense of Online Pornography*, edited by Feona Attwood, 138–54. New York: Peter Lang, 2010.

Phelan, James. "Why Narrators Can Be Focalizers—and Why It Matters." In *New Perspectives on Narrative Perspective*, edited by Willie van Peer and Seymour Chatma, 51–64. Albany: SUNY Press, 2001.

Pinker, Steven. *The Better Angels of Our Nature: The Decline of Violence in History and its Causes.* London: Penguin, 2011.

Pithers, William D. "Empathy Definition, Enhancement, and Relevance to the Treatment of Sexual Abuse." *Journal of Interpersonal Violence* 14, no. 3 (1999): 257–84.

Plantinga, Carl. "Facing Others: Close-ups of Faces in Narrative Films and in Silence of the Lambs." In *The Oxford Handbook of Cognitive Literary Studies*, edited by Lisa Zunshine, 291–311. Oxford: Oxford University Press, 2015.

Porter, Stephen, Leanne ten Brinke, and Chantal Gustaw. "Dangerous Decisions: The Impact of First Impressions of Trustworthiness on the Evaluation of Legal Evidence and Defendant Culpability." *Psychology, Crime & Law* 16, no. 6 (2010): 477–91.

Poythress, Norman, G., Jennifer L. Skeem, and Scott O. Lilienfeld. "Associations among Early Abuse, Dissociation, and Psychopathy in an Offender Sample." *Journal of Abnormal Psychology* 115, no. 2 (2006): 288–97.

Preis, Mira A., and Brigit Kroener-Herwig. "Empathy for Pain: The Effects of Prior Experience and Sex." *European Journal of Pain* 16, no. 9 (2012): 1311–19.

Preis, Mira A., Carsten Schmidt-Samoa, Peter Dechent, and Birgit Kroener-Herwig. "The Effects of Prior Pain Experience on Neural Correlates of Empathy for Pain: An fMRI study." In *Pain* 154, no. 3 (2013): 411–18.

Premack, David G., and Guy Woodruff. "Does the Chimpanzee Have a Theory of Mind?" *Behavioral and Brain Sciences* 1, no. 4 (1978): 515–26.

Preston, Stephanie D., and Frans de Waal. "Empathy: Its Ultimate and Proximate Bases." In *Behavioral Brain Science* 25, no. 1 (2002): 1–20.

Prinz, Jesse. "Against Empathy." *Southern Journal of Philosophy* 49, no. 1 (2011): 214–33.

Prinz, Wolfgang. "Modes of Linkage between Perception and Action." In *Cognition and Motor Processes*, edited by Wolfgang Prinz, 185–93. Berlin: Springer 1984.

de Quervain, Dominique J. F., Urs Fischbacher, Valerie Treyer, Melanie Schellhammer, Ulrich Schnyder, Alfred Buck, and Ernst Fehr. "The Neural Basis of Altruistic Punishment." *Science* 305, no. 5688 (2004): 1254–59.

Ramachandran, Vilayanur S., and Lindsay M. Oberman. "Broken Mirrors: A Theory of Autism," *Scientific American* 295, no. 5 (2006): 62–69.

Reber, Rolf. *Critical Feelings: How to Use Feelings Strategically.* Oxford: Oxford University Press, 2016.

Rice, Marnie E. "Empathy for the Victim and Sexual Arousal among Rapists and Nonrapists." *Journal of Interpersonal Violence* 9, no. 4 (1994): 434–49.

Robinson, Michael E., and Emily A. Wise. "Prior Pain Experience: Influence on the Observation of Experimental Pain in Men and Women." *Journal of Pain* 5, no. 5 (2004): 264–69.

Rogers, Kelly, ed. *Self-Interest: An Anthology of Philosophical Perspectives from Antiquity to the Present*. London: Routledge, 2014.

Rosa, Hartmut. *Resonanz*. Berlin: Suhrkamp, 2016.

Rudner, Martin. "'Electronic Jihad': The Internet as Al Qaeda's Catalyst for Global Terror." *Studies in Conflict & Terrorism* 40, no. 1 (2017): 10–23.

Saarela, Miiamaaria V., Yevhen Hlushchuk, Amanda C. de C. Williams, Martin Schürmann, Eija Kalso, and Riitta Hari. "The Compassionate Brain: Humans Detect Intensity of Pain from Another's Face." *Cerebral Cortex* 17, no. 1 (2007): 230–37.

Schiffrin, Holly H., Miriam Liss, Haley Miles-McLean, Katherine A. Geary, Mindy J. Erchull, and Taryn Tashner. "Helping or Hovering? The Effects of Helicopter Parenting on College Student' Well-Being." *Journal of Child and Family Studies* 23, no. 3 (2014): 548–57.

Schopenhauer, Arhur. *"Zur Ethik."* In *Arthur Schopenhauers Sämmtliche Werke*, 2nd ed., ed. Julius Frauenstädt. Leipzig: Brockhaus, 1919.

Schmidbauer, Wolfgang. *Hilflose Helfer. Über die seelische Problematik der helfenden Berufe*. Reinbek: Rowohlt Verlag, 1977.

Shamay-Tsoory, Simone G., Judith Aharon-Peretz, and Daniella Perry. "Two Systems for Empathy: A Double Dissociation between Emotional and Cognitive Empathy in Inferior Frontal Gyrus versus Ventromedial Prefrontal Lesions." *Brain* 132, no. 3 (2009): 617–27.

Shirtcliff, Elizabeth A., Michael J. Vitacco, Alexander R. Graf, Andrew J. Gostisha, Jenna L. Merz, and Carolyn Zahn-Waxler. "Neurobiology of Empathy and Callousness: Implications for the Development of Antisocial Behavior." *Behavioral Sciences & The Law* 2 (2009): 137–71.

Shoup, Rick, Robert M. Gonyea, and George D. Kuh. "Helicopter Parents: Examining the Impact of Highly Involved Parents on Student Engagement and Educational Outcomes." Paper presented at the 49th Annual Forum of the Association for Institutional Research, Atlanta, GA, June, 2009. http://cpr.indiana.edu/uploads/AIR%202009%20Impact%20of%20Helicopter%20Parents.pdf.

Silberberg, Alan, Candice Allouch, Samantha Sandfort, David Kearns, Heather Karpel, and Burton Slotnick. "Desire for Social Contact, not Empathy, May Explain "Rescue" Behavior in Rats." In *Animal Cognition* 17, no. 3 (2014): 609–18.

Singer, Tania, Ben Seymour, John P. O'Doherty, Klaas E. Stephan, Raymond J. Dolan, and Chris D. Frith. "Empathic Neural Responses are Modulated by the Perceived Fairness of Others." *Nature* 439, no. 7075 (2006): 466–69.

Singer, Tania, and Anita Tusche. "Understanding Others: Brain Mechanisms of Theory of Mind and Empathy." In *Neuroeconomics: Decision Making and the Brain*, 2nd ed., edited by P. W. Glimcher and E. Fehr, 513–32. London: Academic Press, 2014.

Stiegler, Bernd. *Spuren, Elfen und andere Erscheinungen. Conan Doyle und die Photographie.* Frankfurt: Fischer, 2014.

Strohminger, Nina, and Shaun Nichols. "The Essential Moral Self." *Cognition* 131 (2014): 159–71.

Sutton, Jon, Peter K. Smith, and John Swettenham. "Social Cognition and Bullying: Social Inadequacy or Skilled Manipulation?" *British Journal of Developmental Psychology* 17, no. 3 (1999): 435–50.

Tangney, June P., Roy F. Baumeister, and Angie Luzio Boone. "High Self-Control Predicts Good Adjustment, Less Pathology, Better Grades, and Interpersonal Success." *Journal of Personality* 72, no. 2 (2004): 271–324.

Tine, Michele, and Joan Lucariello. "Unique Theory of Mind Differentiation in Children with Autism and Asperger Syndrome." *Autism Research and Treatment* (2012): 1–11.

Todorov, Alexander, Manish Pakrashi, and Nikolaas N. Oosterhof. "Evaluating Faces on Trustworthiness after Minimal Time Exposure." *Social Cognition* 27, no. 6 (2009): 813–33.

Tomasello, Michael. *The Cultural Origins of Human Cognition.* Cambridge, MA: Harvard University Press, 2001.

Tomasello, Michael. *The Origins of Human Communication.* Cambridge, MA: MIT Press, 2010.

Tucker, Corinna Jenkin, Kimberly A. Updegraff, Susan M. McHale, and Ann C. Crouter. "Older Siblings as Socializers of Younger Siblings' Empathy." *Journal of Early Adolescence* 19, no. 2 (1999): 176–98.

Vermeule, Blakey. *Why Do We Care about Literary Characters?* Baltimore: Johns Hopkins University Press, 2011.

de Vignemont, Frédérique, and Pierre Jacob. "What Is It Like to Feel Another's Pain?" *Philosophy of Science* 79 (2012): 295–316.

Voss, Christiane. "Einfühlung als empistemische und ästhetische Kategorie bei Hume und Lipps." In *Einfühlung. Zu Geschichte und Gegenwart eines ästhetischen Konzepts*, edited by Robin Curtis and Gertrud Koch, 31–47. Munich: Fink, 2009.

de Waal, Frans. *Chimpanzee Politics.* Baltimore: Johns Hopkins University Press, 1998.

de Waal, Frans. "Empathy in Primates and Other Mammals." In Decety, *Empathy*, 87–106.

Wahrmann, Dror. *The Making of the Modern Self: Identity and Culture in Eighteenth-Century England*. New Haven: Yale University Press, 2006.

Wallach, Wendell, and Colin Allen. *Moral Machines. Teaching Robots Right from Wrong*. Oxford: Oxford University Press, 2008.

Wegener, Duane T., and Richard E. Petty. "Flexible Correction Processes in Social Judgment: The Role of Naive Theories in Corrections for Perceived Bias." *Journal of Personality and Social Psychology* 68, no. 1 (1995): 36–51.

Wilson, Richard A. *The Politics of Truth and Reconciliation in South Africa: Legitimizing the Post-Apartheid State*. New York: Cambridge University Press, 2001.

Worringer, Wilhelm. *Abstraction and Empathy: A Contribution to the Psychology of Style*. New York: International Universities Press, 1953.

Young, Allan. "Empathic Cruelty and the Origins of the Social Brain." In *Critical Neuroscience: A Handbook of the Social and Cultural Context of Neuroscience*. New York: Wiley-Blackwell, 2016.

Zahn-Waxler, Carolyn, Pamela M. Cole, Jean Darby Welsh, and Nathan A. Fox. "Psychophysiological Correlates of Empathy and Prosocial Behaviors in Preschool Children with Behavior Problems." *Development and Psychopathology* 7, no. 1 (1995): 27–48.

Zahavi, Dan, and Søren Overgaard. "Empathy without Isomorphism: A Phenomenological Account." In Decety, *Empathy*, 3–20.

Zunshine, Lisa. *Getting Inside Your Head: What Cognitive Science Can Tell Us about Popular Culture*. Baltimore: Johns Hopkins University Press, 2015.

Index

CPSIA information can be obtained
at www.ICGtesting.com
Printed in the USA
LVHW041812290519
619461LV00004B/276/P